Psychological Astrology

Tips, Tools and Techniques

By Noel Eastwood

IMPORTANT LEGAL NOTICE

This book is intended as an educational aid for students of astrology. Its contents should not be considered as a substitute for personal supervision or treatment by a qualified medical or psychological professional. The author, editors and publishers accept no responsibility for outcomes if you use the techniques described in this book. For privacy, names of individuals and any identifying details have been changed.

Copyright © 2025. All rights reserved 2025, Noel Eastwood.

Apart from any fair use for the purposes of private study, research, criticism or review no part may be reproduced without written permission of the author.

Please direct all communication to the author, Noel Eastwood.

Email: info@plutoscave.com

Web: www.plutoscave.com

Cover art: original artwork by Peta Fenton

Charts: Solar Fire 9

Books & audiobooks by Noel Eastwood

Psychological Astrology series:

Psychological Astrology an Introduction

Psychological Astrology and the Twelve Houses

Psychological Astrology Tips, Tools and Techniques

Astrology of Health – the physical and psychological health in the natal and progressed charts

Self Hypnosis Tame Your Inner Dragons: clinical and psychic use of trance

The Fool's Journey series:

Book 1 - The Fool's Journey Through the Tarot Major Arcana

Book 2 - The Fool's Journey Through the Tarot Pentacles

Book 3 - The Fool's Journey Through the Tarot Swords

Book 4 - The Fool's Journey Through the Tarot Cups

Book 5 - The Fool's Journey Through the Tarot Wands

Book 6 - The Fool's Journey Through the Tarot Manual

Please visit: https://payhip.com/AstrologyTarotPsychology

CONTENTS

Houses as a story of life
The 4 Key Point Method of Chart Delineations
The Planet of High Degree
The three most common Psychological Disorders
Transits
Progressions and Directions
Cosmobiology and it's Gift to Progressions
Psychology, Family and Michel Gauquelin
Co-dependency—Three Stages of Projection and Romantic Love
Composite and Synastry Charts for Lovers
A Marriage that didn't Succeed - list of Asteroids
The House Systems
Personal Myths and Astrology
The Four Elements as Defences
The Mythology of the Seasons
My Newsletter Has Just About Everything
About the Author

Author's Preface

This book contains more of my approach to astrology with some wicked techniques to better understand your own chart and that of others. I have used both Placidus and Whole Sign house systems because some people don't like using Whole Sign exclusively.

I have tried to get down to the bare bones of astrological calculations by including the Progressions. These are Solar Arc Directions and Secondary Progressed Moon. They do have day-for-a-year calculations and they can be calculated on your computer. I don't think there are computers or software these days that don't do them. Although I don't use progressions very much these days they still hold weight and carry valuable information albeit it is internal and therefore not really visible in the outside world. In other words it is felt rather than seen.

There is a fair bit of love in here too, with progressions, composite charts, synastry charts and an explanation of co-dependency. Co-dependency cannot be fixed with astrology, you will need to see a therapist for that - but it can be fixed, I've see it. There's also Romantic Love, ah, that's the love of your life. Love, yes, humans love to be in love, but there are like six kinds of love, so which is it going to be for you?

You'll also find something on transits which is critical for astrology. Plus there is some material on Michel Gauquelin and his findings on how astrology matches family. You can do your own charts of your own family too, check him out and see what you find. There's a little on Carl Jung too, he pops up now and then in astrology. Did you know that he studied astrology quite extensively? Yep, he did a lot of charts for his clients but never wrote about it, not in his diaries and definitely not in his articles for the psychology profession. He was terrified of being ridiculed by his professional peers, and so he should have been. If they could take him down then his books would never be read and his extensive knowledge lost.

I've often been criticised for not putting enough psychology into my work, and I was a psychologist too. The reason being that no two charts are the same. You can have the chart of a serial killer but be just a normal person living a normal life. So I've included three psychological disorders for those who want more – but remember, no two charts are the same.

Finally I finish with a little on personal myths, those little dreams we have, and on defences. These came from Sigmund Freud and are wonderful guides to the intricacies of astrology, magic and psychodynamic theory.

This volume is a good mixture of practical and theoretical knowledge gained from my 70 odd years of life. Good luck with your studies, and enjoy the book, it is excellent.

Noel Eastwood – March, 2025 here in sunny Brisbane, Queensland, Australia.

Chapter 1: Houses as a Story of Life

Knowing yourself, through your astrology chart, is one of the most important gifts you can give to yourself. Here is a novel way to to view your chart that breaks all boundaries and adds insight for your journey. I find that I am always going back to my own chart to discover features I have either forgotten or wasn't ready to understand – and this is one of those times.

Introduction
1st - birth, delivery and your experiences of the first 2 years of life.
2nd - from 2 years of age to 4 years, learning about security.
3rd - the early school years, learning and communicating, exploring the world up to around 7 years of age.

A simple rule in astrology is to use the Roman names for the Greek Gods and Goddesses. For example: Juno (Roman) for Hera (Greek); Ceres (Roman) for Demeter (Greek); Venus (Roman) for Aphrodite (Greek), but sometimes I like to use the Greek names.

I've always wanted to know more than just the basics, I wanted to know what psychological traits, strengths and weakness I could see in people's chart. Sure, the planets and signs are psychological but what about the houses? I found that by adding the psychological principles of the houses I could delve deeper into someone's psyche than I ever could by focusing on the signs and planets alone.

This concept of the houses as a story of life was presented by my astrology teacher, Chris Turner, principal of the *Chiron School of Astrology*, in Sydney, Australia. That was many years ago and since then I've gone back to her lessons time and again to process them as an experienced astrologer. I now realise this 'story of life' is incredibly powerful and I am excited to bring it to you.

As a psychologist I'll sometimes work with people to develop a narrative of their life. This process is also called their *'personal myth'*. It starts off by discussing their life in sections and it all starts at birth: did your mother, father, grandparent ever tell you what your birth was like? Was it easy, fast, or traumatic?

Let me explain a few things about the 1st house and then tell you about my own birth and link this in to my chart - then you'll see why this method is so powerful.

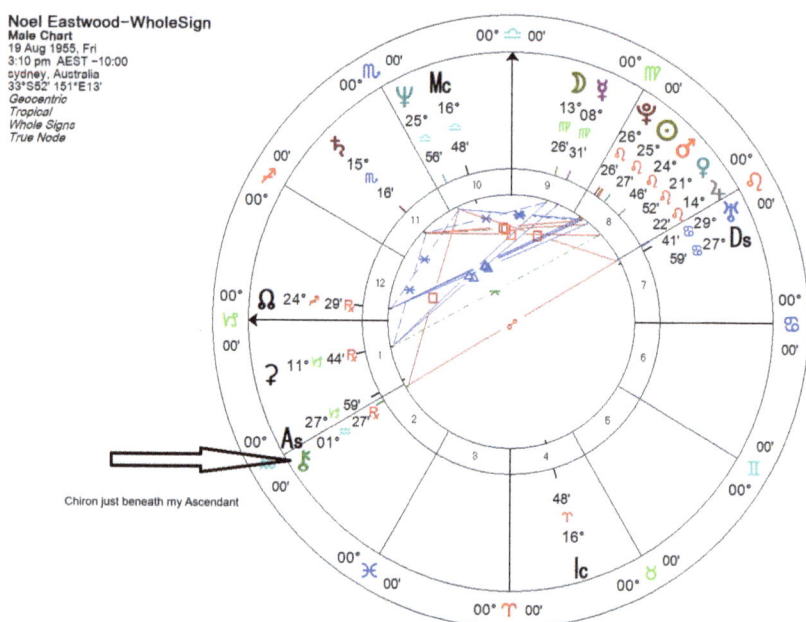

1st house: birth, delivery and your first taste of life

This is the house of the skin, it's what you touch the world with, your physical, emotional and spiritual skin so to speak. It can also become thickened, an armour to protect your sensitive inner self. Your inner weaknesses and sensitivities are hidden within the shell of your Ascendant and 1st house.

      To use a metaphor from the animal kingdom, this armour can manifest as aggressiveness, assertiveness, leadership or as condescending behaviour. I sometimes imagine this as a dog with its tail between its legs, or it can be a dog with its head held high with pride because it's been treated with respect and knows its own worth. Or perhaps one that is smart and confident but still trying to prove its worth in the world of dogs. Your first house is where you connect with the world around you and using this metaphor you can imagine yourself failing, struggling, or becoming a confident human being.

      The Ascendant and 1st house therefore describe your initial unconscious and impulsive reaction when you're confronted with life events. It shows how you react instinctively and without thought. It's also freedom, the freedom from restraint like a baby birthed into this world. It can also indicate your birth experience.

I'll relate my own birth experience: this is also related in my book on the Twelve Houses but I will include it here to emphasis just how powerful the 1st house is.

I have a Capricorn Ascendant, and just 3° away sits Chiron, the Wounded Healer. My mother told me that it took her three days to give birth to me, each time she went into labour it would soon stop. I never gave this much thought, I just didn't want to enter this crazy world, who would?

In my twenties I tried a new-age therapy called Rebirthing. I remember lying on the soft futon and being directed to perform a simple cyclic breathing exercise which dropped me into a light trance and then into my unconscious. I found myself holding and squeezing cold, steel prison bars - and I was being squeezed to death. I could feel the contractions squeezing the life out of me. I had to get out, immediately! I was distressed and overwhelmed from the exertion of trying to get through those cold, steel bars.

My little body was being crushed by each contraction. I felt hot, frustrated, and panicky I was so desperate to escape. I then knew I was fighting for my life, if I stayed there, I would die.

That birth experience had stayed with me, unconsciously, inside my body, so well hidden that I had no idea it was there. Whenever I felt trapped or had to physically struggle I became frustrated, hot, and panicked. I would force my way through this invisible barrier to get to the other side regardless of the consequences, it felt like a matter of life and death and it overwhelmed me.

Maybe this explains why I've always been so determined to continue to transcend consciousness, to go beyond this physical existence. Maybe this is why I live in the borderland of life and death in my meditations, my dreams and in my work with patients and students. Maybe this is why I called my business Pluto's Cave, that place where I still have one foot firmly placed inside the underworld.

Now I know why I take others into their inner world, beyond consciousness, because I nearly died at childbirth. This is just a theory but it fits my loaded and powerful 8th house which contains Sun conjunct Pluto, Mars, Venus and Jupiter.

One side of Capricorn is his ability to restrain, frustrate, hold back, limit and build tension, this was my birth experience. Chiron is the teacher of psychological anguish and he represents my wound. I had to experience it, learn from it and use this knowledge to heal myself and others. Chiron reveals how close I was to dying, his gift was my psychological wound and my desire to transcend consciousness.

To illustrate how powerful our birth experience can be I started to astral travel almost every night when I began to tap into my inner world practising tai chi. Tai chi taught me to move and manifest my life force. Pluto and the 8th house are aligned with this life force, and Chiron conjunct the Ascendant is all about healing that life force. All of these became personal significators for stepping into Pluto's Cave, the deep unconscious and transcending this existence to embrace life and death.

The 1st house can be tough, for me it combined the limits and structures of Capricorn with the anguish and suffering of Chiron in Aquarius. My first few years were tough (very tough) but educational for my soul. It helped form specific psychological programs (belief systems) that led me along my path to study, teach and heal.

Significance of the 1st house

The 1st house is the beginning of your life journey, it shows the zodiac sign pointing to the Eastern Horizon (Ascendant) right at the moment of your birth. Think about it as you read that sentence again, *right at the moment of your birth*. That must hold some significance mustn't it? Your Ascendant and 1st house most certainly are significant.

The 1st house is the first step on your journey of life. Planets moving from the 12th house above it, which is the last house of the 12 house cycle, enter the 1st house. As the planet moves into the 1st house it is now reborn into the start of a new cycle, a beginning, it's actually a birth or rebirth.

Now do you see why the 1st house cusp is so important? It is an ending and a beginning, a rebirth of every planet that moves through your chart. Every month the Moon will cross it, an ending of one cycle and the beginning of a new one. Once a year Sun, Mercury and Venus will cross it ending one cycle and starting a new one. Every two years Mars will cross it, you can see where I am going with this can't you.

When you study **Progressions**, both **Secondary Progressed** and **Solar Arc Directed,** you'll see another reason to go back to your Ascendant and 1st house to study it over and over. *Each house has the same sequence: they all begin with their **cusp**, it's that line which separates it from the house before it. There is always a sign of the zodiac sitting on the house cusp.* When a planet crosses the cusp it triggers something inside you, something within your psyche related to that house, it's cusp sign and it's ruling planet.

Some houses are more significant than others, and this is the trick of delineation, knowing what to examine in great detail and what you can leave to examine later when you have more time. Doing a full delineation will take a professional astrologer at least two full days, sixteen plus hours - and that's just the natal (birth) chart. That's just to know you, your personality and psyche requires an enormous amount of work. A professional astrologer who has studied astrology piece by piece, element by element, knows how to start and where to start. They can then walk themselves through your chart to maximise their time and to extract every scrap of valuable information available.

You have no doubt read some of my readings on the forum (astrologersforum.com) and wonder at how I am so accurate, well, now you can stop wondering. I focus on specific areas of the chart I know will give me immediate feedback and insight into the personality of the person I am reading for. I couldn't do that for many many years, but after reading thousands of charts and devoting my life to the study of everything astrology, psychology and the esoteric it mostly comes naturally to me now.

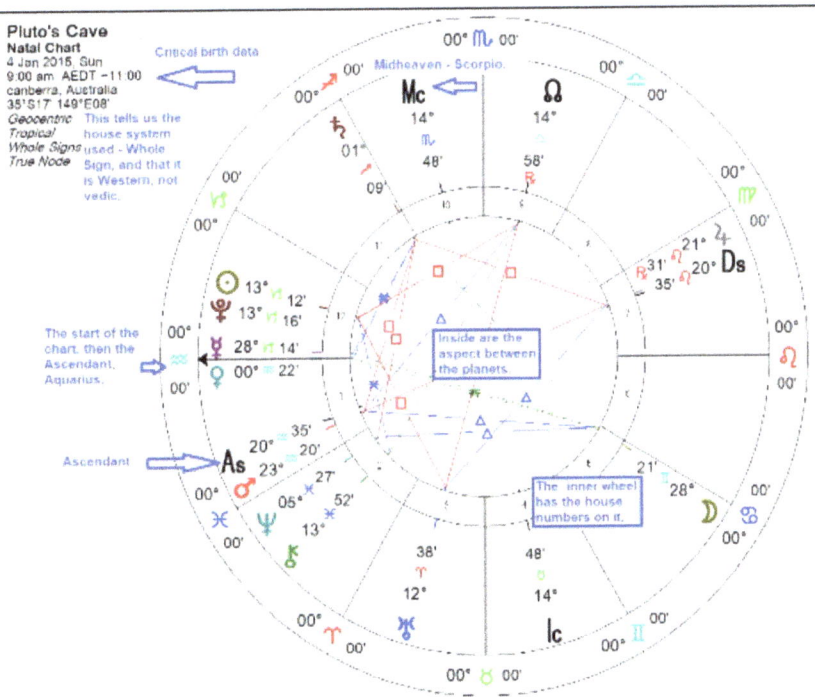

The methods I teach, like the **4 Key Point Method,** provide me with an accurate snap-shot of the person's psyche. If I wanted to I can then dig deeper and deeper into the chart, step-wise, like an archaeologist. I'll then work through the houses, the elements, the planets and the signs in greater depth. When I find something of value I'll carefully dig around it, look at the associations it has with the rest of the chart and link it in with the other gems and gold nuggets I uncover.

But don't think it was easy or that you'll be able to do this tomorrow. I had to earn the right to see into a person's psyche and I was fortunate to have learned some short cuts along the way. That's why I teach, to show you what I've learned, how to trim the fat off the bone and keep the meat.

But enough of me and back to the story of life through the houses. I want you to think about how each house explains certain facets of your own chart and therefor your life. To help you understand this lesson I'll use the number and type of planets in the house described. For now I'm using the **Pluto's Cave chart.**

1st house: birth, delivery and your first 2 years of life.

Please note that I use the Whole Sign House System, each house starts at 0° of each sign and ends at the end of the sign. The 1st house is always the Ascendant sign.

In the Aquarius sign are: Venus, and Mars is conjunct the Ascendant. Baby **Hades** (that's what I'll call the Pluto's Cave chart) has Aquarius as his Ascendant (also called the Rising sign) and this tells us that he is electric, dynamic, easily excited and uniquely interesting. He is also a worrier because he is going to process life through the lens of Aquarius, the electric intellectual mind which is much faster and more abstract than it's Air friends: Mercury, Virgo or Gemini.

How does Aquarius influence Hades' story of life? His birth and first few years of life? It shows that his first reaction is to process intellectually, through this electric life-field with Venus right on his cusp and Mercury right next to it. He'll process information rapidly and differently too looking for angles and ways to leverage information.

Do you know anyone with a strong Aquarius or Uranus in their chart? If you do then you'll notice that they come up with unique ways of viewing the world. Their world is one of possibilities and experiences that others have yet to realise. These people come to realisations and insights way before everyone else. They are our problem solvers, trouble shooters and just know how to use information and insights - they just know.

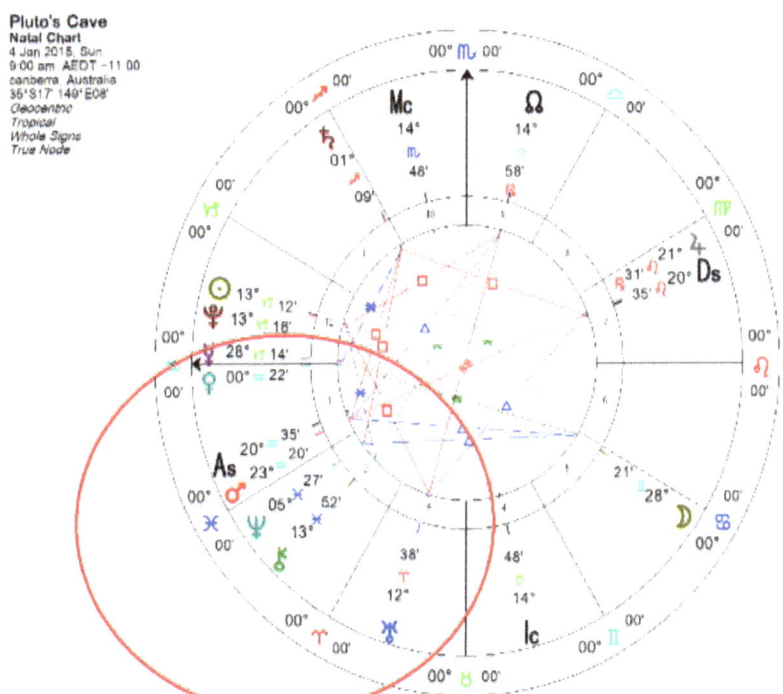

If we extrapolate the above information on Aquarius we know that young Hades entered this world rapidly, intuitively, and uniquely. There may have been bleeding because Mars is sitting right below the Ascendant in the 1st house but Venus has helped make it an easy delivery. Mars is another sign of speed and action, now we have confirmation of what Aquarius suggests - speed and action though it's intellect, not always physical as Mars suggests.

Hades could also have an awareness of himself from a very early age, separating from his mother's aura and psyche without too much difficulty. He is unique in that way, he is himself, but sometimes Aquarius can get lost in his own world. This is not really the case with Hades, I don't see that highlighted anywhere in his chart so we can possibility cross that off the list.

Birth is seen in the 1st house cusp, Ascendant and any planets within a few degrees. I'll use an orb of 3-5 degrees and can see that Venus and Mercury are right on the cusp. So Venus and Mercury are within orb of the 1st house cusp. Mercury is in the 12th house but it is so close it will soon be in the 1st. It is therefore 'out of sign' but within orb of the cusp. Mars is sitting just below the Ascendant and adds speed and blood. I would say that birth was fast, bloody and with lots of love. It also suggests he was a restless, nervy and fairly active baby too. He probably learned to walk and talk early, as well as an ability to talk freely and make friends. It is also likely that he gets along with young females and his mother.

The first thing he did as a small child was reach for the TV remote control, and any video games that made their way into his little hands. He no doubt fell over a lot, had lots of bruises and scratches, fell out of trees and off tables and cupboards, there may have been broken bones too. Insatiably curious? Yes, he no doubt got into some strange and difficult situations, then discovered how to get out of them all by himself. An adventurer in the making with his Mars, Venus, Mercury and Aquarius combination.

One last comment on the 1st house: each planet residing in the 1st house has aspects, those lines joining them to other planets. Venus sits right on the cusp and aspects Moon by quincunx, an aspect that comes and goes, not a major aspect but one that will be annoying. Then there is the sextile to Saturn which is a Generational planet and one that is reasonably good for such a strong individual person. Next there is that lovely conjunction between Venus and Mercury. It is not very strong because planets in the 12th house can be quite weak. Mars is square Saturn and shows structure as well as frustration which is reinforced by his opposition to Jupiter; Mars trine Moon and North Node suggests a nice flow of energy with older females, mothers and society. So Mars is a bit of a mixture with hard aspects to Saturn and Jupiter.

We would consider these aspects in our consideration of the first 2 years of life, particularly the first few months which the 1st house tends to favour.

Rulerships – Venus rules Libra and Taurus which are on the 4th and 9th cusps. The rule is that Venus will draw them into her house. So, the 4th and the 9th houses are drawn into the same house as its ruler, Venus, which is also in the 1st house. It shows that Hades will find that his home and mother, plus the future, travel, law and religion, are his strong points.

Mars rules Aries which sits on the 3rd house cusp and suggests Hades thinks rapidly and is an active processor of information. Perhaps he has some argumentativeness, and he enjoys standing up for himself verbally. Maybe you can add to the delineations yourself? You can do that and see what you come up with.

2nd house: from 2 to 4 years of age, learning about security and preschool.

Pisces sits on the cusp of the 2nd house, Pisces is ruled by Neptune and Neptune sits in the 2nd house - which is very convenient. We could say that Hades infancy is sometimes insecure, sometimes he feels alone and abandoned. There might be periods of temper tantrums and that would fit in with the Martian 1st house and the Aries 3rd house. Chiron does not rule anything, so it isn't included in these rulerships.

When we look at the two planets in the 2nd house, Neptune and Chiron, we have to consider them in light of Hades psychological make up. Remember, anything in the 2nd house is related to possessions – spiritual, emotional, and material. Neptune tells us that he can sometimes get lonely, sad and emotional, but this is only sometimes, not all the time.

Neptune is nicely trine Moon which shows a capacity to love, true love; and a square to Saturn which is generational which adds a level of frustration, but that is minor compared to the Mars square. Chiron has a nice sextile to Sun and Pluto and a quincunx to the North Node which suggests learning through giving and sharing with others. Chiron tells us that he may feel trapped at times, trapped emotionally.

You've heard of the terrible 2's and the terrible 3's? Well Pisces on the 2nd cusp will help to mollify this period of life. Even though the 2nd house is security Pisces will be bothered, just a little, by insecurity. His 1st house does that well enough but when it comes to the 2nd house he'll not really want massive collections of toy cars or Lego. He won't really be fussed by money or keeping things. As an infant he'll grab everything and hold on to it, that's the Mars in her 1st house, but by the time he enters and settles in the 2nd house as a 2 to 4 year old he'll be able to share and let things go quite easily.

3rd house: learning and communicating, exploring the world, early school years, kindergarten and early primary school, 4 to 7 years.

Aries on the cusp, ruled by Mars suggests that he will be quite vocal, and by vocal I mean noisy, chatty, verbal tantrums, yelling and screaming. *"Now that's just great!"* say his parents.

But the other side of the coin, in every facet of astrology there are two sides that shows he will be a fast learner, smart, clever and intelligent. He has a sharp mind and he'll pick up reading and literacy easily. It's possible that he learns foreign languages easily as well with Uranus sitting in the 3rd house. Aspects to Uranus are: opposition to North Node, a square to Sun and Pluto, and a trine to Jupiter. The Jupiter trine is nice as it switches the tension causes by the square to Sun and Pluto into something more enjoyable. The aspects with Pluto and Sun will be a challenge as they cause him to interrupt his responsibilities with the T-square with North Node and Uranus.

His time in kindergarten and early primary school will be robust to say the least. Little Hades will no doubt join every sports group and team he can get his hands on. He'll excel at rough and tumble activities and be the first to the water fountain and tuck shop when he's let out of class. He'll be competitive and dynamic, active and alert and his hand will be up with the answer driving his teachers mad with his accurate answers. The teachers will love him, when he doesn't play up that is.

The 1st years of life - birth to 7 years
Try this little sentence:
House + sign on cusp + any planets inside the house = an astrology sentence about the 1st house.
Aquarius + Venus (+ Mercury, + Mars) = what this might mean

That is a simple recipe but needs a lot of practice because there are so many variables. When you first begin this method don't try to include aspects and rulerships, you'll go crazy. Stick to the basics until you get good at it.

Remember our basics?

Sign = HOW
Planet = WHAT
House = WHERE

Little Hades is quite a live-wire isn't he. He's active, noisy, adventurous and smart. He needs a lot of supervision and has elements of hyperactivity and impulsivity plus some inattention. We can see pointers in his chart that we will be watching for ADHD, (Attention Deficit Hyperactivity Disorder), namely the cusps of the chart which are Air and Fire which are in line for ADHD.

He'll throw big tantrums and want a lot of attention, he'll also need a lot of physical and intellectual activity to keep his mind occupied. He will probably walk and talk early and he would probably pick up languages easily. His birth would have been quick with a lot of blood, and with Mars in his 1st house we might consider it a rather traumatic birth.

In his early schooling Hades would prove to be a quick learner, smart and active, involved in everything he can get into. A great student who would make sure his teacher is busy in keeping up with his mental and physical needs. There appear to be some elements of ADHD and if that's the case lots of activity, sports and responsibility are needed.

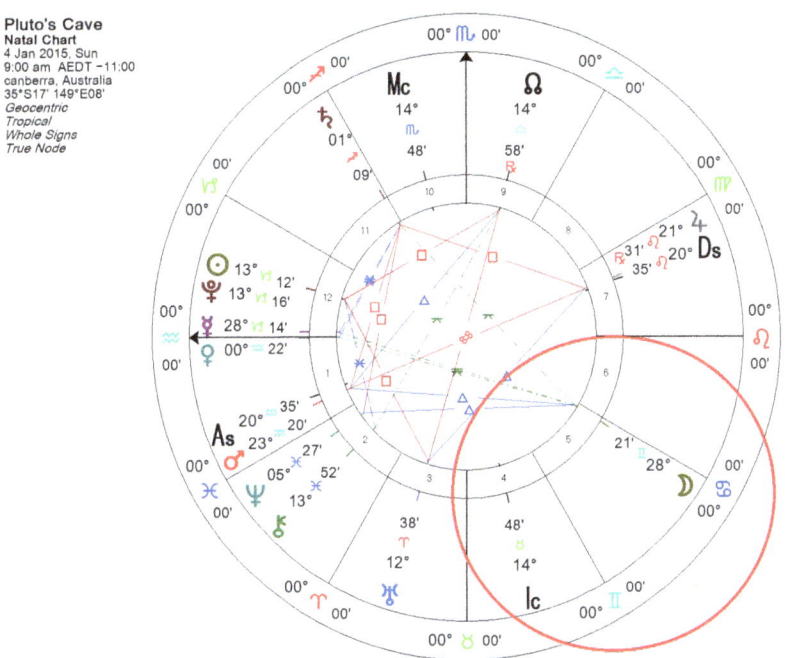

Houses 4th, 5th and 6th: early schooling to starting work, the education years

4th - when you become an individual, family conditioning and Primary School to early High School, I think it is also called Middle School in the USA.

5th - teenage years - as you learn about self-expression, identity, creativity and hobbies, discovering sex, and making friends.

6th - becoming aware of commitments and responsibility and take on a job, ending of childhood and entering adulthood.

4th house: when you become an individual, family conditioning, and primary school to puberty, to 12 years

Pull out your own chart again and I want you to quickly review your 4th house key words: home, family, society, early childhood, conditioning, mother and father but mostly the mother, upbringing, etc.

Now link the sign on your 4th house cusp and fill in your

keywords: house + sign + planet = ???
Blend the 3 together into sentences weaving a complex of traits and possibilities.

The 4th house shows how you were raised, what lessons you learned from your family members and the experiences of childhood. While the 1st house is childbirth, the 2nd house is 2 to 4 years and the 3rd house is kindergarten and the first few years of school, this 4th house shows your early school years.

This section, the 4th house, is designed to show the child turning from mother's skirt to the outer world to announce, "*Here I am world, let's do things.*"

You are now 7 years of age and you want to learn about what is beyond your mother, what about father's world: what is dad's life like?

Children generally spend their first 7 years continually returning to mother's protection and living through mother's expectations. By the time they reach their first Saturn square, around 7 years of age, they have grown more confident and are bursting to explore more of the wonders of the world beyond.

Little Hades has Taurus on his 4th house cusp and it's ruler, Venus is in Aquarius in the 1st house. Even though the 4th house is empty it doesn't mean it isn't active or
important. The sign of Taurus tells us that little Hades will enjoy school, he'll be quite physical and no doubt excel in sports and physical activities. He'll persevere with any task he is given even if it means he has to stay back after school to complete it. With Venus as it's ruler there is a chance that Hades will want to do a music class, study acting and drama, maybe art lesson and probably play in the band or orchestra. Whatever he does he'll do well.

As he moves into early high school he'll continue to be popular, active and enjoy his life at school with his friends and his studies. Taurus is a steadying sign, it's in the element of Earth and like the oxen, Hades will just get on with it. He'll put the yoke around his neck and no matter what task he'll just take each step as it presents at this age. He can be stubborn.

This is also a time of sexual development, puberty, when the individual discovers their sexuality and those bits and pieces of their sexual anatomy. This is the time of discovering the joys of masturbation and what it's like to feel sexual pleasure. It's also a time of extreme guilt and self loathing - of judging oneself against the sexual development of others.

When you think back to your experience of puberty you'll realise that this is an incredibly important period of discovery. Not only does it give pleasure but it also delivers emotional turmoil and distress. This is the age of judgement as we initiate the stage of **Identity Formation**. Who am I really? Am I attractive? Will the boys / girls like me? Will they love me? I'm attracted to both boys and girls so am I gay?

Your family mores and norms, those rules of the household set by your parents and religious rulers, now comes forward into your world like never before. It becomes the age of moral conflict, Freud's phase of challenging your Superego: "*Thou shalt not touch one's private bits! Thou shalt not masturbate! Thou shalt not think rude or impure thoughts!*" The impositions of our upbringing mould our future and our future includes what we teach our own children when we become parents ourselves.

The adolescent Hades has reached puberty, perhaps a little early because we know that Taurus is a sexual sign. He'll no doubt discover sex early, masturbate early and start to seek out girls or boys early. His sexual apparatus will probably develop well and he'll feel quite comfortable in his sexuality.

The Venus rulership throws a bit of a spanner though. Where is Venus? She's in the 1st house. What does Venus do there? She watches and then participates.

OK, now we have a fly in our ointment, Taurus on the 4th says one thing but Venus, his ruler, says another thing. It says that Hades is probably shy in company and so even though an early developer he may just be embarrassed by it. Getting undressed in the sports shed with the other boys could be quite embarrassing because he may be bigger and hairier than everyone else.

5th house: teenage years as you learn about self-expression, identity, creativity and hobbies, discovering sex and making friends.

Hades is now in middle high school and early college years as he struggles with sexual development and shyness. He so wants, no he needs to express his individuality and his sexuality but he's too shy to do it. But, something is here that can rescue him - Gemini sits on his 5th cusp! Gemini, the sign of the communicator, sits on the house of the show-off. His shyness slowly eases as he discovers that he can shine in his ability to express himself. He draws upon his Aries 3rd house and his Mercury in Capricorn in the 12th house.

Let's talk about Mercury. He is expression and mental activity and he is in Capricorn. What does he do in the 12th house? He is easily confused and tongue-tied. Oh dear, just when we thought he was coming out of his shell he starts to say the wrong things at the wrong time. That darn ADHD (Attention Deficit Hyperactivity Disorder) might kick in a bit here too.

This is a period of friendships, drinking alcohol, partying, drug experimentation and finding sexuality and relationships. Young Hades is playing in a band or he might be playing football for the school on the weekends, plus he is doing the drama program for the school eisteddfod. He probably has lots of friends and is a bit of a hero for his many successes in sports and study.

But girls, oh dear, he is still a little embarrassed and nervous with them. He has to get over it somehow so he chooses to talk his way out of it and of course alcohol helps him talk freely with everyone, especially girls. Now we see another side of life forming - his identity with his needs. In this case he needs friends of the opposite sex and he has an interesting sex drive.

Aquarius on the Ascendant tells us that sex is ambiguous - yeah no maybe. '*I like boys and girls but usually not really fussed at all*'. But when we add Mars to the 1st house at puberty he is now driven by an urge greater than Aquarius' ambiguity – lust. Gemini is asexual, too often driven to experience sexual pleasure with anyone of any sexual orientation. The Air signs like sex but it is for the intellectual stimulus it gives them. Other factors of course come into play because I can hear all those Air signs screaming at me.

NOTE: When I talk about the elements I mean 'types' - someone with a dominance in an element not just the Sun.

Young Hades has Moon in the 5th house and now I am going to make this a little more exciting for you. I hope that by the end of this you'll be able to do this with every house in your chart. Hades is now in his teenage years, he is excited about life, the joys of sex and friendships, and he is finally able to gain some level of independence and separation from his family and parents. In short he wants to get out and live a bit.

But, he has Moon in Gemini and on the cusp of the 5th house is Gemini. If you combine and apply the key words for 5th house + planet Moon + Gemini + teenage age years, what do you get? You can see that Hades struggles emotionally as a teenager; he wants so much to join his friends, socialise and have lots of friends. However, he is so very emotional (the Moon) and he needs to find ways to manage his emotions if he's to cope through those turbulent teenage years.

This sheds light on his teenage identity, this emotional, sensitive genius with a depth of shyness he is trying to shrug off – it probably causes him to turns to drugs and alcohol allowing him to do just that. I said 'probably'. The other side of the coin is that Hades gets through his identity years by using his mind and excelling at his studies, sports and music.

6th house: **you become aware of commitments and responsibility and take on a job, the end of childhood and entering adulthood.**

Hades struggles with his school years which are almost over and he begins to look towards making some money to satisfy his Aquarian and Martian needs, and what does he need, a car. To get a car he needs money so he starts working odd jobs - he's always restless because he gets bored too easily.

Hades finds that he's good at fixing other people's problems, computers, computer networks and he knows how to tune in a TV and to set up a mobile phone. He enjoys doing these jobs for his parents and his grandparents. Heck, he's even called up by family friends to come over and set up their sound system and plug in the printer to their computer.

Our young Hades discovers that there are courses he can do to become a computer technician and perhaps he might want to do some software programming. As he starts to make some money he next discovers that girls like him even more now he has a car. His mates revel in the attention he gets and embrace him in their own activities as they get him to drive them around. Now he has what he was after, a girlfriend, a car and a social group. He's still shy but his girlfriend helps with that.

How do we know his girlfriend helps his shyness? Ah, come on, it's his Moon in Gemini. He is attracted to girls who reflect his mother, his mother is Moon and she is in Gemini, and Gemini rarely get embarrassed. Cancer is on the cusp of his 6th house and its ruler is the Moon + his Moon is in the 5th house. His girlfriend is strongly represented here in his 6th house as well as his 5th through its rulership (Moon rules Cancer so Cancer is in the 6th house). You can also see that the house story of the 6th is primarily about Cancer = home, family and the Moon, fun and identity. We might even presume that around this time he has a child or gets married. If we extrapolate further, if he wants to have children and get married, he'll be needing a proper job as well. So now we have a circle forming a semi-ending and a semi-beginning, he is now half way through his 12 house cycle and becoming an adult.

The next question this process demands us to ask is: what about his career? Does the 6th house show us what he does for a living? What career is best suited to his personality and to his chart?

I don't know how many times I've been asked that on the astrology forums, short answer... there is no short answer because as you have noticed by now the clues to his personality and interests are spread throughout his chart. But, what did we discover about him in his 1st house? That tells us a lot about his future interests. Sure he may never grow up to be an astronaut but he'll probably send someone to the Moon with his skills, talents and drive.

What about the 6th house? It's supposed to be the house of career isn't it? Well no, it's actually about diet, good manners and habits, self-discipline, determination, responsibility and dedication. Let me add some more words to this list: reliability, responsibility, application and devotion.

OK, so how do we determine someone's career as a story? To be honest, we don't, we need the whole chart to see that, sorry.

Houses 7th, 8th and 9th: family, parenthood, public eye, philosophy and transformation years.

7th - beginning of adult life, you now enter in legal relationships, moving into the public arena and announcing yourself as a part of society through marriage, working and business.

8th - late 20's to 30's with a young family, the turning point of being a parent showing a return to your family of origin and recognising how your own parents must have felt, a reversal and recognition, the crisis of being a parent with the realisation that you have the power to influence your evolving infant, the spiritual dance of chaos and transformation.

9th - 30's to 40's the children are growing up, going to college and university, some are leaving home as you turn from financial and familial responsibilities to exploring the philosophies of life that you had put on hold while raising your family, a coming of age.

7th house: beginning of adult life, you now enter in legal relationships, moving into the public arena and announcing yourself as a part of society through marriage, work and business.

Hades has now entered and is participating in society and his community. His wife has drawn him closer to her family and his shyness is easing. His work has put him through study courses and his work skills continue to develop. He now has a child and another on it's way but he's still the excitable, introspective yet hyperactive child inside.

The 7th house has Leo on it's cusp and the planet Jupiter is sitting 1° above the 7th house cusp. So what planet rules Leo? It's easy, the fiery Sun of course. So here young Hades has met the community at last. He can no longer hide behind his girlfriend, sports, friends, his car and his interests - he has to confront his fears of being in the public eye. Of course he has Gemini Moon and the attention seeking 5th house, which incidentally, is ruled by what planet? The Sun.

Why is there so much emphasis on Fire in his chart? Let's examine this in some detail:

Mars 1st house = Fire
+ Moon in the 5th house = Fire
+ Jupiter in an Angular House (7th house cusp) and in Leo = Fire
+ Leo on the cusp of an Angular House (the 7th house) = Fire

"But," I hear someone say, *"Hades also has Aquarian Ascendant and that's Air plus his Moon is in Gemini and that's Air too while the Moon herself is Water."*

Aquarian Ascendant = Air
Mars and Venus in Aquarius = Air
Moon in Gemini = Air (yes Moon is Water but I give it weight as Air more than it's Watery element here).

"But," I hear someone say, *"Hades has a Capricorn Sun and that's Earth, if he's a Capricorn doesn't that make him an Earth sign?"*

Hmm, didn't you study my free course on Psychological Astrology where you would have discovered that astrology is not just Sun signs? The Sun is just one of many points in the astrology chart. Yes, the Sun is important, but so too are all the other points in the chart. Go back to the importance of the elements, that is what I use so much – the elements.

To be fair Hades is a Fire fellow who also has plenty of, Air, but only a little bit of Earth and Water. The elements provide us with an enormous amount of information about the individual. What do you think the above information means? What does all that Fire mean? Or all that Air? And why did his psyche give him an Earth Sun?

With so much Air and Fire in his chart Hades needs as much Earth and Water as he can get to ground him and make him presentable to his community.

In our Story of Life the 7th house it tells us about Hades' relationships. Ah ha, now we know who he loves and all about his marriage and his lovers and... sadly no, it doesn't tell us everything about his love life.

The 7th house is about those people who come into his life to teach him be it girlfriends, customers, clients, patients, lovers, the service provider for his telephone, you name it it's there in the 7th. It's like a doorway to the world (7th house) learning through others. The 1st house is learning through oneself.

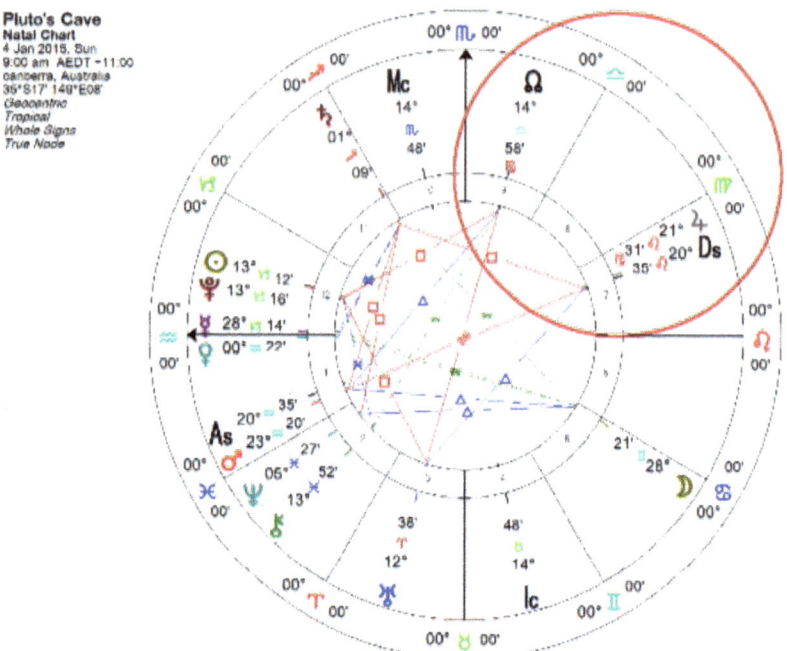

We would say that Leo on this cusp indicates he travels through this phase of life lightly, generously and happily. He sheds sunshine and happiness where ever he goes. His customers love him and his workmates love him. He is jovial and he also attracts jovial types and we all know that Jove is Jupiter. See Jupiter sitting there on his 7th cusp? It tells us that he is larger than life in the eyes of those who are drawn to him.

His wife, of course, is very similar to his 7th house, but then his friends are too even though we have to include details from his 5th house to better describe his friendships.

This phase of entering and establishing himself as a member of his community is critical and from the placement of Leo on this cusp and Jupiter in the 7th we know he will be successful. Jupiter in Leo and Leo on his 7th cusp shows very positive communication with 'others'.

We need to check Jupiter's aspects / relationships to the other planets first though, so let's have a look now. Jupiter is opposite Mars = *people annoy me and I get into arguments*. So, now we see some discomfort in his engagement with his community.

Saturn is square Jupiter suggesting some minor frustration which

I see as the pull-me-pull-you animal from Dr Doolittle. Sometimes things don't move in the direction he wants them to, they stay still, so a little more frustration perhaps. This may manifest as frustration at the lack of progress in his career and with those he depends upon. Jupiter trine Uranus suggests when he is engaged with inspiring and eccentric individuals, they make him excel and feel enthused by them.

These aspects to Jupiter sitting on his 7th cusp suggest that Hades sometimes feels annoyed with people's demands on his time and on his generosity. It also suggests that when he relies on people they sometimes let him down. It could also manifest as wisdom seeking, personal challenges and growth to learn from the interactions between himself and others.

No matter how awkward these aspects are to Jupiter, the Fire and Air still shine through. Sun is conjunct Pluto and is maintaining stability for the people he is in contact with. This shows he transforms those who come to him, those he is in contact with. His is a transformational 7th house because of these factors: Leo on the 7th cusp + Jupiter conjunct 7th cusp + Leo's ruler, Sun, conjunct Pluto in the 12th house.

In some ways he is dancing with others. His generosity is enormous, the Jupiter and Leo combined along with his Fire dominance suggests Hades is dynamic, charismatic and is a leader shining, like a beacon for his followers.

His entry into the community as an adult is dynamic, explosive and charming. He sometimes over-does it and then becomes distressed at the demands placed on him. But overall this is positive, showing he is certainly human and has human weaknesses.

Love and the 7th house
Love is something that comes up time and again in astrology readings and on the astrology forums. Like spirituality love is complex and needs to be synthesised from the entire chart not just one or two points. We look at Venus and Moon and the 7th house cusp but it is way more than just these three points.

Love is not just love, it's probably best described by the word '*nurture*'. To love is to nurture. The sentence: '*I love someone and I want them to love me*' is very close to this sentence: '*I nurture someone and want them to nurture me*'. The word '*nurture*' is a powerful and evocative word just as '*love*' is.

Your first love is your mother, for 9 months you are part of her. When you're born you continue to be nurtured at her breast. *Nurturing* therefore becomes one of your first keys to who you love and how you love. This is represented by your Moon, it's sign, it's house placement and any aspects it makes to the other planets. It is also seen in the 4th house. The Moon shows you how you nurture and how you like to be nurtured as well as how you nurture yourself.

The 7th house and the Moon make 'love' complicated especially when I've added:
(1) how you nurture others,
(2) how you like to be nurtured in return,
(3) how you nurture yourself.

Not many people are good at nurturing others or themselves but enjoy someone nurturing them. The Moon tells us a lot about nurturing and how you experience it. So too does the 7th house cusp and any planets residing within.

Venus is connections, it has a plus sign sitting on a circle ♀. The plus sign draws people to us and connects them, it's the network planet. We look for the sign Venus is in, its house and what planets are in aspect to it, particularly conjunct or opposite. Venus tells us about how you relate, how friendly you are, supportive, pleasant, rude, generous or selfish. Are you demanding in love or giving? Look at those key words though, there aren't many are they and they don't really describe love at all. They are mostly related to 'attraction' and 'connection'.

We have **Moon** as the nurturer, Venus as social attraction and connection, but where is true love? Where is your soul's partner? Ah ha, it's in the rest of the chart and that's where a professional astrologer goes to locate and delineate specific details about your love life. Of course, there are titbits to collect within the chart so don't despair.

The **7th house** is still extremely important in a reading of love, marriage and partners. To better understand the 7th house let me tell you about **romantic love** (more on Romantic Love in another chapter).

Romantic love is like a three legged stool, it's most stable when all three feet are firmly placed on the ground. Remove one and the stool is at risk of collapsing.

The **1st leg** is **Passion.** Passion is like a match, when it's struck into life it flares brightly for a few seconds then slowly burns down to finally turn to ash. A love affair is much like the match stick, it flares brightly, continues to burn while there's fuel (interest, affection, romance, money, good looks, lust). Once it runs out of fuel the flame is extinguished. Romantic love needs passion and passion needs fuel. Candlelit dinners, a weekend away from the children, romantic times together... these are powerful ingredients that can keep the spark of passion alive.

The **2nd leg** of the stool is **Intimacy**. Intimacy is best described as the quiet moments lovers spend together sharing their desires, interests, fears, needs and grand visions. New lovers spend a lot of time getting to know each other intimately. Intimacy is vital in keeping the stool of romantic love upright.

The **3rd leg** of the stool is **Commitment**. Commitment describes a long term relationship in which the partners stay together because they have committed to the relationship for one or for many reasons. It could be financial, it could be that affection and intimacy remains strong, it could be for the children, it could be for companionship, and it could be because they don't want to be left alone.

A relationship generally begins with Passion, it's intense like a bright burning flame. It settles down and the Intimacy gained during those passionate moments can hold the couple together. Finally, as the passion fades and intimacy turns to boredom or disinterest, commitment often becomes the leg that holds the stool upright, it's the glue that holds the couple together.

It's an interesting theory, Romantic Love, and one that you might consider in your professional counselling and astrology work.

Most people think of passion as love but it's just one facet. As you age your concept of love will shift and change shape, just ask an older person if you don't believe me. Where once passion was the centre-stone over time it dies off to be replaced by intimacy and then finally commitment. If you are lucky your three legged stool will keep all three legs intact - but it won't if you don't work on it. Romantic love takes time and effort, it should not be taken for granted.

So what, you ask, does this have to do with the 7th house? The 7th house describes the sort of person you are attracted to and the type of person whom you attract in turn. The sign on its cusp and any planets inside the 7th will also tell you about these three factors: your depth of Passion, your level of Intimacy and your ability to remain Committed.

The 7th house also tells you about your level, tolerance and desire for passion, intimacy and commitment. When reading a chart these three qualities can inform your client of what to expect from themselves and from their partner. Combining these three elements may help them make wise decisions in love.

But, the 7th house is not ALL about love, your entire chart is. Consider the 7th house to be about connections to better understand oneself, and what better way than through close love-based relationships?

Did you work out where this was heading? Yes? Good, you now know that the astrology chart contains information on all facets of romance and love, not just passion, intimacy or of commitment.

In summary the stage of starting a family, establishing yourself in work, and entering and committing to becoming part of the community, are seen in the 7th house.

8th house: late 20's to early 30's with a young family, the turning point of being a parent showing, the crisis of being a parent with the realisation that you have the power to influence your evolving infant, the spiritual dance of chaos and transformation.

Now we enter Hades' very own Cave, the deep unconscious. The 8th house is the house of transformation through crisis and as such precipitates Hades into his own hell and in Greek mythology that's the Underworld.

Hades is now in his late 20's to his early 30's and has discovered that being a parent has its highs and its lows. His dreams of passion, of success and ease, have been put in the attic along with his toys and his teenage fantasies. He has faced the world and succeeded through his journey of the 7th house with the support of his wife and her family, his clients and his customers, his friends and his workmates. He is successful but now he finds himself alone in his own hell which is the House of Transformation through Crisis – the 8th house.

Where the 7th house shows the engagement of Self with the outer world, the 8th house is the engagement of Self with the inner world. Now Hades has to face his demons, his fears, his joys and his reality. A confrontation with reality never leaves you unscathed or unchanged.

Now a family man, Hades is trying to manage his study, his career, long work hours, his financial commitments, plus his community commitments along with his wife and children's needs. Sadly he's lost himself somewhere in between. His health is suffering but more so is his passion for life, his libido and his joy for living. He's even begun to experience anxiety attacks and fits of depression. His nervous system, never all that relaxed at the best of times, is shot and he seeks to find a way to manage. He realises that he needs something more in life: he needs meaning, a reason to live and to push onward. In short, he is having an **Existential Crisis**.

At 30 years of age Hades seeks counselling and starts a meditation course along with some tai chi, yoga, rebirthing and all sorts of weird things in his pursuit of an **existential resurrection**. All through this period he is confronted by a need to challenge his loss of meaning, confusion and self doubt.

With consistent practice he begins to experience periods of time when he is silent within, he begins to relax in his meditations for more minutes than when he started, and he sleeps better too. Hades starts to have strange things happen in his dreams: he wakes up inside them and can interact with the people and environment, like he is a magician. When he tries to talk to others about it they think he's strange, this puts distance between himself and others. His intuition develops.

Hades has gone within his cave of the 8th house to explore his innate potential. His outer world however has to find a balance for these inner changes and he struggles with an increased sensitivity. He finds he needs more time away from others, his kids and wife as well. He can't handle crowds like he could before, and he knows too much about people that he begins to avoid them, to shut down his insights into them.

As Hades discovers himself he also begins to discover his family again. His personal insights reflect the insights he has about his upbringing, his parents and his own parenting. This is the house of crisis and each one becomes a lesson, he transforms his life through each crisis.

We can now see that as he enters the years of his late 20's and early 30's he had reached a crisis point, an **Existential Crisis**. This crisis precipitates change and growth but it can also break people. Hades was lucky, he had a solid foundation of insight and a desire to change, to learn and to explore. His natural curiosity led him to wander inside Pluto's Cave and beyond.

Astrologically he has Virgo on his 8th house cusp. Virgo is ruled by Mercury who resides in the 12th house in Capricorn. What this tells an astrologer is that Hades approach to crisis and transformation is methodical, dedicated and disciplined. He can draw upon his innate Virgoan and Mercurial talents to get him through the tough times.

It could swing the other way of course, the polar opposite to this Virgoan approach is head-in-the-sand and an obsessive methodology of Virgo. In other words he becomes bogged down by rules and structures, which can sometimes lack the flexibility of the other signs.

Mercury in Capricorn in the 12th house suggests that Hades thinks things through, deeply, slowly, cautiously and his approach is similar to Virgo's - slow and steady. The 12th house influence is to take it within first and check it out on himself before suggesting others follow.

Thus we see that Hades' passes through a transformative period of life, as we all do at the time of our **Saturn Return** which this period illustrates. He does it by applying his Virgoan characteristics. His helpers are Mercury and Pluto in the 12th house. They help by engaging him deeper in his inner world than most people.

9th house: 30's to 40's, the children are growing up, going to college and university, some are leaving home as you turn from financial and familial responsibilities to exploring the philosophies of life that you had been put on hold while raising your family, a coming of age.

Let's look at Hades 9th house, you will notice there are no planets, besides North Node, inside the 9th house, notice that Libra is on it's cusp. Now let's look at the life story for the 9th house: the children are growing up and leaving home as Hades begins to explore the philosophies of life that had been put on hold while raising the family, a coming of age.

While he travelled through his late 20's and early 30's Hades wrestled with transformation and coming to terms with the many barriers life throws in our way. Now, as he reaches his late 30's to 40's, his children have grown up and are in college and university, they have boyfriends and girlfriends, some have married. A new set of crisis arise as his home empties and he has to set new goals, a new direction.

He had already studied some of the philosophies of his tai chi, yoga and meditation system while in his 8th house sojourn. But, his studies, which initially led him inwards away from the world, now lead outwards and back into the world.

This stage of life is giving back some of what he has learned. He is teaching classes in tai chi, yoga and meditation and he's studying religion and spirituality for the pleasure of studying. The intensity of his practices have settled down and he enjoys debating his findings with others with similar interests.

Libra is ruled by Venus and she resides in the 1st house in Aquarius, this suggests that his approach to his study of the outer methods of spiritual practice are quite exciting. Rather than confront and bludgeon people with his new found knowledge he now seeks like-minded people to discuss his philosophy of life. His path now fits his 1st house Venus but nonetheless it is still radical which is more in line with the Aquarius side of Venus. This period of life is quieter, less crisis and more transformative that the doing which is the domain of the 8th house.

Oh, before we move on, the 9th house is the house of reckless, non-conformity and may contain some interesting little nuggets if he's not careful.

Houses 10th, 11th 12th: the fulfilment and twilight years

10th – 40's and 50' - you have reached your middle to late years, the peak of your career, your ambitions are now being realised at last, reaping the harvest of the past.

11th - now you're past your peak and dreaming of the future for yourself and humanity, 50's and 60's, becoming philosophical and expressing your wisdom to share experiences with your grandchildren.

12th - this is the last house, the completion of the cycle of life, death is around the corner and you're able to look upon life in a holistic manner with glimpses of the future after you have passed to the next stage of growth - preparing for rebirth into the 1st house to start all over again.

10th house - you have reached the peak of your career, your ambitions are now being realised at last, reaping the harvest of the past.

This is a critical age for Hades, how do we know this, because of the intense Scorpio sign sitting on his 10th house cusp. Let me go back to basics here. The 10th house is another Angular house which helps us identify your ambitions, achievements and goals. You may never fulfil your goals or ambitions but you will strive for them as best you can. Scorpio is intense, passionate and determined to achieve whatever goal Hades has set himself. He will strive passionately, intensely and he'll fight viciously against anyone or
thing that gets in his way. Scorpio is not intellectual, it is not physical force nor is it inspired imagination, but it is pure aroused passion.

Passion can be seen in many ways: vindictive, revenge, violence, love, ambition... the list is long. It tells us that when Hades reaches his middle years he will have basically achieved what he set out to achieve. But will he be satisfied? No matter what is sitting on the Midheaven or what planets resides inside the 10th house itself, we have clues to his crisis.

Hades' Scorpio Midheaven tells us HOW he reacts as he shifts into middle age. HOW does he react is also a function of the ruler of Scorpio, Pluto himself, who sits beside the Sun in the 12th house. We now draw this together and say that Hades reacts passionately by seeking to express his years of work, study and life experience through compassion. Alternatively Pluto, as ruler of Scorpio, will send Hades into a spiral of destruction – messy isn't he. Pluto like all planets has two sides of a coin. On one side he is powerful and somewhat jovial, on the other he is terribly destructive, like the atomic bomb he is know for. Hades just he has to survive through the destructive times to bring out the good in himself.

You see the 12th house is socially barren, it is the 'hidden house' and as such planets go there to rest, recuperate and bliss out as they process their sojourn of the past 12 houses. The conjunction of Pluto with the Sun generally shows compassion and sunshine, love and generosity. He could well be a very passionate philanthropist, generous with his time and money but well away from the spotlight. A person with planets in the 12th house can sometimes need someone to look after them.

If we take note of all the pointers in this house we could safely say that Hades will manage his middle years responsibly and generously but also passionately and in a controlled manner. If he can manage the stress that Scorpio puts him through he will become a nice grandfather.

11th house - now you're past your peak and dreaming of the future for yourself and humanity, you're in your 60's now and becoming philosophical expressing your wisdom and sharing your experiences with your grandchildren.

The age of the philosopher and Hades has Sagittarius on his 11th house cusp. He also has Saturn very early in that house which makes this house one of striving towards achievement of some sort.

Saturn resides in the 11th house and as such suggests wisdom with age. As Hades gets older he smartens up, cuts down on his hyperactivity and impulsivity but remains sharp of mind and spirit. It could also suggest that he becomes very traditional, set in his ways and a 'stick-in-the-mud' not shifting away from his set beliefs. In other words a boring old man.

Saturn, as God of Time, Cronus, indicates order and structure in the house it resides, and here we have him inside the 11th house. We could say that Hades has spent his entire life reaching for Saturn at the top of his chart. His approach to achieving his goals is methodical, logical, ordered and passionately structured. Not much fancy-free here but just down to earth, a hard grind day-in-day-out.

We also look at Scorpio and its passionate desire to achieve all things in striving for its goals. Each step would be structured and its achievement would be with great passion. Saturn is the Planet of High Degree and as such it flies over the rest of the chart. It plays out not only as focal point to the T-square (Mars – Jupiter both squaring Saturn), but as one of the chart rulers.

Sagittarius is the sign of wisdom in its highest form, dynamic, driven and excited, it is perhaps also the sign of 'youth' in our old age.

We would say that Hades waxes lyrical whenever he has an audience. He would sail though his 50's and 60's as someone who enjoyed giving generously of his time and knowledge. He's gone through the boring years of his 40's with Saturn, which sometimes took control, and he was rather inflexible.

We now look at the ruler of the 11th house cusp sign, Sagittarius, and can see Jupiter, the ruler of Sagittarius, is in the 7th house, right on the Descendant to be precise. We know that Hades in his later years will be philanthropic, generous with his time and knowledge but it appears, by this rulership, that he will open up to humanity, but more so to those he is close to. That would be his 7th house, his lovers, his friends, customers and clients. The 11th house is general, the 7th is more specific. But he has both houses highlighted here so we would simply say: as Hades reaches his later years he becomes a happy old man, chatting away freely with anyone who sat long enough to listen.

12th house - this is the last house, the completion of the cycle of life, death is around the corner and you're able to look upon life in a holistic manner - preparing for rebirth into the 1st house to start all over again.

This is the house of the unconscious, the mystical underworld quite different to the 8th house of Pluto's Cave. For me personally the 12th house is both cave and lots of mist. The cave is a resting place for the archetypes, they come here to rest. They recuperate and come to terms with the 360 degree cycle of their existence in my psyche. The mist represents the lack of vision, seeing into the future which is what we all want.

I do have a planet residing in the 12th house, the North Node. The North Node is not a planet as such but it is a point in the chart that we consider a planet, it is the planet of the compass, it points the way for us.

Traditionally astrologers view the 12th house as unexpressed archetypes, instincts and urges. The 12th house holds and hides things, secrets, and it's also known as the house of prisons, hospital stays, dreams, intuition and nightmares. Anything to do with restraint and loss of freedom.

I try to read it in many ways because in terms of the whole chart it can mean different things. In one chart it will mean unexpressed urges and inhibitions, while in another it contains archetypes waiting to be expressed. In a third chart it tells me of urges and instincts at rest or being expressed but more subtly than if they were in any other house.

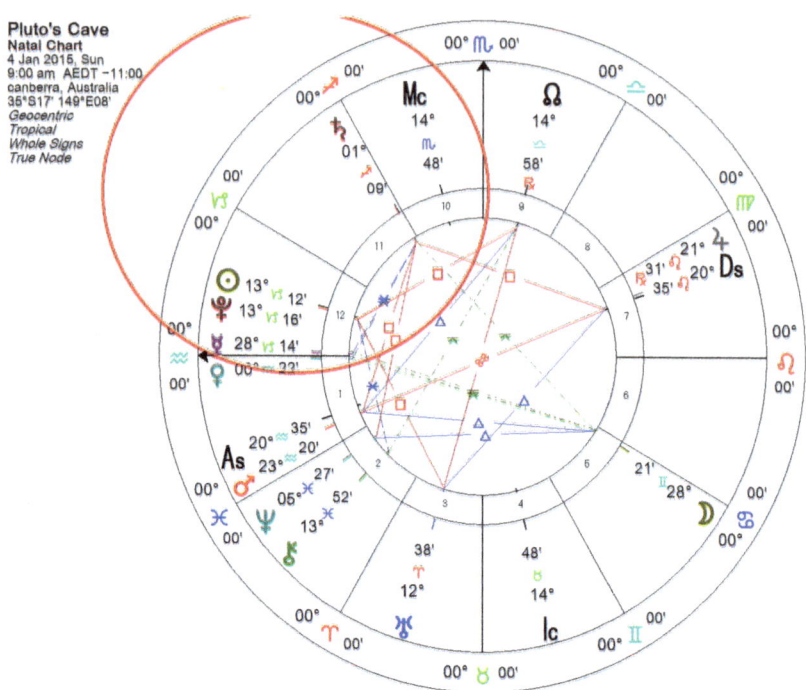

I work with people who have inhibited urges, strengths and weakness originating in their 12th house. I guess that's the way the 12th house is, unconscious and therefore quite unfathomable. This 12th house in our story of life through the houses represents how we come to terms with those urges and instincts that we did and didn't do, and come to express them before out lives are finished. It is our rejoices and our regrets.

Sometimes we need to repress our urges and instincts. Sometimes we need to dig deep and uncover and use them, to bring them into the light of day. These are often the archetypes associated with our 12th house, but not always of course.

In Hades chart we notice Capricorn on his cusp and Capricorn is ruled by Saturn in the 11th house. This tells us that Hades needs to express that which resides within his 12th house cave. Why do I say that? Because Saturn, who rules the 12th house through Capricorn, is sitting right on his 11th cusp: *"I strive to achieve consciousness of my 12th house urges and instincts."*

Do you see how I came up with this sentence? 11th house is goals and achievements for the environment and humanity and Capricorn is ambitions and reaching upwards for something = to strive.

Saturn in the 11th and Planet of High Degree is expressing three things: (1) his own needs as Planet of High Degree; (2) Capricorn's needs; (3) therefore he expresses the 12th house itself.

Complicated, I know, but if you want to be an astrologer you need to learn these things. Maybe not today or next week but if you practice what I teach you, in time it will come to pass.

Hades is driven to express Capricorn, Saturn and the three planets residing within the 12th house, Sun, Pluto and Mercury. But now we have a hitch, can you tell me what it is?

Hint: the 12th house is hidden deep within Hades psyche, it is his unconscious, his underworld, a place of myth and legend. Remember this entire series of lessons is about a 'Narrative' or story of your life and in some charts the 12th house is that story. Remember I told you earlier that I view the 12th house as a resting place, a cave where the planets / archetypes go to rest and recover what their purpose is in the present cycle of life and the next? Some planets can be expressed easily, only dropping into the 12th house for a snack and a nap. Other planets never leave the security of their 12th house cave.

Personal planets, like Mercury and Sun with Pluto riding piggy-back, demand expression, they'll go out of their way to be noticed. If Hades doesn't allow **Mercury** out to play in his consciousness often enough he'll probably create nightmares, disturbed thoughts and obscure his thinking when he wants to write, study or explain things.

Sun and Pluto: if Hades doesn't let these hidden urges and instincts out of his 12th house cave he will draw people to him who make him express them - usually this is painfully so. They will make his life miserable and depressing, lonely and boring. Sun and Pluto are enormously powerful, so powerful that the need for secrecy can be paramount. Sun has Pluto stuck to him, at the same degree, and he can access Plutonic energy in everything his does. They are also the focal point of a T-square between the Outer planet Uranus, and the non-planet North Node, which can screw up his compass.

OK, how does Hades live the final years of his life and come to terms with death, endings and rebirth? How does he approach death? Is he going to be afraid? Will he go gladly into the next cycle of existence? Will he turn to religion? Will he try to buy off the Grim Reaper and demand he live forever? Will he kick and scream as he passes through the curtain and crosses the River Styx?

They sure are good questions and the clues are clearly there in the chart.

Capricorn: perhaps he will seek an orthodox religious path to the other side and go to church daily praying for his soul to pass quietly and without him noticing. Perhaps he will prefer a traditional funeral and so both orthodoxy and tradition rule his ending and passing. I'd say that even though he has Aquarius on his Ascendant he will seek an orthodox funeral, that's exactly what a traditional Capricorn would want - order and structure.

Mercury: he will want to read up on the end of days, what is it like? Is death really the end or is it the beginning? What do people who have had near-death experiences say about the other side? He'll be curious and want to know all about it.

How will Hades die? That's the million dollar question and no one really knows. Some people will dream it, some will see a vision of their death, some don't care, and some have died so many times it just doesn't matter. I've had many many lifetimes and seen some, and I have experienced my death in some of them. How will I die? At this stage I have no idea and I'm not really all that interested. I suppose if I really wanted to I could spend a lot of time and energy trying to find out, but seriously, why bother?

So in summary the 12th house is one of concealment and expression, but it's an expression in small doses for a purpose, not just for the sake of expression itself.

~

Chapter 2: The 4 Key Point Method of Chart Delineations

This is a quick reading method that gives you the keys to the chart.

The 1st Key is the Sun

The Sun and Moon are called the Luminaries and as such they are high up on the food chain of your planets, in fact they are the pillars of human consciousness representing your father and mother archetypes. Just think of these two planets (yes we call them planets just to make it easy) as generalists as well as specific energy forms in your unconscious.

There is a simple reason we need parents, they provide the foundations upon which you grow as an individual. You can learn many things from family members, cousins, neighbours and baby sitters but your mother and father give you something else. There's an entire field of psychology based on these very important relationships between child and parent, it's called **Attachment Theory**.

Attachment basically says that when a parent attaches to their child, they build bonds and form relationships or networks to support and lift the growing individual upwards through life. Those foundations of love, acceptance, belonging and affection are necessary components for a future of happiness, self-management and self-control.

Parents can sometimes lack personal boundaries in such things as over-indulgent behaviours, drug taking, over eating, poor health habits and unbalanced personal habits. These set up their child's future ability to manage their own boundaries in life.

The **overly permissive parent** gives in to their child's whims and creates a similar impact on their household with no boundaries. These are due to the parents poor psychological health amongst many other factors. Teaching a child boundaries, consequences and rewarding appropriate behaviours allows the child to learn to manage their own frustrations later in life.

This is important so let me give you an example. Mid-last century psychologists did what is now known as the **Marshmallow Experiment**. A small child was shown a marshmallow on a plate while chatting with the therapist, usually a psychologist. The therapist then explained that he had to leave the room for a moment. He explained that if the child could just hold off from eating the marshmallow then when the therapist came back he'd give them a second marshmallow.

Of course some kids ate the marshmallow as soon as the therapist left the room, but some didn't and waited for the reward. These children could put off their needs for instant gratification until the therapist returned some time later.

These children were then tracked throughout their lifetime and guess what was the outcome? Those children who ate their marshmallow, the one's who gave in to their need for instant gratification, were more likely to have less secure jobs, they had more divorces, less satisfactory relationships and friendships, less wealth, and poorer health. Those children that managed to delay their gratification and received a second marshmallow had a more gratifying life enjoying greater health, better relationships, fulfilling careers, etc.

Attachment theory holds that a child raised in a family where there are honourable and respectful parents with solid boundaries soon learned to control their own urges, instincts and drives. They learned self-control which is an essential facet of life. They also learned to manage their expectations, their frustrations, to set their own boundaries and to seek help when they needed it.

These qualities are founded on the Sun and Moon in the chart. A good astrologer can see these traits of self control, self management, boundaries, honourable and respectful parents, etc. It's not always only the Sun and the Moon though, we must first study all aspects of the chart.

First of all check out your Sun and Moon, locate their sign, house and then look at what aspects they form with the other planets. Of particular importance are the conjunctions and oppositions to any of the planets. I pay particular attention if they are residing in one of the Angular Houses – 1st, 4th, 7th, 10th. If the Sun or Moon are conjunct (next to) one of these cusps then even greater emphasis is placed on them.

Let's use the example chart below, Walt Disney, the famous cartoonist and animator who created the Disney company. We find Walt's Sun in Sagittarius, in the 4th house and conjunct (next to Uranus) and opposed by Pluto in the 9th house.

The chart already tells us a lot about Walt. Sun in the 4th house tells us that Walt is driven by his need to create, share and communicate with his family and the community he created at his Disney studios. Remember the 4th house is a Cancer house ruled by Moon and so Walt is living through that 4th house of 'family' by sharing his interests and passions with his 'family' be it writing, singing, drawing and movie making. Why else would he be making children's movies?

Born in Chicago in 1901, Disney developed an early interest in drawing. He took art classes as a boy and had a job as a commercial illustrator at the age of 18. He moved to California in the early 1920s and set up the Disney Brothers Studio with his brother, Roy. (https://en.wikipedia.org/wiki/Walt_Disney)

His Sun is in a Fire sign and in a Water house, we combine these to show that he is excited, inspired and driven (all Fire traits) to warmly share with those closest to him, his 'family' (Water traits). For someone with talent, passion and charm, and let's face it, Sagittarian's have charm by the bucket load, this single planet, the Sun, is already opening Walt's chart up to us. The Sun also rules Leo and the 5th house which is 'loaded' which means it has more than 3 or more planets in it.

Uranus is also in the 4th house conjunct the Sun. This is a highly significant placement. It means that Uranus is giving the Sun it's 'unique' qualities. These qualities include intuition, instinct, eccentricity, creativity, unique ways of problem solving and finding solutions, left-field insights and creative talents - every other trait and characteristic you can find in your keyword list for Uranus.

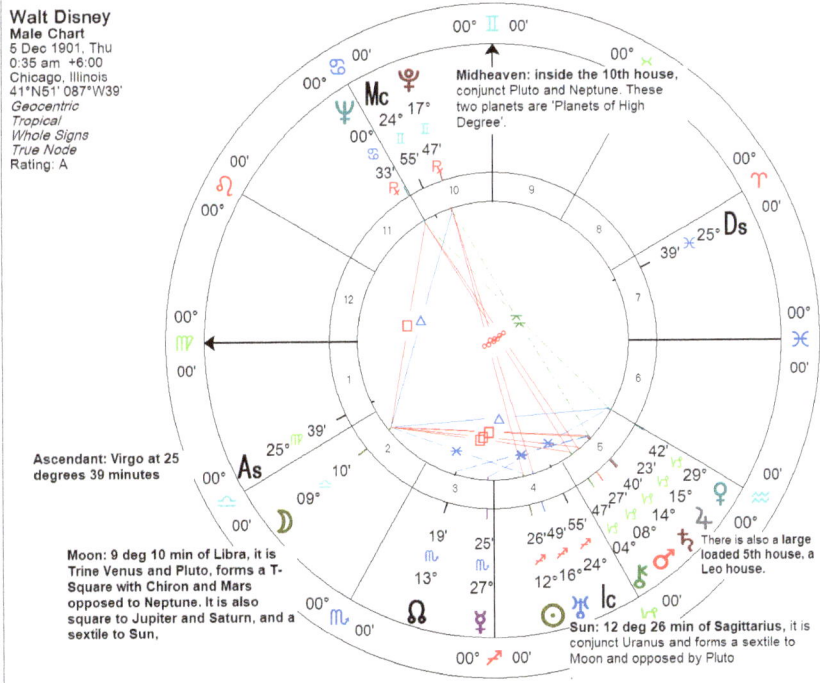

Complete with the loaded 5th house, we now know that Walt had some powerful qualities that would feature strongly in his successes. Imagine Walt sitting before us wondering if he made the right decision to follow his dreams. If other factors in his chart support our hypothesis of success we could safely tell this young man to go for it.

The Sun in the 4th house + Uranus + Sagittarius + his loaded 5th house all point towards a fascination with creating, technology, sharing his good fortune with others. His Uranus wants him to share in novel and new ways, like movies and television, both only recently invented, and he created new ways to present his creations to others. We could predict with the Uranus placed beside his Sun that Walt would be drawn to use innovative techniques to communicate his creations, his products. The Sun in Sagittarius and the loaded 5th house are also highly regarded for innovations and contributes to his overall creativity, especially in marketing.

First Theme: Walt Disney is supremely creative, artistic and has a need to communicate.

Uranus, psychologically speaking, is also a harbinger of stress, worry and excessive thoughts that can, so often, prevent sleep. Keep that in mind when you see Uranus powerfully placed in someone's chart. We could say that Walt would most probably have continuous creative thoughts running through his mind. He would have light-bulb moments all day long, and yes, Walt Disney did have insomnia.

Another facet of this Sun-Uranus conjunction is anxiety. Because his mind is racing continuously it can exhaust the nervous system causing a break down of sorts. Too much mental exertion, too much worry, too much stress can lead to depression and anxiety. Let it be known that Walt Disney was said to have suffered anxiety and depression.

Next we look at that single opposition to Pluto from the other side of his chart. Pluto is associated with death, conflict, doom and gloom, depression and power. It's also sometimes responsible for excessive fear, fear of others. Perhaps his anti-Nazi and anti-communism movies and propaganda during World War 2 were enlivened by this Sun-Pluto opposition.

Sun opposed by Pluto also suggests conflict, serious assault, abuse and violence. It also shows a fear of trauma inflicted upon them. They may have witnessed domestic violence as a child but were not assaulted personally. Having seen it, heard about it, or imagined it is enough to develop post traumatic stress. We would say that Walt probably projected his fear onto others and so avoided mixing too much with staff and outsiders which appears to be the case in his earlier films. Sun opposite Pluto is a common feature in bullies and the victim of bullies, it also contributes to episodes of depression.

These two outer planets, Uranus and Pluto, are keys to his mental health as well as his career and his expression of that powerful 4th house. All this information from just one single planet, the Sun.

The Sun in the elements
Although the Sun is in Sagittarius, it is also in one of the Water houses 4th, 8th, 12th, namely Cancer, Scorpio, Pisces. We would see that this person wishes to express themselves emotionally and needs to communicate this in any way they can. They might be a singer, songwriter, an artist of some type, they might write novels or poetry, and they love to talk about their creations. It is the topics they choose that counts and so his family-style movies show his combination of Sagittarius, Uranus, Pluto and the 4th house.

With the conjunction to Uranus, the **Sun in a Water** house tells us that this person may also experience episodes of being highly strung. They may need some down-time and require nurturing to keep relaxed and rested. Their mind will naturally want to race ahead creating a lot of stress. Relaxation, self hypnosis, meditation and coaching to make best use of his time (and his mind) would be valuable ways for Walt or others like him, to manage their stress, depression and anxiety.

Sun in an Earth sign (Taurus, Virgo, Capricorn) or houses (2nd, 6th, 10th) expresses itself in a more physical way, wanting to do things, act on things. They show dedication, discipline, structure, order, and self discipline. On the negative side it can manifest as hoarding, laziness, over-eating, obsessive compulsive behaviours, addictions to food, alcohol or sugar drinks. They can be boring and want the same old thing every time: same old drink, same old meal, same old TV show, etc. They like set routines, order and structure and don't do well when people change their plans without adequate warning.

Sun in an Earth sign or house suggests the person can be quite successful when they're supported to complete a job; or provided with structure and scaffolding in projects be it to clean their house, to complete a job or do the washing. It can fall down though if they become depressed. They can get stuck down there and be quite resistant to change.

Sun in an Air sign (Gemini, Virgo, Aquarius) or houses (3rd, 7th, 11th). Here we see the Sun shining in an intellectual way. They want to experience life as an extensions of their emotions (or lack of emotion). We look in particular for conjunctions and oppositions to the outer planets to see if there are emotional health issues in their make up.

Sun in a Fire sign (Aries, Leo, Sagittarius) or houses (1st, 5th, 9th)

is where Walt Disney shows some of his qualities. He shines in the 4th house with Uranus inspiring him. And 'shine' is a good word to use for the Sun in a Fire sign or house.

One thing I haven't mentioned yet is that the Sun also represents confidence and courage. Every element and planet plays its role in building confidence, self-worth and self-esteem. Yes, Sun does show us if this person has confidence but only as part of the picture, there are many facets in the chart that contribute to confidence.

The 2nd Key is the Moon

The Moon is the second Luminary but remember that we call them both planets just to keep it simple. The Moon represents your nurturing, your feelings and emotions as well as your social connections. From your free lessons on the planets you should already have a solid list of keywords to draw upon.

Begin by locating the Moon's sign, house and what aspects it makes with the planets. Of particular importance are conjunctions and oppositions to planets and if it's residing in one of the Angular Houses - 1st, 4th, 7th, 10th. If the Moon is conjunct one of these cusps then even greater emphasis is placed on it.

Walt Disney has Moon in Libra, in the 2nd house and its aspects are a trine to Venus and Pluto and there are squares to Mars, Jupiter, Chiron, Saturn and Neptune. This Moon, therefore, has enormous influence over the entire chart, for a number of reasons.

Firstly she is in the 2nd house and shows that it is focusing Walt's emotional energies on his empire, the Disney empire. The 2nd house is all about possessions and security, from finances to his family and its environment. Secondly she is the most strongly aspected planet in the chart. If we consider that the Moon is also a luminary and therefore a pillar of Walt's existence we now recognise we need to look deeply at how she is influencing him psychologically.

I would slow my reading down at this point because the Moon is obviously extremely powerful and busy with all those aspects. Humans are emotional creatures, just look at the decisions we make, can anyone argue that we are purely logical? That humans make rational and logical decisions? No, not at all, we are fiercely driven by the unconscious urges and instincts of our unconscious. We are emotional creatures through and through.

Moon in Libra is the social butterfly, everyone's friend, he wants the entire community to like her. Everyone Walt knows would say what a genial, nice man he was. He knew how to decorate a page and make it presentable, he had a flair for artistic design and presentation. He communicated well and made a career and a business in making people smile.

Libra is the sign of the peace-maker, someone who avoids conflict like the plague. We saw this in his Sun opposite Pluto so we now have two key points saying the same thing. He used a simple strategy to manage this theme - his executives performed any actions he was uncomfortable with performing himself.

Libra Moon can be moody though, she also has an incredibly active and flexible mind adapting and adjusting intellectually with what Walt sees in his mind's eye. Another aspect of the Moon is the feminine. Walt was apparently brought up in a warm family environment. It was reported his mother enjoyed reading stories to her four children. Not much to go on but we can easily see the incredible dominance of Walt's mother on his psyche by the presence of the Moon in his 2nd house. We might say that his mother dominates his chart and therefore his psyche.

Now I want to begin to pull apart this complex maze of information presented by this complex yet powerful Moon in Walt's chart: Moon in Libra. Yes, we know it represents harmony, seeks to avoid disharmony and conflict, and wants to compromise where necessary.

Moon in the 2nd house, is a powerful placement for any planet but especially for a luminary. It tells us how close the feminine is to his sense of 'self'. He needs a female close by his side to be able to emotionally feed his state of being. Is he feeling safe? Is he feeling comfortable in this house? Moon is family and so we see that in his wife and two children. This constant theme of family and wholesome happiness in the America way comes through in his movies, cartoons and his Disneyland theme park.

Moon rules Cancer and Cancer is on the 11th house cusp. This tells us that what he feels most personally is also what he wants for others, the hopes, dreams and wishes for humanity (11th house). This is how we use Rulerships in astrology, you can see this in action in my Coddiwompling Youtube series too.

Moon Trine Pluto and Venus:- now we need to examine the aspects to the planets and this is going to be rather difficult with so many aspects. We therefore need to become thorough and disciplined in our delineations.

Moon trine Pluto suggests an easy flow of energy, harmony between these two archetypes. It can suggest there was a strong bond of affection between he and his mother. Because the Moon also represents older women it suggests he got along well with older women and his wife. Pluto resides in the 10th house so we would say that the feminine presented opportunities to move forward in life. It could also suggest that he was strongly attracted to women.

Moon trine Venus, this is one of the aspects we commonly consider representing true love. We might surmise that Walt was more than capable of experiencing true love. He enjoyed being in love and felt comfortable loving others. This aspect shines in his movies, he felt comfortable with the concept of love in all it's various forms: friendship, love of animals, love between lovers, love of your parents and of spouses, etc. Venus resides in the 5th house so we could say that his lovers were also his friends and they contributed to his creativity. His wife is partially represented by his Moon.

Early in 1925, Disney hired an ink artist, Lillian Bounds. They married in July of that year. The marriage was generally happy, according to Lillian, although according to Disney's biographer Neal Gabler, she did not "accept Walt's decisions meekly or his status unquestionably, and she admitted that he was always telling people 'how henpecked he is'." Lillian had little interest in films or the Hollywood social scene and she was, in the words of the historian Steven Watts, 'content with household management and providing support for her husband'. Their marriage produced two daughters, Diane (born December 1933) and Sharon (adopted in December 1936). (https://en.wikipedia.org/wiki/Walt_Disney)

Moon square Neptune which is on the 11th house cusp which suggests what the native seeks in the world, the well being of its inhabitants, and the planet. We see a difficult relationship with his aspirations for success and that sometimes his sense of love and warmth for the feminine sometimes clashed with his desire to succeed.

Moon square Chiron - the wound, associated with the 5th house where most of his square aspects reside. This shows that he keenly felt the demands and struggles of family life and childhood, they can be painful. We see this in the themes presented in his movies.

Moon square Mars, Jupiter and Saturn in the 5th house - difficulty managing frustration and expectations from his family and his friends. When we say 'family' we look at every aspect of family. This includes his brothers and sisters, his parents, his extended family and relatives, his upbringing and his current family. It suggests that he wanted support but received 'conflicted support'. Sometimes it was great (Mars and Jupiter), sometimes it wasn't (Mars and Saturn). We might say that family and childhood themes in his movies contained some of the conflict and disharmony he experienced in his own life.

At the age of 37 years Walt's mother died after a tragic accident. He felt guilty for neglecting her concerns and no doubt spent the rest of his life regretting this neglect. His mother was extremely close to him, if not physically then psychically.

"Flora died in 1938 in an accident that plagued her son Walt with grief for the rest of his life. After the success of their film Snow White and the Seven Dwarfs, in 1938, Walt and Roy presented their parents with a new home in North Hollywood, near the Disney studios in Burbank, California. Less than a month after moving in, Flora complained to Walt and Roy of problems with the gas furnace in her new home. Studio repairmen were sent to the house, but the problem was not adequately fixed. Flora wrote a letter to her daughter Ruth describing the wonderful new home, but again complaining of the fumes from the furnace. A few days later, Flora died of asphyxiation caused by the fumes at age 70." (https://en.wikipedia.org/wiki/Flora_Call_Disney)

Finally, the T-square Moon square Neptune and Chiron/Mars. The focal point of this T-square is the Moon. The Moon sacrificed its powers to keep the opposition in a state of harmony, or close to it. Chiron and Mars oppose Neptune, their 5th house of fun, creativity and games versus the 11th house wishes for people and places. It is a hard pattern because the Moon is a Luminary and as such it should be free, but it's not.

In this chapter we have seen how incredibly powerful the Moon as a 'mother' can be. In some families the Moon will represent the father when he is the nurturer and mother the dominant parent is represented by the Sun. So not every chart will depict the Sun as father and the Moon the mother, sometimes it's around the other way.

Moon in the elements
Moon in Earth signs (Taurus, Virgo, Capricorn) and Earth houses (2nd, 6th, 10th) suggests that the mother influence is more practical, down to earth and driven to achieve physical security. Affection and warmth are easy and comfort can come in food as well as cuddles. On the negative side it can cut you off from affection by engaging in obsessive compulsive behaviour, hoarding and emotional control.

Moon in an Air sign (Gemini, Libra, Aquarius) or Air house (3rd, 7th, 11th) suggests that the mother influence is very strong and generally intellectual. Thus we can see that it is both Air and Earth according to the chart. Too much Air can strangle the child by rarely being able to express love and lack affection.

Moon in Fire signs (Aries, Leo, Sagittarius) and Fire houses (1st, 5th, 9th) suggests that the mother is creative, excitable, interesting, imaginative and loves playing and acting. This can sometimes be the sign of the 'drama queen' and over-dramatising any ailment or seeking attention for everything they do. If the mother is too Fiery then she can compete with the child for recognition.

Moon in Water signs (Cancer, Scorpio, Pisces) or Water houses (4th, 8th, 12th) suggests that the mother is warm and affectionate showing the child how to nurture themselves and others. It also suggests an easy flow of love providing the support a child needs to grow into a balanced individual. Sometimes the mothers insecurity and fearfulness leads to the child feeling abandoned and this may be projected onto the child as nervousness and depression.

Second Theme: Walt is uncomfortable with disharmony and conflict.
Third Theme: Walt has some mental health issues - though they are not serious.

The themes we now see beginning to form are:
1. We have **creativity with communication and artistic flair** with Sun in Sagittarius conjunct Uranus in the 4th house.
2. Next is a **fear of disharmony and conflict** (Sun opposite Pluto and Moon in Libra);
3. There is another theme that arises and that is his **mental health.** We can see that a Libra Moon in the 2nd house aids his constant worry about everything. This in turn suggests insomnia, racing negative thoughts when things go wrong, and there is some depression too.

These three themes might come up again in his chart so we'll wait to see if this is followed up in the next two Key Points.

3rd Key is the Ascendant and the 1st house

I have shown you how to read the Sun and Moon to give an indication of the individual's personality, therefore in **Keys 1 + 2 we look at the Sun and Moon positions** and what they are up to: their house, sign and element and if they are conjunct or opposed by a planet, particularly an outer planet.

This is now **Key 3 - the Ascendant and the 1st house**. The Ascendant (also simply shortened to as 'Asc') is the zodiac sign or constellation rising on the eastern horizon at the exact moment of birth.

The Ascendant is a point in the 1st house, like a planetary point. I now use the Whole Sign House System and find this to be superior to the Placidus I learned as a student of astrology. Anything residing in the 1st house adds something to the individual's personality. For instance, Uranus in the 1st house will contribute to the way that person thinks and acts. They will tend towards hyperactivity of the mind and nervous system, often verging on genius. But, Uranus in the 1st house can also manifest as nervousness and agitation as well as inspired thinking and intuition. Because it is in the 1st house Uranus would be magnified in importance and its psychological and mental aspects would be quite visible to others - especially to a trained astrologer.

Before I move on to explain the Ascendant, these are our **Psychological themes** that we have uncovered:
1. **Supremely talented and artistic with a need to communicate** - Sun and its associated planets.
2. We also have Walt as **uncomfortable with disharmony and conflict**. With Moon in Libra, in the 2nd house and Sun conjunct Uranus in the 4th house.
3. **Mental health issues** – there is a focus on Air Moon in the 2nd house and other features which can contribute to excessive thinking. This is what we saw when we delineated his Sun conjunct Uranus, in the 4th house opposed by Pluto. This suggests some insomnia, worrying negative thoughts and depression.

Walt's Ascendant is Virgo and inside the 2nd house resides the Moon in Libra. As I've discussed previously the Moon is the most heavily aspected planet in his chart and that increases its power to move and shape his personality. The Ascendant is also considered the 'mask' or face we wear showing the public at large the qualities we want them to see. The mask is the sign of our Ascendant which is Virgo. In this case Walt likes the public to see him as hardworking, honest, honourable, disciplined, respectful, helpful and a servant to the people.

Virgo is the sign of service, the person who makes sure everyone is receiving enough food and enough attention. A perfect host who goes out of her way to be helpful and making her guests feel valued. Virgo is aligned with the asteroid Goddess Vesta, the keeper of the Sacred Flame, dedicated and devotional to all things of high ideal and value.

The mask of the Ascendant is how we hide our vulnerabilities from the world at large. We project a particular personality type that satisfies our particular and peculiar vulnerabilities. For Walt it's Virgo. It's those particular and peculiar Virgo traits that satisfies his need to disguise and protect his particular and peculiar vulnerabilities (and we have already begun to uncover what these might be). In other words Walt uses his drive to succeed, his attention to detail, his work ethic, his service to see that others do a good job, his determination to get things just right - to protect his sensitivity which we see immediately, yes, it's his Moon in Libra.

Walt wears his heart on his sleeve and he can't really hide his sensitivity very well at all. Along with a Virgo Ascendant, his Moon is thrust out for all to see, sacrificed to keep the 4 planets Mars, Chiron, and Saturn as well as Neptune from fighting - it sticks out like a sore thumb. While he projects his self discipline and focused mind to his tasks he is also 'feeling' all the emotions around him. His coworkers, his staff, his wife, his children, the community and his viewing public.

Now we see why he has those 3 themes we noticed in his Sun and Moon. He is super sensitive to criticism (a Virgo trait), to humiliation, embarrassment, rude comments and judgements, to bullies and to anyone who wants to be nasty to him. It's almost as though Walt's psyche created this chart to make his life as easy and secure as possible but then threw in a wild card and that wild card is his Moon.

He already had an inspired Sun in Sagittarius, creative and engaging, charming and successful; he had a loaded 5th house that helped him to strive forward and communicate his zeal to others; he had Virgo Ascendant that allowed him to project a determined, dedicated and professional mask - but then psyche drew the Moon card.

Now we see just how powerful that Ascendant and 1st house are: it confirms my initial hypothesis that Walt had issues with conflict as both Moon in the 2nd house and the Virgo Ascendant will compromise his needs for that of others, giving and giving until nothing is left. It confirms my **1st hypothesis** that Walt was creative, skilful, a communicator and a dedicated worker driven to succeed. It also confirms my **2nd hypothesis** that Walt struggled with his fear of conflict, and my **3rd hypothesis** of a mild mental health issues namely sleep, anxiety and depression.

In the first three key points you can see that Walt's psyche is laid bare for you to read the most important features of his psyche. The psychological astrologer seeks to uncover those urges, drives and instincts that impact on a person's mental health as well as the other personal qualities we have noted above.

Knowing how to do this in such a short time frame allows the psychologist or counselling therapist to shift their therapeutic approach in the direction it needs to head. It saves me countless hours of therapy, question and answer, assessments and evaluations. Knowing the persons psyche like this adds insight and is an incredible value to my practice.

The Mask / Persona / Ego / Shadow - Dr Carl Jung's archetypes

Jung taught us that Archetypes were energy forms which pervade our psyche, in fact everyone's psyche, connecting each of us to every other human being. Every culture shares common themes like father, mother, warrior, housemaid, liar, coward, hero, nurse, chef, farmer... the mask or 'persona' indicates how people seek to protect their vulnerabilities. Projecting a solid persona or mask each individual can feel safer and more secure within themselves. However, most of us have weak masks, astrologers versed in reading the Ascendant and 1st house can see it.

The Ascendant is also known as the 'ego' and we owe Sigmund Freud for that term. It basically means 'strength of character' not 'arrogance'. Ego is strength, and why do we need a strong ego? Because the ego is also our mask, it is designed to protect our vulnerabilities. A weak ego is a psychologically vulnerable one. Some signs are better at managing their vulnerabilities than others. The projection of a solid persona can be seen in Walt's Virgo but we also now know that it has its own weaknesses.

Let's just quickly consider Virgo by itself. A Virgo Ascendant is strong, it's an Earth element so is rather unruffled in the face of adversity, it's not overly emotional and can remain on task and focused for long periods of time. Perfect! But when we begin to look at the other features of someone's Ascendant we start to tease out the threads and can go deeper and deeper into the person's psyche.

Virgo's weakness is that it must serve, must give to others and must bend over backwards when someone needs their service. It eventually makes a Virgo Ascendant person resentful, frothing-at-the-mouth resentful. Can they say 'No!'... nope, they can't unless they have grown through their Ascendant sign and let shine their other planets colours.

Lord Of The Chart - the ruler of the Ascendant sign

The ruling planet of the Ascendant is called the **Lord Of The Chart** which is one of the most powerful planets in the chart. Not only is Mercury the Lord of the Chart but it also rules the Midheaven (his MC is in Gemini).

Apart from the Moon which we've looked at in depth, we now look at the Ascendant sign's ruling planet - or Lord of the Chart. Mercury rules Virgo and Mercury is exalted in its favourite house, the 3rd house. Mercury rules Gemini (Active) and Virgo (passive) and as such shows the intellectual side of Virgo.

We normally consider Virgo as fiercely Earth, but she isn't, she's also very intellectual, which reflects the element of Air. Mercury, as its ruler, fits nicely with the Air side of Virgo, he doesn't say much about the Earth side of Virgo but he certainly does about the Air side.

We see his Air traits in Virgo's need to attend to detail and remain focused, to process intellectually, to stick to the facts and to pick at faults in an argument. Virgo has heaps of Air traits and qualities which sit comfortably beside her Earthy service qualities. After all, Virgos keyword is **Analysis**.

Mercury, the Lord of the Chart, in the 3rd house emphasises theme 2 - creativity, artistic flair and a desire and skill to communicate (with his broad, extended family).

The Ascendant is a rich source of information about the individual. Knowing how to examine and delineate it is a skill that all astrologers need to learn. If your astrologer friend doesn't know how to do this then please, don't call them an astrologer. If I were to give a tarot analogy I would say, "*Never underestimate the single card reading*".

If you also read tarot cards you will already know this maxim: *a single card says as much if not more than any other reading spread.* Once you know what that single card says in depth then a second card may not necessarily add more to that first card. Drawing card after card begins to subtract and dilute the information your psyche is trying to tell you with that very first card.

Jung's Shadow archetype is generally the opposite to what the mask is saying. If the mask is Virgo then the Shadow is Pisces. Where your strength may be attention to detail your Shadow, the opposite, is confusion and lack of detail.

We see the Shadow and what is inside it in the 7th house. By knowing your mask you know what you are projecting to others and what you wish people to see. But knowing your Shadow you can peer beneath that mask to see what you are drawn towards you from that projection. In other words the Shadow is what you draw towards you.

It goes both ways doesn't it, what you push out comes back, what goes around comes around. Virgo on one side is projected outwards while Pisces, other people's dreams, illusions, confusion and loss, is draw towards you. You are attracted to people who project loss, confusion and a neediness.

We see that quite clearly with Walt's work: he projects a personal mask of competency while he attracts people's projects of loss, guilt, confusion, sadness and spiritual needs. We might say that Walt Disney fulfils humanity's projections - he pacifies the projected Pisces needs of the viewing public.

In life there is always a give and take, like Newtons law of attraction, what we project is equally attracted or projected back to us. Examining your own Ascendant in detail in this lesson is a valuable tool to understand what you project into the world and what you attract in turn. Can we change this? Yes we can, but it takes time, discipline and specific meditations, therapeutic and spiritual practices. The first step of course is awareness, once you are aware of what you project and attract you can then begin to engage and modify it.

Ascendant in the elements

If someone has a **Fire Ascendant** (Aries, Leo, Sagittarius) it manifests as inspired, active, intuitive and action oriented. There may be some stress if it isn't projected outwards and expressed physically through sports and physical activity like daily gym sessions.

If the **Ascendant is Water** (Cancer, Scorpio, Pisces) then it express as emotional arousal, agitation, sensitivity, nervousness and be highly sensitised to peoples moods and emotions. These people tend to be highly intuitive, able to read other's feelings instinctively. But they can become overwhelmed when stressed. They need to learn to manage their feelings and stress in particular.

If the **Ascendant is in Earth** (Taurus, Virgo, Capricorn) it manifests as a practical person. They often just know things, like how a motor works, how to open a computer without breaking the lid, how to peel an orange without splitting the soft insides... they do well on the practical plane.

If their **Ascendant is in Air** (Gemini, Libra, Aquarius) it manifests as intellectual. They tend towards being intuitive and approach problem solving without starting at point (a), they can sometimes go straight to point (z) - they might just intuit the answer. These people see a problem and come up with the solution in a flash leaving the experts gasping. Their weakness is also their strength - intellectual - they can become a genius but bordering on anxiety and overthinking things with annoying racing thoughts. These people need to learn to meditate more than anything, even gym work and exercise don't cut it when they stress out. I see a lot of this type in my psychology practice.

Your final lesson will link you to a video clip that walks you through Lucille Ball's chart using the 4 Key Point Method. If you have any trouble with it just email me.

4th Key is the Midheaven and the 10th house

This shows us the direction the person is heading in life, their aspirations, ambitions, goals and how successful they'll be at reaching them. The Midheaven is also called the Medium Coeli or MC for short - Latin for 'middle of the sky'. This points directly above you at the exact moment of your birth. In other words when you were born the constellation directly above you, in the middle of the heavens, is called the Midheaven.

Let's consider someone with a Capricorn Midheaven. In other words Capricorn sits in the 9th, 10th, or 11th house. We will also give the person Mercury and Venus in the 10th house (the 10th house is considered almost equivalent to the MC).

Firstly consider Capricorn, he is the mountain goat who notes where he wants to go and then sets off slowly and carefully taking one step at a time. Not like the impulsive Aries ram which wants to race up as fast as it can go and generally gives up when things become difficult.

That old mountain goat is crafty and wise, it knows just where to place its feet, which rock is solid and won't give way when he places his weight on it. We can tell that this person has enormous potential to grow slowly but surely through life. They may not be successful in their early years but they sure have a great opportunity to put things together as they get older and wiser. How do we know they'll be successful? Because they have two lovely planets, inner planets too, in the 10th house - Mercury and Venus, and we'll make it that these planets are in good aspect.

Mercury tell us this person engages their conscious mind, they think and they communicate. Venus is social relationships, charming and attractive. People see this person as someone they want to hang around with. They are witty, intelligent, charming and know how to work the crowd to get what they want. This combination, given other points in the chart, is highly successful and we would support this person with meditations and psychological strategies that scaffold their goal setting and goal achievement.

Lastly, we turn to the ruler of this example chart's Capricorn Midheaven, Capricorn's ruler is Saturn and we might just place Saturn in the 5th house.

Without knowing any of the planetary aspects to Mercury, Venus or Saturn we can still understand how Capricorn moves and drives this person forward towards their goals. We know that Capricorn is slow and steady, and well, so is Saturn. However, Saturn has other qualities, he loves order, structure and managing life issues before they get out of control. He has lists of things he wants to do, he has certificates and licenses all over his walls, he has investments and his finger in every pie.

Capricorn's ruler, Saturn, is in the 5th house of creativity and imagination, friendships and parties. This tells us that this person doesn't waste time and money on frivolous fancies, she wants to go forward dominating his desires for addictions to games, internet, drugs, alcohol, parties or buying clothing because they won't help her achieve her goals. Instead she invests wisely, has solid but few friends, she enjoys going out but to traditional and moderately priced events and restaurants.

That is an example of the information the Midheaven and the 10th house provides us with. It is an enormous amount of insight into our client's drives and goals and that's without any other point in the chart.

Let's now examine Walt Disney's Midheaven and 10th house and see if our hypothesised themes of the first 3 Keys lay out one more time.

Walt's Midheaven (MC) and 10th house.

Walt's Midheaven is in Gemini, and we know that he already has a Gemini theme with (**1**) the Moon in Libra is an Air sign, and we saw it a second time with (**2**) his Virgo Ascendant, and Virgo is ruled by Mercury as is Gemini which is number (**3**). There we have confirmation for in our **1st hypothesis** of creativity and communications.

Gemini on the MC tell us a lot. It tells us that Walt strives to communicate, to shout out to the world, *'look what I've got!'*. His Sun is in Sagittarius so there is some of that attention-seeking behaviour of the Fire signs too. Even though we know he wants to guard his sensitive side, his Moon in Libra, he still wants to be noticed.

Sitting next to his MC is Neptune, and that makes things

interesting because Neptune is the planet of dreams, illusion and fantasy. How about that, it's everything Walt Disney is famous for, presenting and fulfilling peoples dreams. Neptune also rules his Shadow, his 7th cusp - Pisces.

Isn't it interesting how Walt's chart just oozes confirmation for these themes we've uncovered? But look at Neptune's oppositions, it's opposite Chiron and Mars and it's square Moon. In fact we have a T-square here: Neptune opposite Chiron and Mars and they all square the Moon. Moon now becomes the focal planet of the T-Square pattern. It means that his emotions are frozen, sacrificed to allow the harmonious function and flow of the opposition between Neptune and Chiron / Mars.

Let's look at this for a moment. The opposition raises issues of his 4th house - family, childhood and early life foundations. He loves his family and he had what is described as a normal childhood, so what gives? Well, he might not have had such an easy childhood at all. This little boy, third eldest of his four siblings, is artistic and obviously quite sensitive. His Sun opposite Pluto suggests he may have been bullied, perhaps at school or by his siblings.

His 10th house tells us he had ambitions to express himself and maybe the Neptune opposing Chiron / Mars placed barriers against him achieving this. Maybe his psyche used the emotional energy of the Moon in Libra to pacify this underlying stress. It allowed him to overcome whatever issues he had in childhood to achieve his successes – the opposition of Neptune to Chiron and Mars.

Now that's fascinating isn't it. We can see that trying to achieve his goals would have been like trying to grasp a beach ball in the swimming pool while treading water - it's impossible. Every time you reach out to grab the ball your fingers just push it further away. His foundations, the 4th house, were compromised. It appears that he hid his emotions, maybe through denying his emotional needs, which comes from the Air element. Suppressing his emotional needs allowed him to stretch forward and achieve his goals.

Let's look at the ruler of Gemini, the Midheaven, and we know it's Mercury. Isn't that incredible, we have both Walt's Ascendant and the MC ruled by the same planet, Mercury. It is exalted in the 3rd house saying the same thing over and over again - "*I am a creative communicator.*"

Walt, like anyone else with Virgo Asc and Gemini MC, has Mercury as one of his chart rulers. In fact Mercury is the *Lord of the Chart* and we can see evidence of Mercury in everything Walt has succeeded in throughout his lifetime.

Planet of High Degree

The highest placed planet is called the *Planet of High Degree*. This placement is not often discussed in astrological circles, but simply put it's the planet sitting at the top of the chart in the 9th or 10th or 11th house. It is at its most powerful when conjunct the MC, in fact the closer to the MC the more powerful it becomes.

Neptune is in the 10th house conjunct the MC by 6°. Pluto is close by 7° but it is **Neptune which is the Planet of High Degree**. Neptune now takes on greater significance and power. I see the Planet of High Degree much like a light bulb sitting at the top of the chart, it shines its particular form of energy right through the entire chart.

We could say that Walt Disney was heavily influenced by the placement of Neptune for this reason: because it is the Planet of High Degree. We see it in his visions, his presentation of family values, his adoption of modern methods to produce mass marketing of his dreams fulfilling the hopes, dreams and fantasies of the world community. Let's face it, few people have not seen or heard of at least one of Walt's Disney's characters.

MC and it's foundations - Imum Coeli (IC) or 4th house cusp, is Latin for 'bottom of the sky'

This is something I sometimes do during a reading, I look at the persons foundations, where they came from and their upbringing. That can be seen in their 4th house. We know from **Attachment Theory**, that a persons foundations begin in childhood, therefore a healthy functional family is essential for a person to reach out and touch the stars.

Sometimes you'll find a chart that looks promising for a highly ambitious and successful career by what they see in the 10th house yet the person never quite achieves what they set out for. That's when you would look at the opposite house, the 4th house. Here lies the person foundations. Builders never build on soft, shifting soil or lay weak foundations, they always dig deep until they strike solid ground. The higher the building the deeper the foundations. The same goes for achieving greatness, the greater their achievements the deeper the foundations need to be.

If their childhood shows weaknesses by the IC's sign, sign ruler and planets inside the 4th house, then they probably need to go and talk to someone. Perhaps they will need some counselling, perhaps psychotherapy, or maybe a good mentor. So that's a little trick you can try when you do your readings, check out the opposite house. In this case it's the 4th house, and see what's supporting their growth and forward momentum.

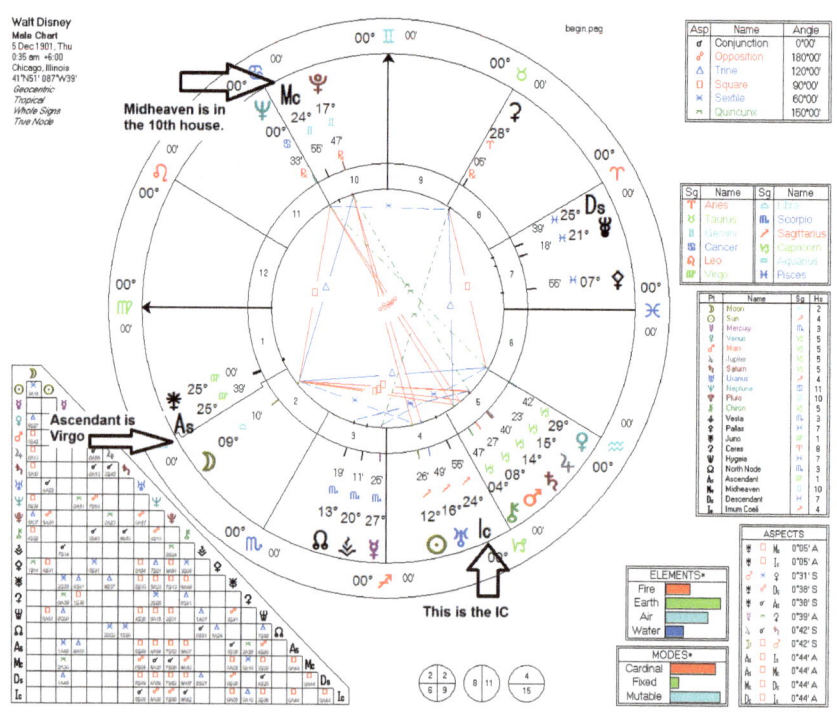

The Midheaven in the elements:
An **Air Midheaven** shows the native aims to express themselves through communications, critical thinking, intuitive and unique ways of solving problems. They have drive and desire to be noticed for the information they share not so much for personal recognition like the Fire signs but because they just love shifting information about.

Earth Midheaven suggests the native aims for success in physical and material ways such as career, material goods, hoarding, security like a house, and will go to great lengths to attain it. They have enormous patience, fortitude and determination to succeed in the long term.

Fire Midheaven strives to achieve success by being 'out there' which could mean as a drama-queen constantly crying 'look at me', being the centre of attention. Whatever it is the Fire signs love recognition and being noticed for their achievements. Usually shows success and the drive to succeed.

Water Midheaven is less easily defined because it crosses into the emotions and feelings. Probably the best way to describe them is to say they seek success through forming and remaining in a relationship, having a family and connecting with people emotionally.

Final Summary of the 4 Key Points Method:
Key 1 - Luminary, the **Sun** and if there are conjunctions or oppositions to it and which house it resides in.
Key 2 - Luminary, the **Moon** and if there are conjunctions or oppositions to it and which house it resides in.
Key 3 – the **Ascendant** and the **1st house**, it's element and it's ruling planet.
Key 4 – the **Midheaven** and the **10th house,** it's element and it's ruling planet.

How did we go with our hypothesised themes?
1. We found Walt to be **creative, have artistic flair and a need to communicate** it with Moon in Libra and Sun conjunct Uranus in the 3rd house - **yes for all 4 Key Points.**
2. **Fear of conflict** (Sun opposite Pluto and Moon in Libra) **- yes for all 4 Key Points.**
3. **Mental health** and we can see that an Air Moon in the 1st house which can contribute to excessive thinking and worry. We saw it when we delineated his Sun conjunct Uranus, in the 3rd house opposed by Pluto too. This suggests elements of insomnia, anxiety, worrying negative

thoughts and depression. When we look at the 4th house we can see dysfunction and insecurity but I might give this a half point for the Midheaven. **Yes, for all 4 Key Points** (but only a 'half-a-yes' for the Midheaven}.

~

    So there you have it, the 4 Key Points that will provide you with a simple, practical and fast astrology reading. From these 4 points I can work with someone in a short space of time to bring their strengths forward and develop strategies to heal their weaknesses and their conflicts. It's not the end of the reading, oh no, it's just the beginning and you'll learn more about the rest of the chart if you stick around. Remember this 4 Key Point Method gives you a very accurate snap-shot of the person, but it is not the whole person, that comes after some experience.

Now please view the **video clip** on my **Coddiwompling page** as I walk through female comedian, **Lucille Ball's** chart using the 4 key Point Method. It's certainly worth watching even if just to see how I try to find the best House System to use for the reading. The star and creator of '*I Love Lucy*' deserves a thorough examination as so much came out of this 4 key point reading that even I was amazed.

~

Chapter 3: The Planet of High Degree

The planet in the upper half of the chart and closest to the Midheaven is considered extremely important as its 'light' shines upon every planet, house and sign beneath it. The qualities of that planet can influence your entire psyche. I like to think of it as a glittering disco ball that radiates its multicoloured sparkles throughout your chart. Not everyone will have a planet at the top half of their chart, in which case astrologers use other techniques.

The history behind the naming of the Planet of High Degree
I was taught that the highest planet in the chart was known as the *'most elevated planet'*. On becoming a professional astrologer I soon recognised just how important that planet was, so I decided to give it a more fitting title. I called it the *'Planet of High Degree'* to celebrate its innate power.

The name I chose reflects the special role of the Australian Aboriginal *ngangkari*, sometimes called a sorcerer or medicine man -- but I'll use the more accurate term 'shaman'. The shaman caste is a select brotherhood within aboriginal society that reinforces and upholds the spiritual life of their tribe. Each takes on apprentices, training them in the arts of shamanism. Sometimes talented men and women will also be trained in the higher degrees of magic, healing and walking with the spirits, even though they are not destined to be part of the shamanic caste. These are called men or women *'of high degree'*. They form a cadre of highly respected individuals within the tribe who, though not full-fledged shamans, have significant knowledge and are certainly not to be trifled with. It is this tradition of passing the shaman's magical knowledge to selected individuals that I wish to honour in my astrology work.

How does this shamanic model fit into psychological astrology?
Every planetary archetype has specific traits and characteristics. When placed at the top of the chart, that planet's power pervades your life in unique ways; in particular, it supports you in manifesting your destiny. It is your life purpose to recognise its importance and draw down its power into your daily life. This represents the shaman's quest and what I seek to identify when I do a reading.

Your shaman's quest is not limited to this point in the chart. Many other points, planets and signs support your spiritual development. For example, I would consider the placement of Pluto as an indicator of shamanic power. The powerful forces of Pluto (and by association the 8th house and Scorpio) can drive the individual to seek answers found only in the inner worlds - the unconscious, which I call 'Pluto's Cave'. One could say that the Planet of High Degree does not force the native to go within as Pluto does. Instead, it lends its particular form of magic to those who seek to walk the path of the shaman in other, less demanding ways.

The Planet of High Degree *eases and encourages* your personal power into consciousness, while Pluto *forces* it upon you - ready or not.

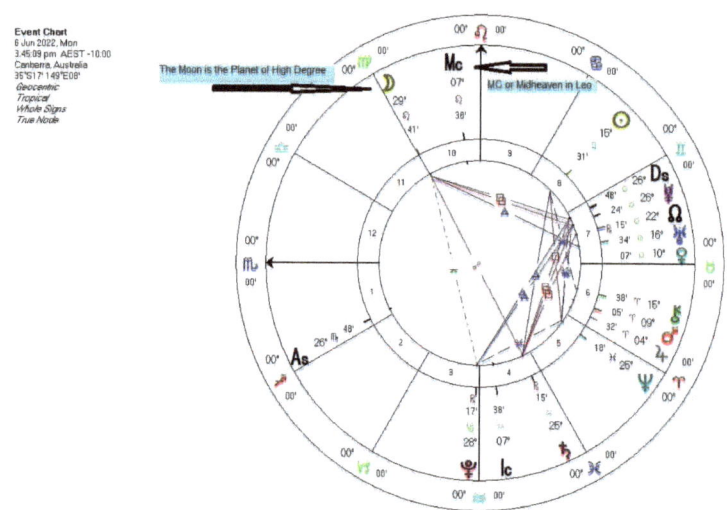

How does it help me to walk the shaman's path?
The Planet of High Degree guides you towards your destiny via its particular qualities. You might be guided by Neptune, Sun or Venus to be a musician, writer or artist; by Mars, Saturn or Jupiter to become a business person; by the Sun or Moon to be a generous and caring person no matter what your career is. The Planet of High Degree does not force you to be the best, instead, it lends you the gift of insight into your destiny, for example:
* Sun lends his divine light to shed happiness and warmth along your path.
* Moon wishes to assist your personal development by giving you emotional insight.
* Mercury lends his communication skills and clarity of thinking to assist you in presenting your ideas to others.
* Venus assists in forming and maintaining relationships.

* Mars lends his drive and energy to your projects.
* Jupiter lends his sense of adventure and charm to anything you want to do.
* Saturn is solid and centred; he seeks to lend you his sense of order and structure.
* Uranus has the ability to help you intuit the answers to problems in unique ways.
* Neptune lends his dissolving and melding qualities to help you see beyond your limitations.
* Pluto, of course, will open you up to the underworld that he rules, your unconscious.

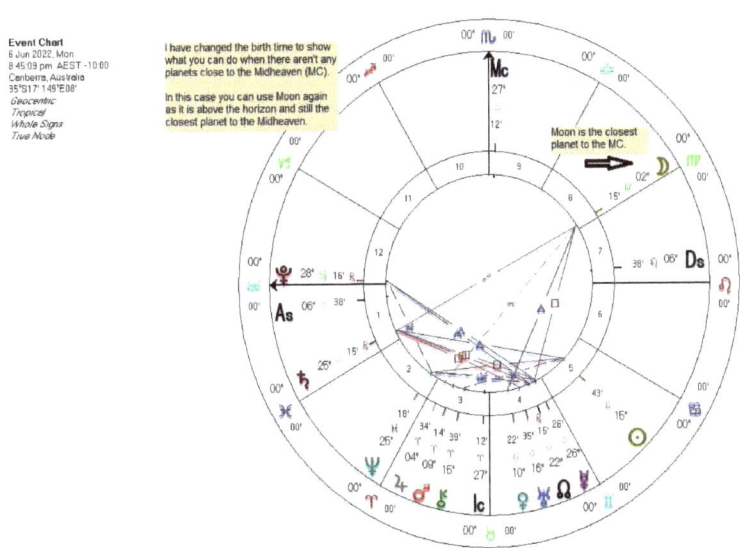

How do I find my Planet of High Degree?

If you look at the chart above you will note that the Moon, although not within a 10 to 15 degree orb to form a conjunction with the Midheaven, is the Planet of High Degree. Please remember, I use the Whole Sign house system in which each house is the same size and anchored at zero degrees of the Ascendant sign. If you use other house systems they can deform the house sizes. I consider a Planet of High Degree if it is within about 60° of the MC.

In the chart below I have changed the birth time so that there is no obvious planet close to the Midheaven. If there is a planet within an orb of two signs, up to 60°, it is more powerful than if it is outside that orb (greater than 60°). The closer a planet is to the Midheaven, the more powerful it becomes. I tend to limit my orb to 60°, a planet outside this orb is technically the highest planet of the chart but it doesn't have the strength of a planet within the orb of 60°.

In the chart below, the Moon remains the Planet of High Degree because it is above the horizon and closest to the Midheaven more so than Pluto, on the other side of the chart. At this distance, the Moon is not overly powerful, but should still form part of your meditations for personal growth.

If every planet is below the horizon (in the 1st to 6th houses) I would use the ruler of the Midheaven. In the chart below, the ruler of the Libran Midheaven is Venus. Venus is in Taurus in the 4th house. Venus is thus elevated in importance as the ruler of the Midheaven, however, it is NOT the Planet of High Degree. The ruling planet of the Midheaven also plays a role in determining the path your life takes.

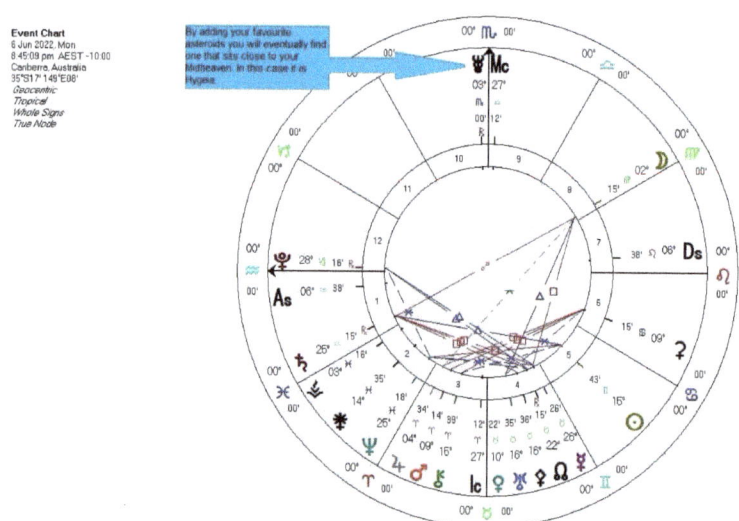

There is, however, another way to determine your Planet of High Degree and that is to add the asteroid goddesses or other astrological points that you like to use. In the chart below I have added my favourite asteroid goddesses: Vesta, Hygeia, Juno, Ceres and Pallas. Of these, Hygeia sits right next to the Midheaven, making it easy for me to say, "*Hygeia is your Planet of High Degree*". As such, the asteroid Hygeia will play a major role in guiding that person's shamanic quest.

How does the Planet of High Degree impact your life?
This depends on many factors such as: the Lord of the Chart (the planetary ruler of your Ascendant sign), where your Luminaries lie in your chart and their aspects to the other planets (Sun and Moon), stelliums in houses and signs, and any aspects to the Planet of High Degree.

The Midheaven itself, along with the 10th house, is associated with ambition, a beacon that points to what your life goals are and therefore what you aspire to reach upwards to grasp in life. One could say that your Midheaven represents the 'stars' you reach for. The nature of those stars is hinted at by its sign and any planets in the 10th house.

The power points in your chart (Lord of the Chart; 10th house, Midheaven, Planet of High Degree, Luminaries) support each other in guiding you towards the realisation of your destiny. I would add that your destiny is also your shamanic or mystical quest.

Using the top chart as an example: in this chart (where the Moon is the Planet of High Degree), the Moon must blend her lunar energies with Leo, which is the Midheaven sign, and her own sign. Leo is one of my favourite Moon signs -- generous and honest, often a little hyperactive but always there to help a friend. Moon lends its happiness and kindness to the native's entire psyche, attracting like-minded people. The native's destiny is to manifest these Leo Moon qualities in her life, doing everything possible to help those in need of assistance, nurturing, or emotional support.

If I were to analyse the rest of the chart I would highlight the many psychological traits displayed by the native: the Taurus stellium in the 7th house creating the need to be friendly and in peaceful relations with others; the Sun, ruler of her Leo Midheaven, in the 8th house of spiritual evolution, healing and the occult; the T-square formed by the Moon opposite Saturn squared by Mercury and North Node; the Scorpio Ascendant and its ruler, Pluto, the Lord of the Chart, in the 3rd house conjunct the 4th cusp highlighting an intense desire to understand and share the hidden secrets of life and death. These aspects of the chart are moderated and supported by the glowing Leonic energies of the Moon, the Planet of High Degree.

How does this planet inform you of your mystical quest?
The Planet of High Degree helps identify what you are reaching for - which is sometimes described as 'reaching for the stars'. What are those 'stars'? This is your shaman's quest, to find out. Your guide is your Planet of High Degree.

The excellent article linked below discusses the Midheaven and its impact on the chart and the person. It also explains the roles of both the Midheaven and its ruling planet:
https://www.astro.com/astrology/tma_article180419_...

Chapter 4: The Three most Common Psychological Disorders

What is Adjustment Disorder?
(Definitions extracted from https://psychcentral.com/)
　　　　Adjustment disorder affects both children and adults. The condition, sometimes called 'situational depression', involves a severe emotional or behavioral reaction to a specific life stressor or series of stressors (causes).
　　　　The life stressor can be a negative event or, it can be an event that is generally considered positive but is emotionally charged and changes your routines.
People with this condition can also experience physical symptoms:
- relationship problems; getting a divorce; being diagnosed with an illness; having a baby; getting married; starting a new job; changing your job.
- causing: fatigue; headaches; indigestion; insomnia; not wanting to go to school; picking fights with siblings; having frequent crying spells; feeling deeply sad; hopeless; overwhelmed.

Causes of Adjustment Disorder
A significant life event always triggers adjustment disorder, **these common life-events or stressors** may include: marriage; divorce or relationship problems; death of a loved one; moving; having a baby; losing a job or unemployment; retirement; illness or health issues; financial difficulties; being discharged from the military; parents' separation or divorce; school stressors, including social or academic difficulties; moving to a new house, neighborhood, or city; health or sexuality issues, such as being uncertain about sexual orientation or gender identity; death of a close relative or friend.

*Astrology – this is quite a common disorder for adults as it encompasses almost everything. When a situation (get a new job, the ending of a relationship, lose something, etc.) changes and you cannot cope it may be called an Adjustment Disorder. When I say '**cannot cope**' I mean you feel like falling down onto the ground and crying every day. In astrology you will find that transits to the natal chart from a generational planet (Saturn, Uranus, Neptune and Pluto, and Chiron) in conjunction or opposition with Sun, Moon or Ascendant. This is very standard, a generational planet conjunct or opposed to a luminary or Ascendant. It can, however, include a generational planet conjunct or opposed to a personal planet: Mercury, Venus and Mars. In this case you would expect* *it to be a more moderated form and not as obvious than conjunct or opposed to a luminary or Ascendant. In the natal chart you will find this is more serious if the person has a generally weak chart, in other words they already have Sun or Moon in poor aspect which can be triggered by events. An Adjustment Disorder lasts for around 6 months, if longer then it is becomes Post Traumatic Stress Disorder.*

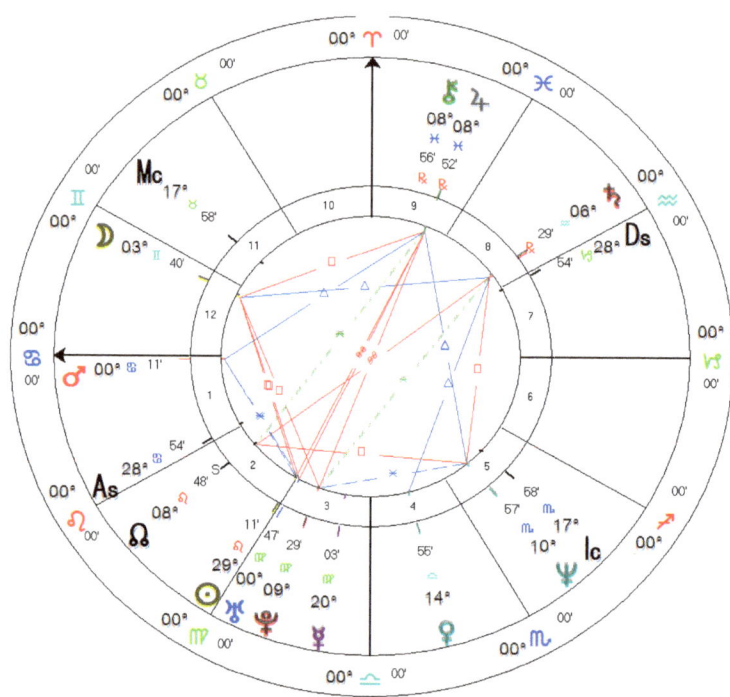

Chart: B (female, Adjustment Disorder)

B (female, Adjustment Disorder) – *here we can see the Sun conjunct Uranus and Pluto opposed by Chiron and Jupiter. This is a very hard aspect and one that can spin her out just by itself. Then we have the focal point of a T-square from Sun and Uranus opposing Jupiter and Chiron and they all are square the Moon. It is not as bad as the previous aspect but one that leaves that native feeling slightly less normal than others – in other words she feels imperfect. Moon carries the responsibility of managing the T-square and is heavily aspected, it also rules her Ascendant, which is Cancer.*

Now we have two more aspects, an unaspected Mercury, and Venus is a singleton with only one aspect. Sometimes a planet that does not have an aspect or has only one aspect, is going to cause trouble. It tends to drop in and out at any moment and can cause significant distress. Mercury is possibly going to cause trouble by influencing her

Scorpio mind. This can happen at any time and makes her very distressed when it happens (and fearing when it doesn't). The Venus is okay, it isn't as bad as Mercury but it can turn on and off seemingly at will. Not every person you see with this aspect will have an Adjustment Disorder, so please be mindful when reading someones chart.

What is Reactive Attachment Disorder (RAD)?

For most children, bonding begins in the womb. Research shows that they can hear their parents' voices and their mother's heartbeat from an early time. They're born with an attachment that's already begun, and it grows stronger in those early months of life. As time goes on, secure attachment can form, initiated by the parent. That is if the infant has caregivers who are emotionally and physically available.

Attachment with caregivers is a crucial part of a child's development. When this is disrupted to the extreme through abuse or neglect, a child may develop Reactive Attachment Disorder (RAD). When those early attachments are disrupted, most often as a result of child abuse or neglect, attachment disorders can develop and Reactive Attachment Disorder (RAD) is one possible outcome.

A child with RAD is less likely to seek comfort when they feel distress. They may show limited positive emotions, but they can show more irritability, fear, or sadness when they come into contact with their caregivers. Although attachment disorders can be very difficult to navigate, healing is possible. With effective treatment, care, and coping methods, children can bond and develop healthy childhood and adult relationships – but this is not all that common.

Reactive Attachment Disorder

According to the **American Academy of Child and Adolescent Psychiatry (AACAP)**, RAD forms as a result of negative experiences with adults in a child's early years. Children with RAD may exhibit behaviors such as: trouble calming down; a refusal to seek comfort from caregivers; an apparent lack of emotions and emotional attachments; disruptive emotions, such as irritability, sadness, fear, or anger when engaging with caretakers; reduced brain growth in the left hemisphere, an area that specializes in logical and rational thought; increased limbic system sensitivity, an area related to emotion regulation; reduced hippocampus growth, an area important for memory; depression; anxiety; learning and memory impairments.

Research suggests that a RAD diagnosis is more common in socially deprived populations and is also higher in children who've been placed in foster care. When left untreated, symptoms of RAD and trouble forming attachments can carry over into adulthood. In other words we see RAD in children who have had very **bad experiences**.

Symptoms

According to the **Diagnostic and Statistical Manual of Mental Disorders (DSM-5)**, RAD is a condition that's induced by trauma or stress in early childhood. Contributing factors may be neglect, maltreatment, and abuse. Symptoms of RAD include:
- rarely seeking out or responding to comfort when upset; withdrawing socially and isolating oneself; showing limited emotional responsiveness to others; having a negative emotions; being irritable; being fearful; being sad; showing extreme responses to stress; having working memory impairments; showing executive functioning impairments; exhibiting undeveloped or underdeveloped social skills; showing increased aggression, fear, defiance, or rage; showing psycho-motor restlessness including hand-flapping or rocking.

Astrology – *this is generally seen in children up to the late teenage years at which time they can become a social misfit who commits serious crime - against others or against themselves. It can go on to become Conduct Disorder as a youth and finally as an adult it becomes Anti-Social Personality Disorder (a criminal).*

"Antisocial personality disorder (ASPD) describes an ingrained pattern of behavior in which individuals consistently disregard and violate the rights of others around them. Individuals with antisocial personality disorder may behave violently, recklessly, or impulsively, often with little regard for the wants and needs of others."
https://www.psychologytoday.com/us/conditions/antisocial-personality-disorder

This disorder can split into two groups, one group 'internalise' and self harm: cutting, biting, punching or drugging themselves. The other group 'externalise' and take out their frustrations on others or their property through violent assaults and/or smashing up property. This is a serious disorder and one that is hard to treat. I would try EEG Biofeedback but that may fail if they don't stick with it.

What I would look for in the natal chart are conjunctions and opposition from Neptune, Pluto or Chiron to the Sun, Moon, and Mars. If I were to add the narcissistic side of Antisocial Personality Disorder (which is it's externalising form) then I would add the sign of Sagittarius, the 9th house and Jupiter. These children are capable of crossing the *boundary of good behaviour and frequently turn life into chaos for their sufferers, that is their family and friends.*

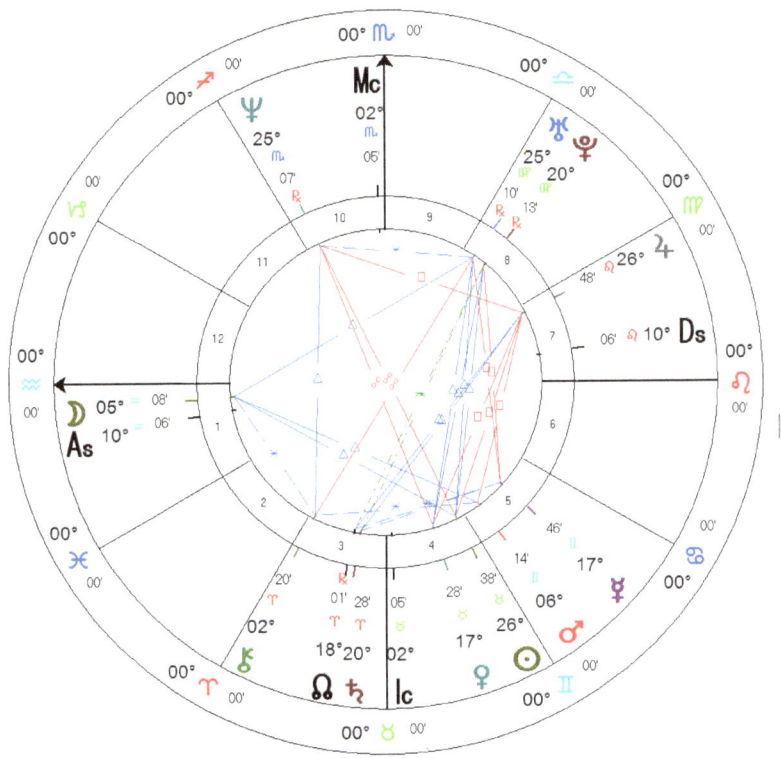

Chart: BP (male, Reactive Attachment Disorder)

BP (male, Reactive Attachment Disorder) - *BP is a male and someone that I made considerable gains with but I lost contact and don't know whether it continued. He*
too was alone and uncared for, all he wanted was to have a girlfriend. Looking at his chart you can see that he has an Aquarian Ascendant and his Moon is conjunct the Ascendant. Although Moon is beautifully placed with trines to Uranus, Sun and Mars, and a sextile to Chiron, it is still a tough aspect because of its placement which is conjunct and Applying to the Ascendant. There are also hard aspects to Uranus from Chiron and a hard aspect from Mercury to Uranus and Pluto, and Neptune to Sun and Venus. There are also elements of ADHD with Air and Fire on the cusp of Air and Fire houses. Actually it is an unusual chart for RAD

This is a person who 'internalised' his RAD, he didn't seem to exhibit many of the externalising symptoms. What was it that caused him to feel alone and turn his self-harm onto himself? It is the T-square from

Neptune to Venus, Sun and Mars all squaring Jupiter that is causing him to turn inwards. I don't think he was serious in his self-harming, I didn't see any marks on him... but I know that people with this disorder can hide it by cutting in secret places like the inside of the thighs, so maybe he was serious. All in all he came good while in therapy, but what happened later I just don't know.

What is Post Traumatic Stress Disorder (PTSD)?

Post-traumatic stress disorder, aka PTSD, is a serious mental health condition once attributed only to war veterans. Today, we know that it's so much more. Many of us are familiar with that near-miss feeling. Whether it's a car that comes a little too close or a medical scare in the emergency room, that near-miss is a memorable experience.

When we go through a traumatic event, several systems in the body kick into high gear. The hypothalamus and pituitary gland both send out a rush of stress hormones, preparing us to fight, flee, or freeze. It is an escalation of symptoms that make it must bigger than an Adjustment Disorder. An Adjustment Disorder lasts for around 6 months, if longer then it is becomes Post Traumatic Stress Disorder.

When the danger passes, many people can move on and "shake it off," so to speak. Yet for some of us, that feeling of being on high alert can persist for weeks, months, or even years, and occur alongside other symptoms.

If this resonates with you, know that you're not alone. Post-traumatic stress disorder (PTSD) is not a rare condition, and with the right management plan, including trauma therapy and EEG Biofeedback, you can manage and reduce the severity of your symptoms. With determined and long term therapy you may no longer exhibit the seriousness of symptoms.

PTSD is a mental health condition that may occur as a result of witnessing or experiencing a traumatic event. It was added as a diagnosis by the American Psychiatric Association (APA) to the third edition of the Diagnostic and Statistical Manual of Mental Disorders (DSM) in 1980. **People who live with PTSD experience an elevated 'fight or flight' response (you can add 'freeze' and 'fawn' to this list).** Perceived threats trigger the autonomic nervous system, which leads to chemical alternations in the brain. This creates a sense of danger and other symptoms, even when there is no actual threat.

Causes of PTSD

PTSD was formerly called 'shell shock' or 'battle fatigue

syndrome', and many people may be familiar with the condition through its association with war veterans. However, PTSD can develop from a range of different scenarios. What ties them together is a real or perceived threat of danger, which may involve a possible loss of life.

Some PTSD causes include:
- natural disaster; crime with violence; serious medical event; near-death experience; loss of a loved one; physical or sexual abuse; transportation accidents (car, plane, etc.); witnessing or experiencing Domestic Violence. In general, any stressful event where you feel fear, shock, horror, or helplessness can cause PTSD.

[T - Post Traumatic Stress Disorder, female.]

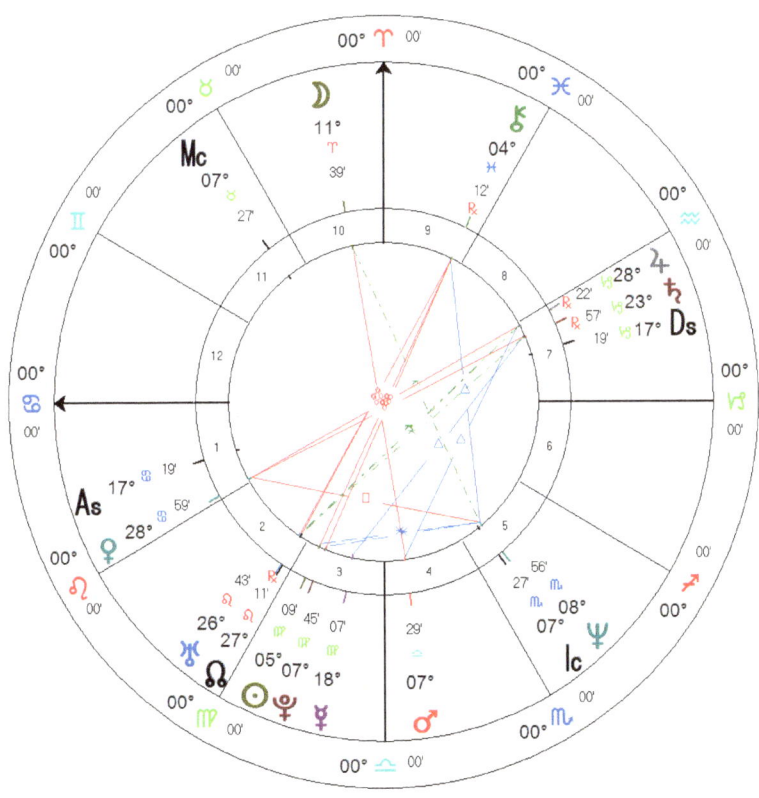

Intrusive symptoms
These symptoms, referred to as re-experiencing symptoms in older versions of the DSM, are those that take you back to the trauma.
- flashbacks or dissociative reactions; nightmares or distressing dreams; intense, unpleasant memories, images, or thoughts; emotional or

physical distress when you think about the traumatic event; irritability; feeling on edge; difficulty with concentration; heightened startle response; sudden bursts of anger; negative self-talk; feelings of guilt or self-blame; memory issues; lack of interest in things you love; sweating; shaking; dizziness; headaches; chest pain; upset stomach; unexplained aches and pains; fatigue from nightmares or sleep disturbances; bed-wetting; nightmares; increased clingyness with adults; expression of trauma through art or games; low self-worth; fear, sadness, isolation; aggression; abnormal sexual behavior; self-harm; alcohol or drug abuse.

Astrology – *one of the more common disorders that encompass the entire spectrum. It is generally more specific to physical injuries that impact the native with intrusive thoughts – consider pain as one of these. The patient is in pain and all they can do is take it out on objects or partners. When the severity of this disorder goes beyond what is normally expected then it is given a name – Post Traumatic Stress Disorder (PTSD). You don't need to be a war veteran to have a diagnosis of PTSD.*

Not always can a single natal correspondence be given to PTSD. If you were to look at the native's chart you would see that it is possibly caused by a minor transit but particularly trines. An abundance of trines can make you very insecure and sensitive. Major transits will do it, but that is uncommon unless it morphs into something else. The best the person can do is work on their strategies and do them properly and regularly. There are aspects natally which will make it more serious. PTSD is a damaging disorder, please take its diagnosis seriously. **Unfortunately you can't see these disorders in the chart because they can affect anyone. There isn't a sign or planet that is immune from a neurological disorder. However, the chart does show the depth to which these disorders can affect people.

T (female, PTSD) - *Sun conjunct Pluto has put enormous pressure on her thinking processes and causes her to over think and second guess herself. One who lived in fantasy land she certainly had the symptoms described by PTSD. When the symptoms are extreme and almost beyond help they call it Complex PTSD. This is hard enough to manage but she also has Sun and Pluto opposed by Chiron in the 9th house. Sun conjunct Pluto, Uranus, and North Node opposed by Chiron is very dangerous in PTSD as it opens the native up to their pain.*

Moon opposite Mars and no other major aspect to Moon: this places excess tension on her Moon and the trine from Mars to Jupiter is not enough. The opposition from Venus to Jupiter and Saturn is a difficult one as is the Jupiter and Saturn conjunction. These are all very hard to manage but if she had a nice family she would be able to manage this just a touch better.

Chapter 5: Transits

Cycles

I practised as an astrologer for many years before I studied psychology. These days I can sometimes look at a chart and see the person's soul. I am not as good as I would like to be but it does get easier the more charts I read and the more I study and meditate. One thing I had to come to terms with was that astrology is all about cycles. The chart itself is a circle, a metaphor for the movement of the planets and constellations around us. Its beauty is its simplicity

I read the chart by turning the planets into people, the house is where they live and act and the sign is the personality they adopt. Thus a Cancer Moon conjunct (next to) Saturn in the 8th house demonstrates how the person acts emotionally (Moon in Cancer), where they will be emotional, and as the 8th house is the house of transformation and crisis they will act emotionally to most life situations. Hopefully they will work to transform those events and emotions into life-changing events. They will also remember every crisis they have ever had, because it hurt so cruelly.

Saturn sitting next to the Moon, that dark, sober, and depressing bring-you-down-to-earth planet, indicates that this person has great difficulty sharing emotions, so they lock their tender feelings inside, no matter how much they hurt they won't show it.

If I see this configuration (and there is much more in their astrology chart than Moon conjunct Saturn, of course) then I know it will take a lot of trust before they open up and share. They, however, have a depth of understanding of emotion and will have an intuitive understanding of that pain and emotion. This person, if they survive life's challenges, will slowly become a deep thinker and have a deeper understanding of life than most. As they grow older they'll be able to teach others how to manage life because they have lived the pain and suffering and learned how to manage themselves.

This is just the birth or natal configuration but of course the planets and constellations never stop, they are in perpetual motion in the heavens above us. Eventually Saturn will have moved until it appears opposite its natal position, across from the 2nd house (the house which is opposite the 8th where Moon and Saturn reside). What happens now?

This individual's 'cycle' has moved to bring new lessons. transiting (or moving) Saturn opposite the natal or birth Moon triggers all sorts of nurturing issues (Moon) under the doom and gloom personality of Saturn. Saturn is the God of Time, Cronus, and his influence on this person is to challenge them to address the long-standing issues they have with nurturing. This could be their own mothers controlling behaviour as a child, belittling and humiliating, or their own marriage in which nurturing plays a big part. It's also their own ability to nurture others and themselves.

These are now being challenged in many ways, some on the surface, such as friendships start to break down. Or it could be deeper in the subconscious in which they feel they have never been nurtured, not even in childhood, and become depressed and needy.

What happens when the cycle ends? It starts another, a new one on another 'dimension' that was not addressed previously. Cycles exist to allow us time to work on things that need to be worked on, then they shift gears and change to the next issue that needs addressing.

The Inner Planets

Before you do any predictive work with transits or progressions, always thoroughly understand the native by studying their natal chart.

The Personal Planets are Mercury, Venus, Mars and includes the Luminaries Moon and Sun, they make up our 'visible' personality characteristics. The two luminaries are not quite as visible to outside observers as the other three inner planets. The Moon shows our emotional make-up and emotional reaction to stress and affection, while the Sun is our urge to continue in this incarnation, why we are here and what we are aiming to do with our life. These two qualities of our personality are quite deep, most people will notice our Moon qualities when we show emotion but the Sun is most noticeable when we let our guard down with those we trust.

In this section we will concentrate on the three inner planets as they transit across our natal chart. These planets define most of our short term opportunities and dreams, though there is still much of this in our two luminaries as well.

Mercury shows others what we are interested in, what we enjoy intellectually and our sense of humour. The books we read, the magazines we buy, the movies we watch, the TV shows we enjoy, the music we relax to and the level of conversation that we use are all characteristics of Mercury.

Venus is of course our affection barometer, it shows how well we relate with others, who we are interested in, how we show affection, who is interested in us, those we are attracted to and how nice we are in mixed company. Venus is most noticeable in social situations.

Mars is our drive and ambition, it is, in some situations, our aggressive energy. Mars shows how we go about getting what we want, our sports interests and how we react watching sports on TV. It is seen in our sex drive and energy levels in sexual activity, it is also visible in our movement and manner at work and at play. It can be seen in our love of blood sports or interest in sports shows.

The important thing to remember at this stage is that although we have these raw urges, Mercury, Venus and Mars, they are always modified by the powerful and very subconscious outer planets (Saturn, Chiron, Uranus, Neptune, and Pluto). An inner planet, not in contact by major aspect (especially the conjunction & opposition) will present a clearer representation of its energy than one in close aspect to an outer planet. The outer planet in close major aspect will always modify, deepen, hide or forcefully express the inner planet's energies.

For instance, Venus in Libra is seen as a love of beauty and an interest in art, music and decorating, a nice taste for beauty. If Venus is not conjunct or opposite an outer planet it will generally be quite clearly Venus in Libra, relationships will not be overly stressful and they will generally be quite successful.

If Venus in Libra is square, quincunx or trine to an outer planet it will take on qualities or be modified by that outer planet. So if Venus in Libra were square Saturn it will show as a love of beauty and art (Libra qualities), perhaps a need to express artistic talents but with some stress involved, and there may be some frustration in personal relationships. If it were trine it will show more success in relationships but the native will be more demanding and perhaps lazy in expecting her partner to give more, thus there may be some distress involved here too. If Venus were conjunct or opposite Saturn then it may show bigger relationship issues, failed relationships and friendships that end badly and a sense of failure in love. It could also indicate affairs rather than true love.

This example does not mean that everyone with Venus in aspect with Saturn will have poor relationships, it is designed to illustrate the effect of the deeper subconscious outer planet on the more conscious inner planet. A positive aspect of Venus / Saturn aspects in the natal chart is where the native works very hard at keeping the relationship together.

If an inner planet is in aspect by another inner planet they will generally modify each other in a less dramatic way. There is a degree of enhancement of the two even in traditionally negative aspects. Mars-Venus conjunction is seen as enhancing the sexuality of Venus and enhancing or easing the sexual inappropriateness of the Mars. The key to this is to know your natal chart **first** by looking at placement of the inner planets in relation to the outer planets before looking at transits.

Transits with the Personal Planets – use a 1° orb

Why don't astrologers use inner planet transits very much? It is because they travel so fast around the zodiac that they simply don't have time to do much. The Moon travels up to 13° per day, thus a transit only lasts a few hours. It must go from a 1° orb to exact, then 2 hours to move back out of that 1° orb. We don't normally use Moon transits except in fine tuning a single day or hour. One example of using the Moon this way is to determine the winner in the Melbourne Cup race, it lasts only 3 minutes.

Sun, Mercury and Venus all travel roughly 1° per day, thus it takes one day to get into orb and then one day to move out of orb - the transit lasts only two days. Mercury and Venus sometimes slow down and stop (Stationary and Retrograde), their speed varies around the zodiac but it averages out at one degree per day. The Sun is the only planet that has a regular 1° travel per day. Watch for Stationary, Direct and Retrograde motion for Mercury and Venus.

Mars travels about one degree each week and spends a little more time on a planet or point, but it is still very short. Retrograde motion transits for Mars can last up to a month or two, though generally about a week is average.

The most sensitive points are: Ascendant, Midheaven, Moon, Sun, Mercury, Venus, Mars, the Descendant and IC. Don't forget that conjunctions, oppositions, squares, quincunxes and trines have to be calculated. Personally I don't do aspects to house cusps, but some other astrologers may.

Transits of the Outer Planets – use a 10° to 15° orb

Astrologers use a number of methods to predict the future but like weather forecasting astrology is not easy. This is like a newspaper astrologer predicting events for large masses of people, (e.g. *all Pisces will have a nice day today*), or like predicting specific general events - like at election time. It is not easy nor is it very successful.

Astrology is, however, excellent at predicting '*trends*' for individuals. By this I mean that we can safely say that someone, a client, is going to experience difficulties or major changes in their relationship when Saturn, Chiron, Uranus, Neptune, or Pluto moves across or makes an aspect to their Venus or 7th house cusp. Predictions or forecasting is most accurate for a specific individual, for a specific time period, and in a specific manner. Just don't think that it will tell the name of your next lover, see a clairvoyant for those details.

We can project our predictions into the future quite easily because we use an ephemeris which has the planetary positions for the next 50 years or so. An ephemeris is the little book that has the planets position for every day of the year. Astrology will also give a time-line for events. It will give the beginning of the events, when the pressure will peak, and when it will end. All this is calculated using the ephemeris, and if you don't have it on paper your computer can do it for you.

Case study one – Bill
A man who went through a very stressful period in 1995 when I was counselling him, he had Uranus and Neptune transiting his Ascendant. Turn to your ephemeris now or use your astrology software (free or otherwise), look at June 1995, look backwards to find when Uranus first crossed his Ascendant at 27° Capricorn, then ahead to when it makes its final crossing of the Ascendant. You should find when Uranus applied to the Ascendant. In April / May 1994, this is a building up of energy or Uranian tension but it is not released, like a boil or blind pimple, not ready to be picked. It then retrogrades back a few degrees and rushes ahead and crosses in February 1995. This is its initial transit of the Ascendant, but wait, there's more! Uranus, like all the other planets, retrogrades and dilly-dallies about placing added pressure on Bill. It transited the Ascendant three times.

If we look at **Bill's** panic attacks they began building as Uranus applied to the Ascendant. In April 1994, **Bill's** relationship was going through a bad time, his girlfriend left him when Uranus moved into aspect with the Ascendant for the first time.

1) Stress in **Bill's** personal life begins as Uranus applies to the Asc.

2) Stress manifests as panic attacks and relationship problems.

3) His girlfriend says good bye as Uranus crosses / transits his Asc.

4) Relationship see-saws on-again-off-again over the next 12 months.

5) Relationship ends when Uranus finally crosses the Ascendant.

6) All the while **Bill** is unable to get rid of his panic attacks while Uranus is doing its thing on the Asc.

7) This is also an opportunity for **Bill** to get to know himself deeper, to get some counselling and to work on unresolved personal issues revolving around abandonment and relationships.

8) **Bill** sends a Christmas card in Xmas 1996 to say that he is doing well.

9) Therapy lasts 6 months, June 1995 to December 1995 with a few sessions through 1996.

10) By showing **Bill** the time line of expected stress, looking at real life issues as shown in his natal chart, and then tying them together with the transiting planets he was able to handle it much better. Uranus always provides opportunities in life like job options, real life rewards as a gift after he has put us through hell. I had my first book published and completed my psychology degree when Uranus transited my Ascendant, but he put me through hell first. This is a real life situation and one that is just so common. Let's look at some of the issues in **Bill's** life.

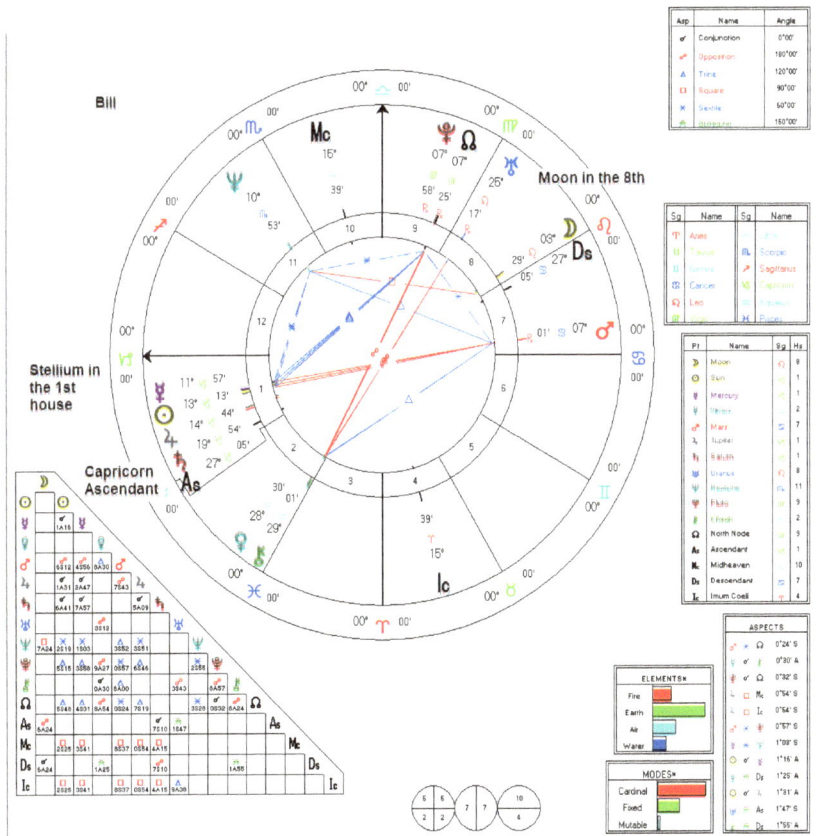

Bill's natal chart - possible problems to look for:
1) Saturn applying to Capricorn Ascendant – susceptible to depression with Saturn applying to the Ascendant. Saturn would also suggest issues

of abandonment. We could summarise right now and say that Bill has abandonment issues.

2) Sun, Mercury, Jupiter and Saturn in Capricorn in the 1st house – already we see issues of loss, not being in control, feeling abandoned, especially by his father. His girlfriend was the strong guiding influence in his life, like a father figure. But it also raises issues of **Bill** growing up and being a father are shattered when his girlfriend and future mother of his children leaves. But, with Jupiter, Sun and Mercury in the 1st house we would expect to see some happiness and joyfulness. Yes, he has the potential to be jovial but I don't see people who are happy, just sad. This will come out more and more as he slides away from Saturn's melodrama. Saturn also rules his Capricorn Asc which makes him that much more controlled and sad.

3) Moon in Leo – another buoyant planet, in the 8th opposite Ascendant, shows that he is in need of love and nurturing, loss of nurturing means loss of meaning. The 8th is the house of crisis and chaos as he transforms into the person he wants to become. This is a Singleton and has the single aspect to Neptune, and that is a square. I would say that this causes obvious trauma when it is triggered by transiting planets as they cross it (and the Ascendant). His normally jovial Moon in Leo is poorly aspected but he will try to smile when it is expected of him. His Moon is very important and confirms what we thought of him.

4) Venus conjunct Chiron (2nd house) opposite Uranus (in the 8th), North Node and Pluto in the 9th house. That's a dead give-away for the wound he is experiencing. Bill is wounded in love and any threat to his love (or object of love) is like bumping an old wound. Second house is security issues too. This in itself gives us Bill's major problem and also the direction therapy should go. This is a big aspect and one to watch for as it involves nurturing (and the Moon is all about nurturing too).

5) Mars Retrograde opposite Sun in Cancer – not a comfortable sign for Mars, it is too watery, too emotional, Retrograde focuses on unresolved anger or Martian issues and so instead of getting angry and yelling he gets angry, suppresses the anger and feels guilty, frustrated and depressed afterwards. Mars (anger) without expression = depression. Fortunately Bill is involved heavily in martial arts.

We don't need to look much further for clues, and his chart has a mixture of good and bad, but you should be able to find a few more. There are strengths of course, and these are used in therapy, but it is the weaknesses, the painful wounds that are our best indicators of where we should work in therapy (or psychological astrology). These are constitutional, they are what **Bill** is born with and are therefore deep psychological wounds that require healing. Our examination of Bill's natal chart shows his possible problems, an examination of the transiting planets shows what is hurting, where it is hurting and why it is hurting.

The outer planets in transit – we start with Uranus

In transits we use the outer planets initially because they are slow moving and therefore act on sensitive points in the chart over a longer period. Uranus can be rather rough, creates stress and tension. Panic is one of its manifestations, though panic is a keyword for all the outer planets.

* Transiting Uranus rules Aquarius – Venus is in Aquarius and so is affected by what Uranus does in the transiting chart. Its effect is to stress Venus' activities, stress in Bill's love-life. Venus is a key player though we cannot see it in action right now.

* Uranus is in the 8th house natally, it is close to the 8th cusp and so is a little weaker here. This natal placement opens up issues of crisis and transformation through crisis, 8th house activities. It is also karmically placed, in other words it is placed in the 8th house showing that when it is triggered by transit or progression it will manifest as a crisis in preparation for transformation at a deep spiritual and personal level. Uranus is also a Singleton (one aspect).

* Uranus rules Aquarius which is on the 2nd cusp of security, security is being threatened.

* **Uranus is transiting the 1st house stellium and Ascendant**. The 1st house and Ascendant are a microcosm of the macrocosm, it is a miniature soul, so what happens to it will affect the entire being, it is a very sensitive point in the chart.

* **Uranus has already transited Sun, Mercury, Jupiter and Saturn** over the past few years weakening Bill's resistance to stress and so he is ripe for a major stress attack. We could safely say that Bill has been stressed for some 4 to 5 years while Uranus worked through his Capricorn stellium.

* Uranus is opposing the natal Moon – this is an applying aspect and thus building up, it can be a frightening aspect as it opens wounds of love, nurturing and abandonment that are part of the 8th house.

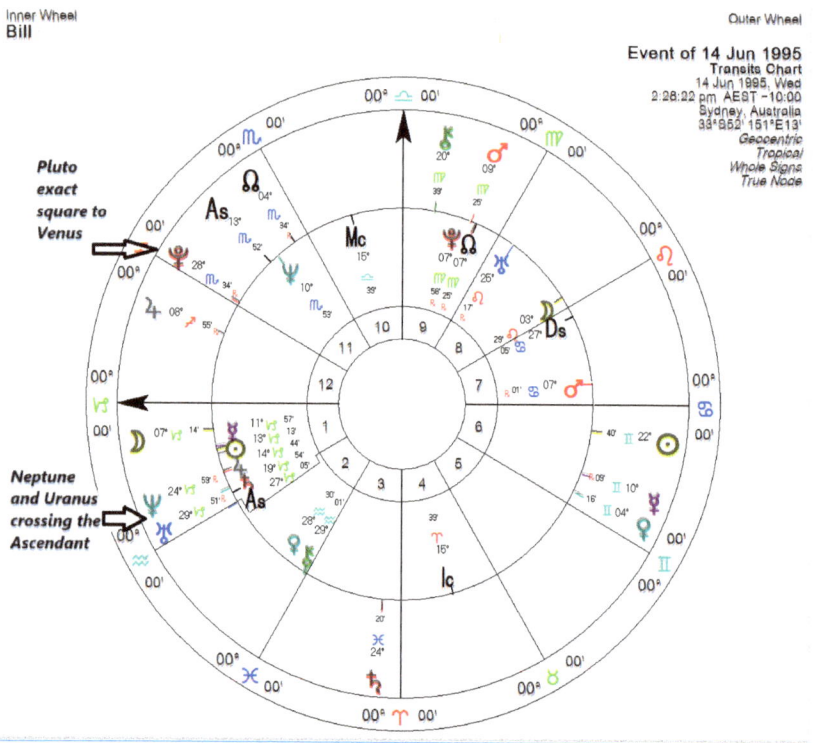

* **Transiting Neptune** has also worked through the stellium, it is also applying to the Ascendant. Neptune is preparing to dissolve the Self, this is frightening because everything Bill thought was safe and secure is no longer. Neptune is confusion, disillusionment and abandonment, all part of Bill's panic attack issues.

* **Transiting Pluto** is squaring natal Venus – now we see another pointer or clue to where the stress is happening. A square could manifest as denial, *"My relationship is fine."* while it falls apart, or it could manifest as not noticing the relationship falling apart because he is too busy working on other issues.

* **North Node squaring Moon** – applying as it retrogrades back through the zodiac. This places extra stress on Bill to resolve Moon issues (mother and nurturing) and shows that this is destiny, it is serious stuff and there is a reason behind it. When the North Node is involved with these major transits you know that it is for a reason and will have an effect on the person for many years to come.

Bill did therapy for 6 months then off and on for another 6 months. He came through
nicely but it was a very difficult time for him.

Transits by Outer Planets – why do we use the outer planets first?
The outer planets are powerful, they are REAL and they represent deep psychological traits and issues of the individual. They awaken us to our own power from within. In transit, the inner planets don't last very long, two days for Sun, Mercury and Venus. The Moon lasts only about four hours and Mars a week or two. They don't put pressure on us for very long, we can shrug them off quite easily. The outer planets however, stay around and sit on those sensitive points and planets for ages, in some cases it is years, they won't let up until we acknowledge them. We need to recognise what it is that needs fixing, if we are smart we then do something about it - they won't be shrugged off.

The outer planet transits are major transformers of our psyche. Just think of your holiday in Fiji, no worries, no $$$ problems, no stress, no reason to transform. We could be the world's biggest and nastiest person and while thing goes well, you are not forced to make changes. Then along comes an outer planet like a Cyclone (or Hurricane in the northern hemisphere). It tips you out of your hammock, the wind blows sand in your face and your wallet is stolen, what do you do? You have to acknowledge, accept and then work to better your situation. That is what astrology demonstrates, the dynamic process of self development, be it spiritual, material or emotional and what causes it.

How Do We Calculate Transits
It's all in the software, simply click on the natal chart, then go to the transit button and click that. You need to select the place, date and time for the transit you wish to project onto the natal chart. All transits must be connected to a natal chart unless all you want is a chart for that time, in which case you would select a transit or natal chart with that time, date and place.

Outer planet transits - how they work
The energy builds up as it applies to the natal degree, like a steam train slowly climbing a hill. The pressure builds up to boiling point and is released as it crosses the peak and goes down the hill. The issues involved with the planet (or point) begins with a nudge, then it gets painful, then it bursts out in agony and is finally released as the last carriage reaches the crest and begins its way down the hill. To show this better we use the bell curve showing that as the planets gets closer the pressure increases (applies) and decreases as it leaves (separates).

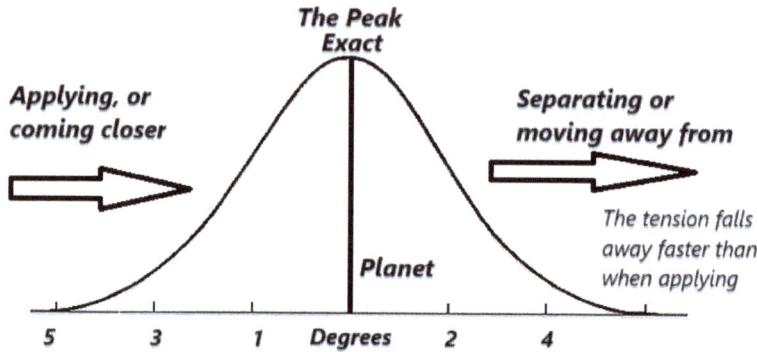

The Bell Curve – as the planet gets closer to the exact degree (Applies) the pressure increases. The pressure lessens as it moves away (Separates).

The problem with most transits is that they don't just move across smoothly, they stop, go retrograde (moves backwards), stops again, goes direct, stops, retrogrades, stops, goes direct, etc. Often they will cross the exact degree up to 5 times before finally moving away. In these situations the pressure is tremendous initially, the first few transits or crossings, the wound is fresh. The second feels almost as bad, the third not so bad and forth and firth are just a nuisance, *"Hey, I've been here before but now I'm getting used to it."* Finally when it moves off the lesson is generally well on its way to being resolved. At least we hope or else it will resurface again under another outer planet transit.

Looking at a transit as a lesson in life we could say:
The initial transit is the awakening stage, it yells loudly, *"Listen, you've got a problem here, pal."* This makes you sit up and take notice. It then retrogrades backwards across the exact degree again and feels like, *"Not again, I don't think that I can handle this!"*

It then stops, goes direct and crosses a third time, *"Oh no, not this again? I thought this was resolved, damn it!"* It stops and goes retrograde and crosses/transits the exact degree for a fourth time, *"Yeah, I know, this is what it feels like. I'm getting used to visiting this space. I think I better get some help or maybe I'll try that bottle of Black Label again."*

The transiting planet now goes direct and makes its final transit of the planet. In **Bill's** case it is his Ascendant, and so we say, *"Well, if it isn't that same old feeling again, I think I will just ignore it."* By this stage you are fed up well and truly, battle scared and weather beaten, slightly lame and stiff from sitting being depressed. Or, you could be well on the path to insight and transformation. You could use this transit as a kick in the rear to seek help in some way.

Planets – key words for transits
Jupiter – expansion, making things appear bigger and better than we first thought, opportunities, biting off more than we can chew, risk taker, greed, narcissist, situations blowing up in our faces, speed - things going faster. It seeks to illuminate, expands consciousness of the house that it is transiting. Jupiter is both a good guy and a narcissist, he has two distinct sides to his coin. Be careful in translating Jupiter because he can be either.
Saturn – depression, limitation, frustration, fear, worthlessness, anxiety, things stop,
time stands still, consolidation if used wisely, taking real situations and making them work. Remember this though, Saturn seeks to consolidate, organise and stabilise the house it is transiting.
Chiron – the wound awakens, pain, fear, anxiety, frustration, anguish, a seeking for meaning and insight, the quest. It seeks to heal the affairs of the house it is transiting and usually does it in an uncomfortable manner.
Uranus – stress, tension, nervousness, hyperactivity, opportunities, rebel and revolution. It seeks to release the inhibitions and limitations of the house that it is transiting.
Neptune – abandonment, fear, loss, betrayal, grief, illusions, disillusioned, confused, daydreaming, unable to grasp why it is happening to me. Neptune seeks to soften the issues associated with the house that it is transiting but it can cause confusion and despair.
Pluto – the depths of despair, fear, panic, extreme worthlessness, pain, down in the gutter, black depression, betrayal, power awakening because nothing can hurt me more than I am feeling right now. It seeks to transform the issues of the house that it is transiting through holding you down until you are ready to let go of everything. Yes, he is like an 'all-or-nothing' guy.
North Node – indicates that this is a seriously soul developing moment in life and very important to get it right. It seeks to show us what is going on and just how serious this is.

Transits – Bill's calculations
By looking at the orbs (and applying or separating, please work them out yourself from your ephemeris) we can see immediately that the planets within a 2° orb using major aspects only to the Outer Planets, are:

Tr. Jupiter – quincunx Mars
Tr. Saturn – quincunx Uranus
Tr. Chiron – trine Saturn
Tr. Uranus – conjunction Ascendant
Tr. Neptune – conjunct Ascendant
Tr. Pluto – square Venus and Chiron, sextile Asc.
Nth Node – square Moon, conjunct Neptune

Aspects – only tells part of the story, we do need to get outside and see the weather with our own eyes, not just sit in front of the TV and watch the weather man. Looking at the chart shows what is brewing, Neptune is working his way towards the Asc., Uranus is moving across the Asc. Pluto is looking to go exact square Venus, etc.

Houses – where are the powerful outer planets? What houses do they occupy, what are they transforming? Apply your key words to these houses too. Are any of the planets moving into a new house or sign? Do any of the planets fall on house cusps, this will emphasise house and planet issues.

~

Case study two - Joe
Joe has recently divorced, an ugly one too. He now lives with his mother, a demanding and demeaning woman, he is coping but unhappy. His ex-wife has remarried and has trouble coping with the demands of her three ADHD teenagers. In fact she swapped one dysfunctional partner for another. Joe is an average Aussie bloke, he has a car, works as a plumber, drinks home-brew, has three kids and a dog. But his family situation in not all that 'crash hot'. His three children have ADHD (like him), his wife has a pituitary problem requiring life-long medication. His mother told him she wanted him to divorce his wife if he wanted his inheritance, and he is an alcoholic. By applying your knowledge of personality development you can glean more information from his chart that describes the best way to treat his problems in therapy. Look at Joe's Fire chart:- Leo Moon, Jupiter conjunct Sun and 3 planets in Aries, and the Personal Planets, Venus & Mars, are in Fire houses. Then there is the Grand Cross and Moon conjunct Pluto.

Object Relations Theory, which is basically about how we manage life through objects, tells us that Joe has issues with love and abandonment. This can be applied using astrological symbols (basically a combination of Jung and Objects Relations) which states that for every astrological symbol (planet, sign or house) there is a corresponding 'object'. For instance Moon would represent the object of 'mother', Venus of 'money' or 'lover', Mars of 'drive' or 'aggression', etc.

Joe, has Sun in Aries conjunct Mercury and Jupiter, opposes Saturn and Neptune and squares Uranus and Chiron to form a **Grand Cross** (Sun + Mercury opp Saturn and all 3 square Uranus and Chiron). Sun also trines Pluto, quincunxes Mars, resides in the 2nd house of security and rules Leo on the 6th cusp.

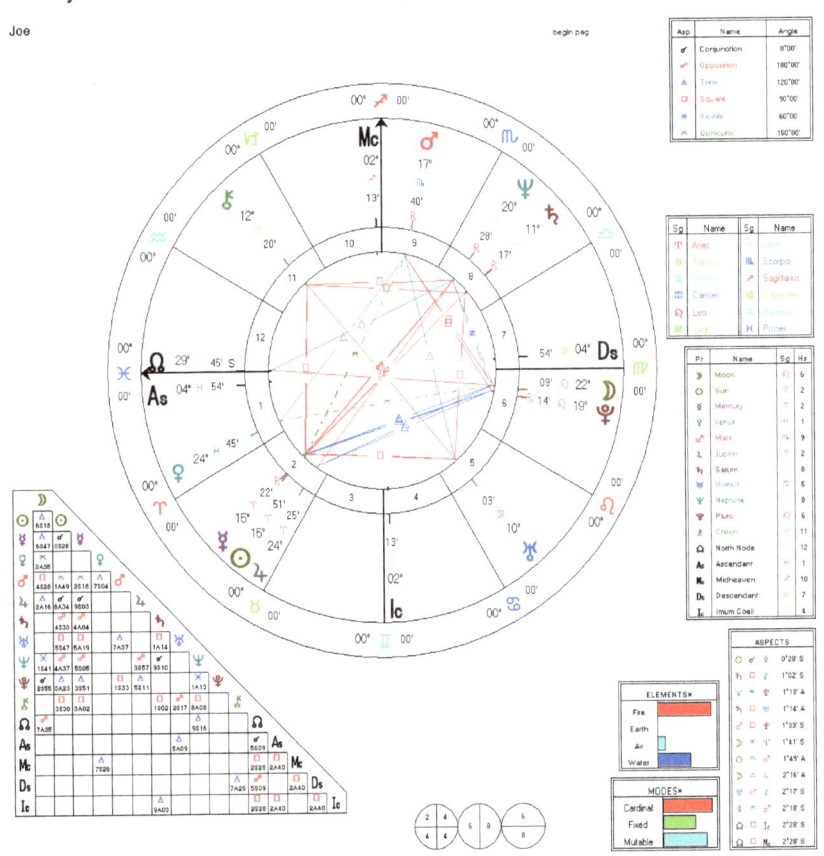

As you can see the Sun is a very active and influential planet. Using your knowledge of the Elemental Defences (last chapter) we can see 6 points in Fire: Venus and Mars in Fire houses (1st, 9th) and the two luminaries, Sun and Moon, both in Fire signs, and the Midheaven in Fire.

Then there are Mercury, Jupiter and Pluto all in Fire signs. It is possible that Joe had hyperactivity, anger outbursts, self-centeredness, episodes of manic joyfulness, Attention Deficit Hyperactivity Disorder (ADHD), a racing mind, and sleep disturbance.

Already we begin to see the 'objects' he will relate to in a dysfunctional way. Fire is heavily emphasised so immediately we see that he needs stimulation, attention and affection. He will compete for the attentions of those 'objects' that support his needs. We can now see that this level of attachment is manifesting in alcohol abuse.

Planets powerfully in aspect in Joe's chart:
Sun / father is in great need - in Aries in 2nd (physical insecurity), quincunx to Mars and square Chiron, square Uranus, opposition to Neptune and Saturn, part of a Grand Cross. Its conjunction to Mercury and Jupiter increases his needs for security and affection (and if he can't get that some alcohol will do).
Moon / mother / wife - in 6th in Leo is attention seeking and needing to serve, square Mars, conjunct Pluto, opposite North Node all point to basic needs for affection. There is also a need to express himself in some way, usually inappropriately.
Venus / wife / lover / money - Pisces, 1st house and needs to be expressed as it has a lot of love and libidinal energy, quincunx Moon and trine Mars.
Mars - Scorpio and 9th house, quincunx Sun/Mercury, square Moon, Square Moon/Pluto. It is also the Planet of High Degree and needs to be expressed, mainly with his children, having fun and laughing and I don't think he has enough of this.
Chiron - in Capricorn in the 11th house, opposite Uranus, part of Grand Cross squares Sun/Mercury and Saturn/Neptune and is very bothersome standing out like a sore thumb.
North Node - conjunct Ascendant, Pisces, opposite Moon / Pluto.
Uranus—Cancer in the 5th house, square Sun / Mercury / Saturn, opposite Chiron, trine Mars. It is an awkward planet with only one good aspects, the trine to Mars.
Saturn—Libra in 8th house, forms part of the Grand Cross too.
Neptune – is significant in that it is the Lord Of The Chart and helps form a pattern with North Node + Moon/Pluto so helps them stabilise on some way.
Pluto – conjunct Moon and that is one of the most significant signs for us as it sits on his Moon and manifests some positive aspects with its trines to Jupiter, Sun and Mercury. In many ways it is a difficult planet as it

conjuncts Moon, but it also has positive aspects.

Looking at the pivotal role of the Sun in Aries and the Fire emphasis we see that **Joe** needed a lot more attention from his father. Why father? Jupiter conjunct Sun shows that father was somewhat influential and giving, and if powerfully aspected it can show that father did not 'give' enough of himself. Now this is complicated, Sun is heavily aspected, it is insecure in the 2nd house, over emphasised in Fire, it needs attention and affection, is competitive (for recognition), is aggressive and argumentative.

Jupiter shows a conjunction, but not a tight conjunction, so there was some attention from father, but the other aspects show that Sun/father was not a good 'object'. Immediately we find conflict—the object of 'father' was not good, but was good! Jupiter conjunct Sun is the good bit, while the other poor aspects show it was not good.

Moon is his controlling but charming mother, is conjunct Pluto square Mars and nicely trine Sun / Mercury / Jupiter. It's nicely aspected but that conjunction with Pluto... hmm, I'm just not sure. Using an *Objects Relations* approach we would say that the internalised object of father (self-esteem, vitality, support, guidance, mentoring) was one in which:-

Conjunct Mercury in Aries — father argues with me or ignores my intelligence.

Square Uranus — father creates tension and stress, 5th house shows he is not fun though I wish he were.

Quincunx Mars — he creates tension, is aggressive and can make me angry.

Opposite Saturn — he limits and inhibits me, fathers take my freedom off me, they dominate, discipline and frighten me.

Opposite Neptune — father betrays me, he is never there for me, he is not trustworthy.

Conjunct Jupiter — father mentors, guides and gives to me on an older mature level (like an uncle).

Part of Grand Cross—a Cross is a strong Earthy Defence, a planetary pattern that indicates fixed views or fixed opinions. It is unable to let go of thinking patterns and is stubborn yet it also gives the strength to complete what he has set out to do. Patterns play a dual role, one shows the weakness it causes yet within that weakness is strength, in this case it's to lock on and not let go. It also manifests in society as being available to the community when difficulties strike.

History

When **Joe** was 12 years old his father left home and mother took up with a new man. This new guy was Jupiter, an 'uncle' or mentor figure who fulfilled the 'idealised' father figure that Joe needed. Neptune in the 8th house opposite Sun, shows Jupiter's idealisation. There is one positive aspect to father, his Sun trine Moon / Pluto. He both hated and loved his 'father' object.

The Sun trine Moon / Pluto is interesting. When he was a child mother was everything, she ran the household and told Joe how important he was. She also said that father was 'no good'. So the 'object' of father was conditioned by the original relationship or 'object' of mother, his first 'love' object. Joe listened and believed his mother's version of reality, to do otherwise would be to betray his 'love object' (mother). But, he unconsciously knew that his mother didn't always tell the truth, she could also be domineering, aggressive and controlling (Moon conjunct Pluto, quincunx Venus, square Mars). She also inhibited his personal and spiritual growth (opposite North Node) by destroying his relationship with his father.

We now have Joe believing his mother (his 'love' object) when she says that his father (his 'support' object) was 'no good'. He was fortunate to have a step-father enter the picture while he was still a young man to fulfil the Jupiter / Neptune aspect. Joe then projected his 'support' needs onto this step-father who was a positive and supporting person (Jupiter).

Object Relations shows that the two main objects in Joe's life, Sun / father and Moon / mother, are very powerfully placed in his psyche. Astrology shows that they are also very complicated in their 'objects' of:- support, self-esteem, vitality (Sun); nurturer, wife, lover (Moon).

Joe's Moon was later projected onto his wife, who took up on his need to be controlled (conjunct Pluto), to be nagged and dominated (square Mars), and to have unsatisfactory sex (quincunx Venus in Pisces). He was already disillusioned by the betrayal from his father (opposite Neptune) and so his self-esteem dropped, and with all that stress in his chart he began to drink heavily.

This fulfilled two roles: (1) to avoid the responsibility of acting like a man because he felt that he was a failure. (2) To take the edge off his bitter disappointment with his 'love' object and 'sex' object (mother—wife).

His wife wasn't interested in sex with him so he drank every night to escape his disappointment. She put him down and ignored his needs. She devoted her attention and affections on their three children possibly creating an Oedipal Complex between father and eldest son.

He failed her by showering her with unwanted affection and gifts, he would not leave her alone when he was home during the weekends. His wife, his 'love' object (replacing his mother) avoided him. His manliness was unattainable, he felt unworthy of being a man, impotent (powerless), so he escaped by drinking. His ADHD impulsive behaviour was also a turn off. He was moody, angry and aggressive when upset, this was getting out of control especially when his three children were also ADHD and had their own needs and problems. Thus the mother, the 'love' object (his wife), could not cope with four ADHD kids at home so she switched off.

Finally, they sought counselling for their marriage problems. I worked with each individually, and because we lived out in the country we began to deal with their individual needs in their own individual style. The first thing we worked with was Joe's relationship with his father. He discovered that his father really loved him and that in hindsight his mother was the one who disciplined him while father stayed away as much as he could (drinking and working). Her controlling temper tantrums were just too much for poor old dad. Dad 'escaped', leaving the step-father to be the hero in his place. He then adopted his 'objects' from his mother, she taught him who was good and who was bad. It was not until he sought counselling that he found out the truth about his father.

This is where astrology comes into the picture. How else could we explore Joe's relationships without the aid of astrology, without months of expensive therapy? Psychological astrology pointed out swiftly and with such clarity his *Object Relationships* with his parents. By resolving his issues of abandonment and betrayal from his father, Joe was able to claw back some of his self-esteem. He was able to see his mother for what she was, manipulative and domineering. Is it normal to tell your son to divorce your wife so that he could get his inheritance? By exploring his foundation objects, 'father' and 'mother', he was able to make decisions, he had power now, to decide to leave or to stay and change.

Joe didn't have to make any decisions in the end. Remember that his wife received therapy too and we were able to put her foundations into perspective. She found that she wanted out, that she didn't want to replay her own parent's marriage all over again, so she left him. Did I feel a failure? Not really, the outcome was much the same as it had been for ages, they had both achieved what they came to me about, their life.

Astrology provides the 'objects' or 'archetypes' that we have founded our lives upon. Jung used archetypes, I also use archetypes, while *Object Relations* use 'objects'. I think they all say much the same thing.

This is what I'd do. I would look at the role of Pluto in Joe's women for each generation (grandmother, mother and child, and any other family members I could gain birth data for). I would then explore a psychological theory which could explain issues such as:- domination, power, sexuality, anguish, abandonment, hurt, wounding, violence, etc. all the key words that go with the Pluto archetype. I would then explore Fire, Sun, Jupiter and Pisces on the male side. The Ascendant and its ruler Neptune are playing such a powerful role of betrayal and need to be explored.

Next I would look at Joe's parents and his own children's charts and compare and contrast the major elements, planets, signs and houses that flow through each. By combining astrology and psychology of the family we can get a more complete understanding of ourselves, our families and our clients.

~

Chapter 6: Secondary Progressions and Solar Arc Directions

How do astrologers attempt to tell the future? They use predictive astrology. Astrologers use three main methods to determine future events or trends, Secondary Progressions, Solar Arc Directions, and Transits.

Progressions and Directions
Progressions and Directions are generally called 'progressions'. They are considered 'internal' because they are not outwardly visible, they happen in the person's inner / unconscious world, as part of their emotional or personal growth. Transits, on the other hand, are visible. we can actually see that the planets in the sky have moved, and are therefore considered 'external'. They happen in the outer or external world as real events, real experiences. Therefore Progressions and Directions use the inner planets perhaps more than the outer planets.

The difference can be simple, transits, like transiting Saturn square natal Mars = frustration and anger. Their outcome in the real world is through actual temper tantrums or being accident prone. If it was Progressed or Directed Saturn square natal Mars = frustration and anger, the outcome would be more likely internal. It would manifest as resentment, turned inwards as stomach ulcers and passive aggressive behaviour (pretend to follow orders but sabotage when no one is looking), headaches and insomnia.

"Day for a Year"
Progressions and Directions both use one day for each year of progression. Secondary Progressions use the ephemeris to advance your chart one day for each year of your life, while the Solar Arc Direction (Directions) advances the Sun one day for each year. **Remember**, the Sun in a Solar Arc Direction, moves ALL the planets one degree for a year.

Apparently there is some mention in the Bible to uphold this method. I don't consider the Bible to be a sound source of scientific empirical methodology but I believe that this method has been used for centuries and is still in use. It is taught by the best astrology schools and backed up by evidence at a personal level.

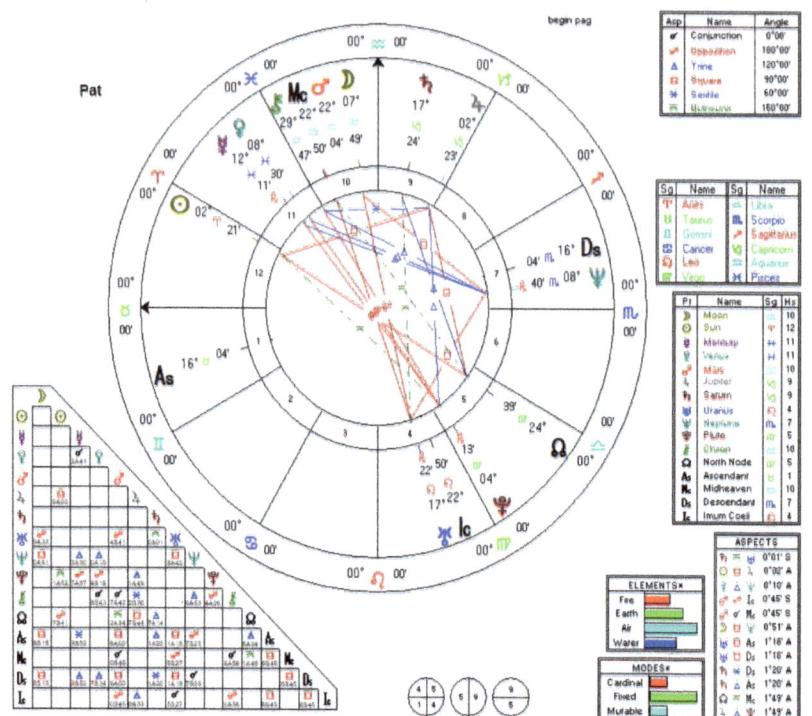

[Image: Pat, natal chart]

The real proof is when I have done a reading for a client and I see the same theme repeated in three ways: **Transits (Tr), Secondary Progressed Moon (SR or progression)** and **Solar Arc Directed (SA)**. For example: a lady in the middle of personal relationship problems has Transiting Pluto and Tr. Saturn aspecting Natal Venus and 7th house cusp; Solar Arc Directed show Directed Saturn aspecting Natal Venus and Directed Moon aspecting Natal Pluto; the same is repeated with Secondary Progressed Moon conjunct 7th house cusp - all point to a crisis in her relationship. By the way, the methods used to calculate these progressions are different, so statistically there is no way that this would happen by chance.

Secondary Progressed Moon / Solar Arc Directed Orbs—keep them tight, to within 1/2 to 1° only

Keep orbs tight for Progressions and Directions. It only takes one degree for a whole year so a half degree orb is better. If Saturn were progressing Venus, we would say that it builds up, from 1° applying to exact, and then separating for 1/2°. I describe to my client a 12 months period of tension (depends on the planets of course). I tell them that it takes 6 months to build up to an exact aspect (half a degree). It becomes its most intense at about two months before exact (applying), after the exact degree (separating) it is still intense for another 1 or 2 months, it then eases off over the last 4 to 5 months. In other words 6 months applying and 6 months separating.

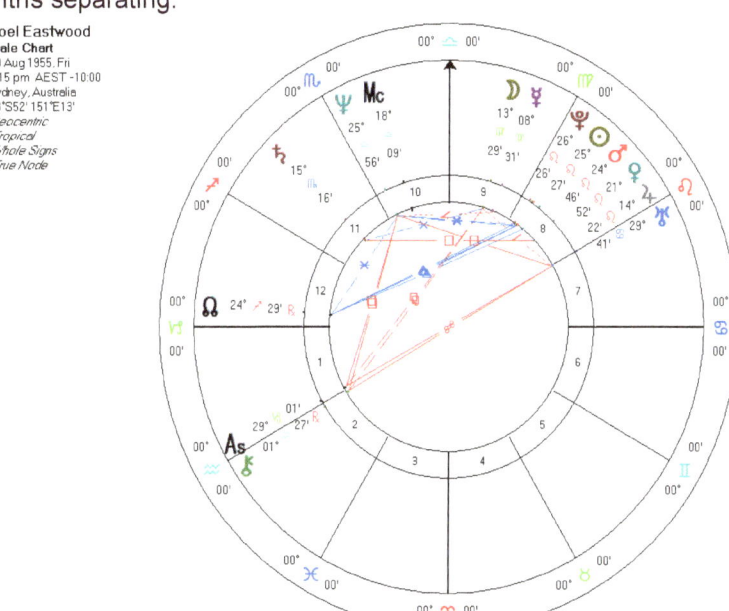

[Image: as you can see that's my chart up there. We use the 90° Dial when doing Solar Arc Directions. The chart is drawn up using my natal chart and adding the number of degrees for my birthday which makes 69 days ahead in time for 69 years – one day for a year. The inner wheel stays still while the outer wheel moves one degree per year in an anticlockwise direction. All the planets move the same degrees which is 69. Both my charts can now be draw into one chart using a 90° Dial.]

Solar Arc Directions—they are put into a 90° grid

When we use the day-for-a-year system of progression we look at how far the Sun has moved and **move all the planets by the same degree**. In other words if you are doing a chart for a client, Patricia (Pat), and she has presented for a reading in August 2024, she wants to know what is in store for her. You will calculate, amongst all the other things you calculate, her Solar Arc Directed. She is now 63 years old, her Sun has travelled 63 degrees, therefore the Sun (and all the planets) has made an Arc of 63 degrees.

Illustration: Venus is square Uranus - but it looks conjunct

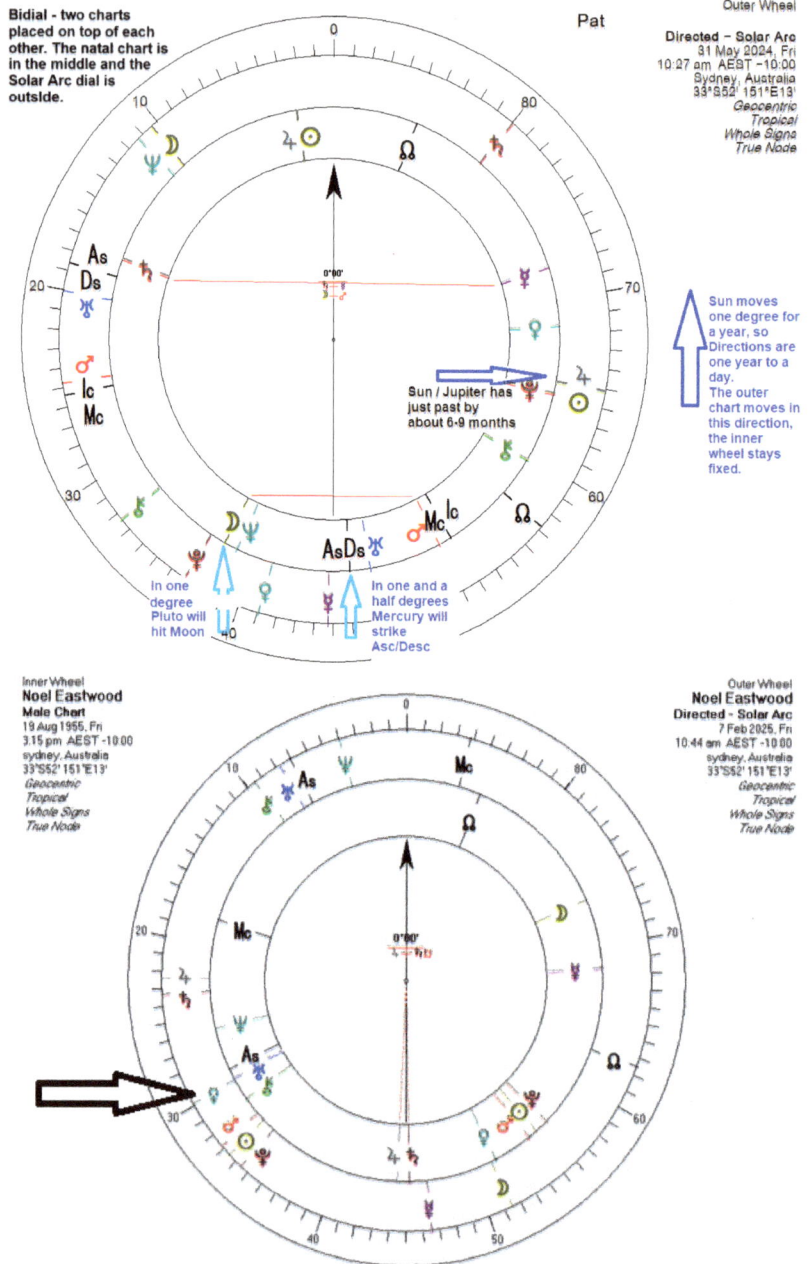

[Chart: we have used my chart to demonstrate. This method cuts the *chart into one 90° dial. We have my natal chart on the inside, it looks different now that it is shrunk down to 90° and not 360°, and my new chart is on the outside. Look, Venus on the outer rim is square to my Uranus although it looks like a conjunction].*

In Solar Arc Directed we simply progress ALL planets forward the same arc as the Sun. Don't forget to calculate 60 minutes to one degree and 30 degrees to one sign. Now we plot **Pat's** natal planets against the progressed planets to see which ones are in aspect. We can see that her Directed Pluto is about to crash into her Natal Moon then Neptune within 12 months; and Directed Mercury is about the crash into her Natal Ascendant within 12 months. This will make her feel very low. In 12 to 18 months Transiting Pluto will come into Moon's orb and starts playing up. This happens about 6 months or so after the events described by the Directs chart. Then there is Neptune and Saturn also crossing the Natal Sun at the same time. Something will go wrong for her before the event hits the fan. That, my friends, is a bad sign. Please note that this chart is a Dial of 90° not 360° so they look like conjunctions but the are really squares.

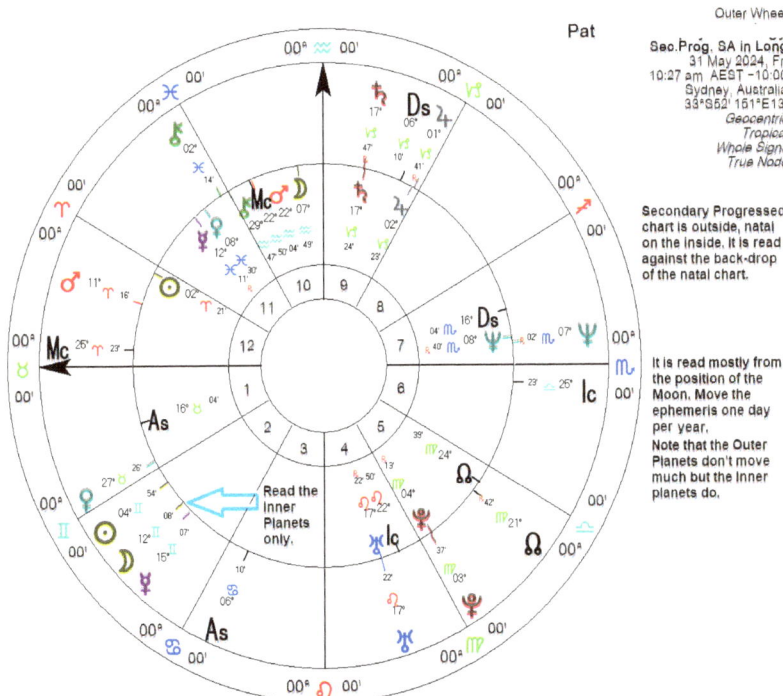

Secondary Progressed Moon – Progressions don't use the Dial
This is the most popular method of determining future events next to

transits. It is quite simple, again we move forward the number of days for the years that have elapsed between birth and the event. **Unlike the Solar Arc Directed chart they are not fixed to the Suns orb** but keep their position. That's why we only use the inner planets.

The Moon travels the fastest, about 12 degrees per day compared to the others (Sun, Venus and Mercury - the next fastest move about 1 degree per day) and can trigger minor events. The Solar Arc Directed Moon moves one degree per month and you'll see what I mean in a minute. It is a great predictor all by itself.

Looking at Pat's Biwheel we can see if there are any house changes for the Sun, Mercury, Venus, Mars and Moon. They would only be important if they changed house at the time of our reading, then we could tell Pat to take notice. The only thing this chart highlights is that there is stress in her 2nd house of security. The next big exercise is to progress the Moon for each month of the year that you are calculating.

Calculations of the Secondary Progressed Moon Monthly motion— Pat meets her future husband

First of all we need to adjust for our Moon's placement because we didn't have an exact midnight birth time and remember that the ephemeris only shows planets at midnight. To adjust we simply use the same method we did to calculate the natal planets. We see that the Moon travelled 14 degrees and 36 minutes in the day, but for our progressed calculations we say that it travelled this far in one year (year-for-a-day).

[Image: the Secondary Progressed chart is usually done as a wheel. The inner wheel is the natal chart and stays still, while the outer wheel has the Solar Arc Directions and moves one degree per year of life in an anticlockwise direction.]

Our most accurate calculations in progressions are the Secondary Progressed Moon. With the Moon moving roughly one degree per month we can see what is transpiring every month, using a one degree orb we can be pretty accurate. This method of using the Secondary Progressed Moon for prediction is most commonly used in early infancy, looking at our experiences in the very important first few years. Each month the Moon moves about 1 degree. We surmise here, of course, because the only way we know what happened as a child was from reports from our parents or siblings. It is worth exploring this fascinating area, read Howard Sasportas and Liz Greene's *'The Development of Personality'* for more on Secondary Progressed Moon.

How to read Secondary Progressed Moon charts
The house position of Secondary Progressed planets is important. When you have calculated the progressed planets place them in the natal chart and see if they have moved into a new sign or a new house. Use a one degree orb and see if they are applying to a new planet. We look specifically for change, does a planet change signs or house? Are there new aspects being made? As Secondary Progressions rarely change in the first 20 to 30 years of life, look mostly at the Moon's position for younger clients.

Meanings: is the same for both Solar Arc Directed and Secondary Progressed Moon.
Progressed Sun — general health, father, heart, back, important men, bureaucracy, ego and self, vitality and personal needs. If the natal Sun is aspected by progression it is similar to transits but is internal or subconscious. It may indicate that this is an important year for the native. Look especially if the progressed Sun changes sign or house, this represents an important period in the natives life. This means that the person will take on some of the personality characteristics of that sign.
Progressed Moon - important mother influences and emotional times. The Secondary Progressed Moon is particularly important as it moves through a sign and/or house every 2 and a half years, which is much the same as Saturn's movement through the zodiac. It parallels Saturn so watch when the two aspect important planets. The house that the Secondary Progressed Moon travels through is the focus of the native's life for that period.

The Moon rules breasts, female organs and stomach so these could be triggered during progression of emotional points in the chart. It also affects females in the natives life: mother, society at large, emotions, nurturing, etc. In fact, whenever the Secondary Progressed Moon crosses a planet or cusp you can bet that an emotional moment is about to take place. If the natal planet is stable then it will be fine, but if unstable then it will be the focal point for the month leading up to its exact aspect (applying) and one month leading away from it (separating).

Watch for progressed **New Moon** (Secondary Progressed Moon crossing natal Sun) and progressed **Full Moon** (Secondary Progressed Moon opposite natal Sun), these will show important events and feelings. Yes, Secondary Progressed Moon aspects are minor psychological awakenings, they can be easy or difficult but rarely severe as they only last a month and does not have the supercharge of an outer planet.
Progressed Mercury - not a great or exciting show when Mercury

aspects from progressions. May indicate mental activity to stimulate hobbies and interests. Friendships and parties may flourish and communication may be at the top of the list. Children could also be triggered by a natives progressed Mercury. Retrograde progressed Mercury is a time of introversion, looking inwards, a great time for meditation and dreaming. Health areas to watch are nervous system and mind, keep meditating and Earthing if mental activity gets too much. Watch for Retrograde, Direct and Stationary movement in the ephemeris.

Progressed Venus - relationships of all kinds. Look at art and music, decorating and changing house colours, look at glands and organs as well as fluids, kidneys and large intestine for water flow, what goes in must come out. It is also money and cash flow so it could indicate good times or tight times. Look at when it goes Retrograde or Direct, change of sign or house and aspects to Moon and Sun in particular as they may indicate some love involvement, good or not so good.

Progressed Mars - Secondary Progressed Mars can aspect natal planets for up to 5 years. Watch when Retrograde and going Direct as well as change of sign and house, aspects to inner planets and luminaries. Indicates drive and energy, but could also show aggression, frustration and health like high blood pressure. Health is cuts, wounds, bleeding, surgery, accidents, blood and fevers.

Progressed Jupiter - can aspect for up to 12 years when in aspect by Secondary Progression. Rules law, morals, religion and travel, health is nutrition, gall bladder and liver, so if aspecting a personal planet or angle watch the alcohol intake. On a negative note watch for narcissistic behaviour, selfishness, greed and criminal behaviour.

Progressed Saturn - shows limitations and where the native needs to consolidate the lessons learnt in life. Often Saturn will make us feel under the heel of a powerful force when all he wants is for us to pay attention to life and to what we are doing. Saturn will often ask of us to slow down, or else we may crash. Look at skeletal structure, inhibition, consolidation, teeth, exercise, facing up to responsibility.

Progressed Chiron - wounds of all sorts, but most will be psychological wounds. Openings and closing of wounds, making them conscious is the role of Chiron's directions and transits. The best thing about Chiron is that he gives you a handle on what he is doing, you will 'see' the problem before it gets too large. Use these progressions to work on your personal emotional issues, learn that the real issue is to "let it go" if it is not working for you. Very similar to Pluto.

Progressed Uranus - can come as a rush, activity, hyperactivity, opportunities and adventures. However, he always asks for payment for his gifts: hard work, honest attention to personal integrity and he will demand a high price of your mental and physical body. Watch nervous system and take nutrients that will support high levels of stress, tension, mental and physical activity.

Progressed Neptune - this is often subtle and hard to understand, basically because Neptune is subconscious, in the astral and in dreams. It manifests as an inability to 'see' direction, "*Where should I go now, what should I be doing?*" It will appear as though the native has no direction, that destiny has been taken out of their control and they are left stranded and abandoned. Neptune transits and progressions can be quite demanding and frustrating basically because you have no way of knowing what is going on, like being in a fog. Watch infections and mystery illnesses that come and go. Fluids and mucus linings, lungs and addictions, it is best to wait for it to pass. Apply your Taoist philosophy of "*non resistance, go slowly but safely, non-doing*" until it is out of orb and the fog clears.

Progressed Pluto - a time to call upon the powers of rejuvenation, also a time for seeking counselling because he will not let up until you have cried 'uncle'. "*Giving in*" is the key phrase for Pluto progressions and transits. The problems faced are more obvious than Neptune's, less exciting than Uranus, and much deeper than Chiron's. Health is sex organs and can be severe life-threatening illnesses that force us to reflect upon our lives. Pluto wishes us to think upon our meaning and purpose of existence, and if it is time to let go take up yoga or painting until it shows itself – don't be impatient because he is serious.

Progressed North Node - this indicates that whatever you are going through is a very valuable and insightful period, best to take note of it and go with the hard road instead of giving it up. When you see this activated in the chart you can bet that events beyond our understanding are occurring in the deep subconscious driven by destiny.

Progressed Ascendant - when it changes it shows a new mask for the native to wear, perhaps indicating that they have grown up or matured. May also show new health problems or weaknesses as well as psychological problems with the new mask / sign.

Progressed Midheaven MC - shows career and work, ambitions and achievements when aspected by transit and progression. Watch for new activity when it changes sign.

Summary

Progressions show internal psychological states and stressors that will show what the native is thinking and coping with but not necessarily talking about. If the same planet, house or cusp is aspected by progression and transit then what is happening in the real world (transit) is affecting them at a subconscious emotional level (progression). Thoughts, emotions and actual changes in the outer world, could manifest as change in job, getting sacked, affecting emotions and thoughts.

Important Note:- For Solar Arc Directed use all the planets. For Secondary Progression Moon **do not use** Outer planets, because they are so slow they rarely move away from their natal position in a lifetime. Only use Inner planets (plus Asc. & MC) for Secondary Progressions. Look for repeats of a theme with all three forms of prediction, and remember our **Rule of Three**: if it occurs once it is a '*maybe*', if it occurs twice in the chart it is a '*possibly*', if it occurs three times it is a '*definitely*'.

Chapter 7: Cosmobiology and it's Gift to Progressions

Cosmobiology is a method of astrology developed by Reinhold Ebertin in the 1920's. Cosmobiology eschews the use of traditional house systems and uses a complicated charting method to develop a cosmogram of heavenly objects that places special importance on midpoints. A midpoint is a point half way between two planets, or other points. For example, the distance between 0° degrees Aries and 0° Cancer is 90°. Half of 90° is 45°, so the midpoint would be located at 15° Taurus.

Cosmobiologists consider 'indirect midpoints' to be important, too. The point opposite 15° Taurus is 15° Scorpio, this is an indirect midpoint. In fact, it is common to use all indirect midpoints at 45° or even 22.5° intervals. Indirect midpoints carry nearly the same energy as a direct midpoint.

Reinhold Ebertin, 1901-1988, came to Uranian astrology, and, according to the story, was denied permission to use the new TransNeptunians in his work. So he reduced the Uranian system to the 90° dial, 45° graphic ephemeris and half sums (eg, midpoints). His use of these materials was brilliant. For those of you who don't know what these 45° or 90° things may be, the short answer is that they are methods of reducing all hard aspects to conjunctions on a wheel or graph. We can see it with our dials and wheels.

Traditional astrology bases its interpretations on the interplay of the planets, their aspects and their positions in the signs and houses. Cosmobiology does not use the house divisions, the house system was discarded as it was not considered sufficiently reliable to give a precise interpretation of the chart. Some astrologers use the Equal House system to overcome the problems with Placidus and other systems which create differing sized houses, Ebertin solved this by dumping them all, no houses. Most people do not have an exact time of birth, and it only takes a difference of 4 minutes of time to move a planet from one house to the next. Ebertin along with Australian cosmobiologist Doris Greaves, decided not to use the chart with house divisions but to interpret the chart only by the known and proven facts of planetary position and containment of aspects and midpoints.

Cosmobiologists use a cosmogram, a 90° dial where 1° represents 4° of the zodiac. These days most astrological software packages draw charts represented in a 90° dial. Numbering begins at the top of the dial and moves in an anti-clockwise direction. **The first 30° represents all of the Cardinal signs**, the **next 30° all of the Fixed**, and the **final 30° the Mutable signs**. When all of the natal planets are placed around the dial, the conjunctions, squares and oppositions can easily be seen. Semi-squares, (45°), and sesquiquadrates (135°) appear on opposite sides of the dial. They focus on the hard aspects which are the major squares, conjunctions and oppositions, this is the 90° dial. It is the hard aspects that create the most obvious 'events' in our lives. **This is what you use for your Solar Arc Directions**.

Ebertin's cosmogram was devised to show these 'hard aspects' as these aspects were useful in interpreting the basic tenets of cosmology, namely to determine the effects of stellar bodies on the native. In the Ebertin midpoint system he gives special attention to any sensitive point which falls on the midpoint between two others. Ebertin wrote the ground breaking book, *The Combination of Stellar Influences* in 1940, he gives interpretations for all possible planetary combinations and midpoints.

Cosmobiology is an astrological school which has done away with the houses altogether. It still uses the Ascendant and Midheaven but due to the considerable inaccuracy of birth times and in cusp calculations they don't bother with cusp lines. In fact if we look at house systems we could safely say that the Whole Sign House system itself is probably the best house system as it doesn't need any calculations besides Ascendant and MC.

I'd suggest that you stick to Placidus or Koch or Equal and when you feel safe then start to use Whole Sign. As I said earlier the only reason Placidus is used more than other system is because it was the only house system available in table form. Up until then only mathematicians and astronomers could be astrologers.

The Whole Sign house system uses the simplest system that was devised in the Hellenistic period. It was used in the university that was attached the Alexandrian Library (roughly 100 BC to 600 AD) by our early astrology ancestors. It appears to be the earliest written method for astrological projection. Although it took me a few years to test, I now use it because I believe it works better than the Placidus house system.

Cosmobiology has some great methods that we can use, such as midpoints and the dials. To make up a 360° dial just draw up all the planets in a circle, just like a normal chart, but don't put in any house cusps, easy. To draw up something a bit more useful, use a 90° dial. **Here is how you do it**. You place all the planets in Cardinal signs on the dial from 0° to 30°, these go in the first third of the 90° dial, the second 30° is for the Fixed planets then the last 30° is reserved for the planets in

Mutable signs – and that's the Dial you have for your Solar Arc Directions.

A simpler method is below, just use a strip instead of a dial.

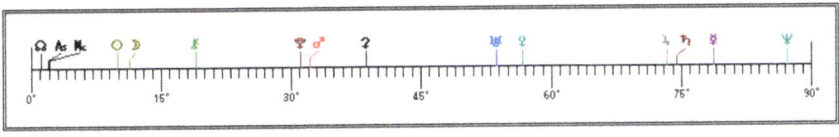

90 Degree Dial - Strip

Cosmobiology Conversion Table and the Meanings of our 90° Dials

Planets in the Cardinal Signs—starts at 0° and ends at 30°
ARIES, CANCER, LIBRA, CAPRICORN

Planets in the Fixed Signs—starts at 30° and ends at 60°
TAURUS, LEO, SCORPIO, AQUARIUS

Planets in the Mutable Signs—starts at 60° and ends at 90°
GEMINI, VIRGO, SAGITTARIUS, PISCES

How to use the 90° Dial

The 90° Dial as a strip above, shows the 1st 30° from 0-30° are the **Cardinal house planets** North Node, Mars, Saturn and Ascendant; the next 30° from 30-60° are the **Fixed house planets** Neptune, Jupiter, Moon, Chiron, and Uranus; the last 30° from 60-90° are the **Mutable house planets** Pluto, Venus, Mercury and Sun.

This shows by which planets are Square to each other. We use 90° bi dials for Solar Arc Directed charts to the natal chart to determine the hard aspects, anything that is conjunct on the bi dial is actually at a 90° angle, a square. Thus to use a 90° bi dial in prediction, we set it up to have the birth chart on the inside and the transits on the outside, Secondary Progressed, or the **Solar Arc** on the outside.

NOTE: for the Solar Arc directions versus natal chart all the outer dial planets move counter-clockwise to the stable inner dial. Only the outer dial moves (Solar Arc Directed), the inner dial stays still (natal).

Another dial is the 45° dial, which shows all the Semi-Squares, nice for those with lots of time to spare when doing charts, but too time consuming for me. It is the same as for the 90° dial, but divided in half again. Most astrological software can do these charts with ease, it is the interpretation that hurts!

A point to remember is that you can also determine midpoints this way. Either the computer does it for you, as in these charts, or you can use a ruler and compass (the same one you used in geometry from school).

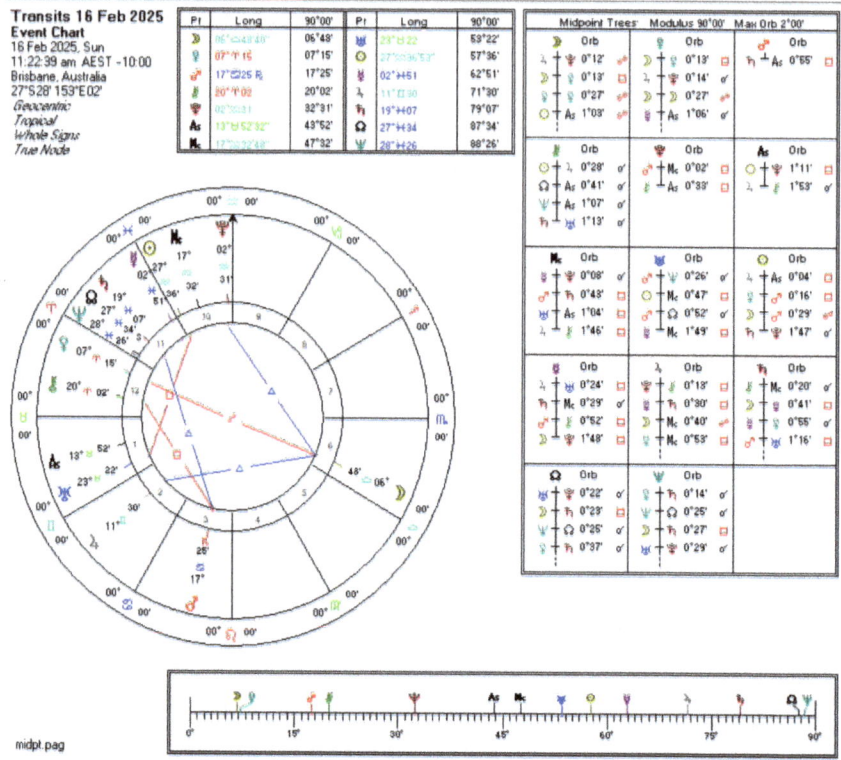

[Image: Cosmobiology chart with midpoints]

Sociology and Astrology

As cosmobiology is so aligned with society I thought I'd add it to this section. Astrology, sociology and psychology do go hand in hand, they compliment each other nicely. Looking at how groups influence individuals and visa versa is a sociological study, while looking at inner motivations and influences is psychological too. What moves a person is a combination of their inherited genes, their inner drives and outer influences, thus we are a combination of genes, childhood experiences, upbringing and influences from the outer circle of peers and society as a whole.

So what identifies society in the chart? The houses we would look at are:

* 1st a mini whole chart with everything in it and showing how we influence everything outside of us.
* 2nd how societies values and attitudes impact on our sense of material, spiritual and emotional scrutiny—what we hold dear to us like owning our

own home is valued in Australia, but not so highly valued in other countries.
* 3rd how we learn to communicate, the impact of siblings and school.
* 4th society and family as a whole.
* 5th friends and people we play and party with.
* 6th work mates and people we associate with at work and the community.
* 7th others, we are attracted to and who are attracted to us.
* 8th society in its dark nasty ways, representing the underlying urges and instincts underpinning a society or culture, such as racism or its religion.
* 9th teachers, people we admire and mentors.
* 10th those people we connect with to achieve our most pressing goals.
* 11th groups and institutions, clubs and organisations for the betterment of our culture and the environment.
* 12th hidden institutions, prisons, hospitals, representing societies secrets, those things society wishes to keep hidden and secret, and most importantly what we want to keep secret.

The planets are:
* Moon and North Node which directly reflect society pressures and influences, values and attitudes.
* The Sun is more personal though, society enters through the wise father figures who mentor us.
* Mercury is the mass media we watch for an average of three hours each day, social media, the magazines and the newspapers – influence of society.
* Venus is society reaching through friends and lovers, we connect to society through the people we relate with.
* Mars represents society through our personal drive to affect change on the world, it may not reflect society directly though.
* Jupiter is the society's morals through religion and law. The philosophies of a society are transmitted through Jupiter, without the good side of Jupiter civilisation would break down leaving anarchy, narcissism and fascism.
* Saturn reflects societies attitudes and values, its beliefs and structures. Saturn continues our traditions and perpetuates the norms of society from one generation to another, as unchanged as possible.
* Chiron reflects societies wounds and our attitudes to healing, the accepted medical model, whether it be greed based as our western model is, or traditional as in many eastern countries.
* Uranus reflects the rebel in society, the urge to change and renew, to

move forward and embrace freedom of expression.

* Neptune reflects societies dreams and wishes, the mystical as well as the 'wishful thinking', the smoke screen of the new age and the bull-dust of the self proclaimed guru, it is both visionary and delusion.

* Pluto reflects societies need to renew at its deepest level, through destruction. It reflects the personal Shadow, that which is inside needing to come out. We see Pluto on our TV and at the cinema thus we can play out our shadow needs in the computer games and by watching it on the screen. Pluto / Shadow needs to be expressed safely so we do it through plays and theatre. If someone else does it we don't need to do it ourselves to fulfil our Shadow expressions.

Here we see that everything basically reflects society back to us in some way or another. We are therefore influenced by society at every turn of our lives. At home, at school, at work and at play. Everyone we connect to brings with them something from their society, as we do for them. People often say that they wish to run away from society, from the evils out there, but society reflects our inner evils too, as you know, you can never run away from yourself.

Chapter 8: Psychology, Family and Michel Gauquelin

In the mid to late 20th century Michel Gauquelin examined the natal charts of thousands of people in various professions, and only those who excelled in their profession. He found that certain planets were dominant in these people within the confines of their profession. We should not be perplexed at this, it is sound astrologically and scientifically, the evidence is in the natal chart. This is the story of a French psychologist who spent the later years in his search for the elixir of life and astrology.

The Scientific Validation of Astrology
Michel Gauquelin was trained as a psychologist and statistician, but is widely known for his revolutionary work on what he sometimes called neo-astrology or cosmobiology. This is the scientific measurement of the correlations between the position of certain planets at birth (Jupiter, Mars, Saturn in particular), an individual's fame in various professions,

and their personality. He published many books on his research, mostly of course in French, but some have been translated into English: his last, *Neo-Astrology: a Copernican Revolution*, was published by Penguin-Arkana.

Introduction to Michel Gauquelin and his scientific research - extract from Michel Gauquelin, *The Cosmic Clocks*, Chicago, 1967.

The observed effect whereby a person is deemed successful in one of more endeavours of life, such as a doctor, or army general, appeared to be related to the diurnal (daily) movement of celestial bodies of the solar system: the Moon, Mars, Jupiter and Saturn. At the moment of birth of successful professionals, planetary positions are distributed in a way which differs significantly from the patterns obtained with control groups of ordinary persons. In particular, the individuals who later become renowned in a professional activity tend to be born shortly after one of these bodies rises or culminates during its diurnal (daily) movement.

The professional activities studied correspond to large categories of human interests (science, art, literature, politics, army, sport, and so on). The statistical correlation varies according to the different groups and planets. But for a single group, the results were the same in all attempted experiments, first in France, then in four other European countries: Italy, Germany, Belgium, and Holland. These observations were submitted to numerous men of science. Till now they have not been able to find an artefact (an error) which would explain the observed effects other than by the intervention of an exogenous (outside) cosmic factor.

The birth and astronomical data of professional groups showing planetary correlation, i.e. more than 15,000 births, form the first series of volumes of this publication. The planetary effect of heredity: A statistical study made from 1959 to 1965 on more than thirty thousand deliveries has shown, in accordance with this hypothesis, that there is a hereditary tendency **for children to be born under the same cosmic conditions that prevailed at the birth of their parents**. *This is a feature of the 24 hour revolution period of the Earth, and involves the closest or heaviest bodies of the solar system, i.e. the Moon, Venus, Mars, Jupiter and Saturn. At the moment of birth these lie in the same diurnal position that they occupied at the moment of birth of the parents. In particular, there is a tendency for children to be born after the rise or culmination of one of the celestial bodies, if the same circumstance held for the birth of one of the parents.*

This phenomenon was called **the planetary effect of heredity.**
All details about the methodology and numerical data of these experiments were published several times. Let us point out only that the effect does not appear if the delivery was not natural; and that the statistical correlation decreases according to the distance of the planets from the Earth. It is very marked for the Moon, Venus and Mars, it becomes less important for Jupiter and Saturn, and it is impossible to detect for the more distant planets Uranus, Neptune and Pluto. The correlation disappears also for Mercury, the smallest planet of the solar system. Such an effect, apparently related to distance and mass, suggests the physical nature of the phenomenon.

The fact that the planetary effect seems related to the geomagnetic activity leads one to look for other possible physical explanations. The Moon and the nearest, most massive planets could provoke a diurnal (daily) disturbance in the solar field, sufficient to be felt by the child during the crisis of birth, and this proportionally to the solar activity. The nature of such disturbances and their specific biological repercussions remain unknown. Howeversome recent observations could lead to the first steps towards a future explanation in astrophysics and in obstetrics.

Discussion – from: *Michel and Françoise Gauquelin, Paris, 1949-1969*
In conclusion, the planetary effect of heredity presents itself, in our opinion, as a particular case of the relations between solar and terrestrial factors in biology. Here heredity and environment appear to be linked: at the moment of their birth, individuals of the human race react to changes of the cosmic environment according to a specific sensitivity which they have inherited from their parents.

Summary so far - *Planetary Heredity*—Michel Gauquelin (1966)
1) Successful people have a significantly high chance of having certain planets conjunct Ascendant (Asc) or Midheaven (MC):-
Jupiter on the Midheaven or Ascendant:- actors, politicians, military leaders, top executives, journalists.
Saturn :- scientists, physicians.
Mars :- physicians, military leaders, sports champions, top executives.
Moon :- writers, politicians.
Venus :- was not significant for successful people, but was for parents and their child's common planet (**Finding 2**).
2) When both parents have the same planet conjunct Ascendant or Midheaven there will be a significantly high occurrence of having children

with the same planet also highlighted.

Therefore, if both your parents had Jupiter conjunct Ascendant or MC you have a significantly higher chance of also having Jupiter in a strong position. When we use the word, 'significant' we use it scientifically, that is, it must occur more often than if by chance.

3) There is no correlation between Sun, Moon or MC sign, house or aspect (Sun—Sun, Moon—Moon, MC—MC) between parents and their children. In other words, if your parents have Sun in Gemini, in the 4th house with a trine to Pluto, having children with the same pattern, by itself, is only by chance that it could ever occur.

4) People with planets conjunct Ascendant or MC at birth will die with these planets in the same position more often than expected. In other words, if you have Saturn conjunct Ascendant, the chances of dying with transiting Saturn conjunct your Ascendant has a statistically significant chance of occurring - more often than if by chance.

Career

How does one go about providing information on a person's most suitable career? This is another one of the big questions in astrology. We are told that astrology can do just about anything, that it is good at predicting career and interests and hobbies and these sorts of things. But what about elections, country and business charts, astrology is supposed to be good at that too? Well the truth is, from my experience, and I could be perfectly wrong here, is that astrology is great at contributing useful information in addition to question and answer and other forms of research. With practice you will get better and better at understanding these themes in the chart.

If we do use astrology then the first place to look of course would be the 10th house, the MC sign, the 6th and the 2nd, the Earth and 'work' houses. These all provide some information on their interests, their security needs, their ambitions, work ethics and whether they make good work mates, working as part of a group, a self starter, work independently, disciplined, dedicated, reliable, responsible, have the ability to follow instructions, etc. But it still does not show their career as such, just parts of their personality. I would suggest that you also need to know the full chart, all qualities need to be considered because this is a full and complete person, not just their Earth houses.

First of all we look at the basic principals of personality, Ascendant, Sun and Moon, Midheaven, the personal planets, and any planets conjunct the Asc. and MC. We study the basics of introversion and extroversion: is he/she the person most comfortable with people, would they prefer to work alone? We could see this with the outer planets, are they conjunct or opposing the personal planets? Are the personal planets in outgoing signs such as Gemini, Leo, Sagittarius, etc. If so then there is more chance that they will be interested in working 'with' people. Look closely at the 1st house, are there planets there? What are they? Outer planets are deeper and more powerful than inner planets here, therefore would the planets indicate any field of interest?

Did you notice that I missed square and trine aspects? They don't have quite the same impact and therefore are not as 'visible' as oppositions and conjunctions. It's quicker and it makes things easier to get started when doing a quick reading. This is the method I use in Chapter 2.

We then consider Gauquelin's research:- the social planets, Moon, Venus and Jupiter are more outgoing and harmonising than the others. Mars is more driven and successful as is Saturn in a career. Jupiter is best acting out, selling and performing, Moon is social and emotional, etc. You could make a list of the planets and signs and houses that would suit various careers and interests for your client, does the chart suggest the same thing 3 times? Remember the **Golden Rule**, once is '*maybe*', twice is '*possibly*' but three times is '*probably*' and sometimes I would say that it is '*definitely*'.

One major point to make here is the role of Applying and Separating aspects of the planets to the Angles. If Mars in the 9th house is applying to the MC, why is it more powerful than Mars already in the 10th house Separating from the MC? Any planet Applying is always stronger and more demanding than a planet Separating. It stands to reason that Gauquelin hit upon this in his research - all the '*Gauquelin Degrees*' are Applying, the planets are all in the Mutable house approaching the Angular house cusps. We know that the Angular houses are the most powerful, thus a planet Applying to their cusp will be emphasised. Therefore if your client has planets Applying to their Angles they have a greater drive and determination to succeed than those natives with planets already in the Angular houses.

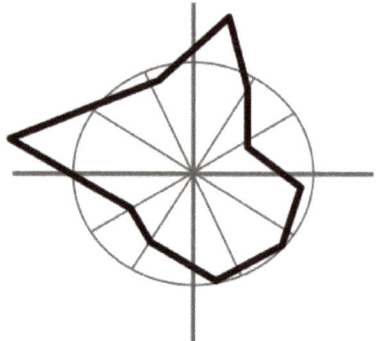

[Image: Mars effect]

, planets in the Angular house and thus Separating from the cusp, show that the native is more comfortable with their achievements though not as driven. They handle success and work placements and problems with greater ease than those with planets Applying. Remember this distinction, Applying are driven, Separating are more comfortable and laid-back but can be just as successful.

A word about Gauquelin's **Mars Effect**—simply put it refers to Michel Gauquelin's research on the effect of astrology on elite athletes, and Mars is the predominant planet in their charts. More as you read further.

Frequently Asked Questions & Frequently Voiced Objections About the Gauquelin Planetary Effects

Careers, success, leadership—we turn to Michel Gauquelin and his research which we have discussed before, a short excerpt from Ken Irving's article -
https://planetos.org/mmf.html

Objection: *These "effects" only seem to show up when the Gauquelins are involved in the experiments. No one has replicated them independently.*

Answer: *Not true. First of all, Suitbert Ertel and Arno Müller, working separately or together, have replicated findings including a study of members of the Académie de Médecine (done entirely after Michel Gauquelin's death), Italian writers and German physicians. Secondly, data gathered by three sceptic groups on athletes shows the Mars effect as specified by Gauquelin. Though some members of organized sceptic groups still contend at least two of these studies failed to support*

*Gauquelin, a growing number accept the **Mars effect**, as a genuine anomaly (i.e., not due to simple explanations such as bad statistics or data manipulation), while rejecting any "astrological" explanation.*

Objection: *The Gauquelin effects are too small to be of much consequence, amounting to a deviation of about 5% from the expected number in the case of famous athletes.*

Answer: *First of all, the total range of the Gauquelin effects is much larger than often supposed. Since this criticism is usually based on the positive Mars effect for sports champions, it doesn't take into account the fact that there are both positive and negative Mars effects for 8 of the 11 professional groups studied by the Gauquelin's. Even more interesting, however, is the fact that when just the sports champions are used and they are ranked according to the number of volumes in which they are cited (done by Ertel, using a specific set of references, as mentioned above), the range from the lowest-citation athletes to the highest is about 8%. However, if we consider the range from the highest ranks in "Mars effect" professions such as sports to the highest ranks in "anti-Mars" professions such as writing and art, using Ertel's citation counts we find it to extend from 32% down to 17%, or about +/- 7.5%. In other words, the numbers are often assumed (incorrectly) to be small because a particular effect is being viewed in isolation from the others. But when we look at relationships between groups, and between coherent classes within those groups, we see a quite different picture.*

Career	Positive Correlation	Negative Correlation
Actors	Ju+	Sa -
Doctors	Ma+ and Sa+	Ju -
Sports	Ma+	Mo -
Military	Ma+	Ju+
Executives	Ma+ and Ju+	
Politicians	Ju+ and Mo+	
Journalists	Ju+	
Playwrights	Ju+	
Scientists	Ma+ and Sa+,	Ju -
Writers	Mo+	Ma—and Sa -
Painters	Ve+	Ma—and Sa -
Musicians	Ve+	Ma -

The Gauquelin Research—Professions (see grid below)
From the grid showing the planets that Michel Gauquelin found to be correlated with various professions, we can see that Moon, Venus, Mars, Jupiter and Saturn are described, but no mention of the outer planets Uranus, Neptune, Pluto or Chiron. Gauquelin found that these planets (Moon, Venus, Mars, Jupiter and Saturn), in particular, were the ones with the highest correlations both positive and negative.

Mars is energy and drive, it's easy to see why it is involved with sports, the military, executives and science, but why doctors? My thoughts are that the medical profession is dominated by energetic and driven intellectuals, to gain entry to a medical university course you have to be in the top 1% of intellects, and to be that successful in your studies you need an enormous amount of drive. So does Mars indicate or correlate with medicine? Probably what this grid shows is that Mars correlates with driven personalities, success and physical expression.

Moon, positively correlates with writers and politicians, but not sports stars. Moon is society, emotion and empathy, it is easy to see this with those professions that want to get across thoughts and ideas, plus emotion is used to sway people's thoughts. Sports stars aren't all that interested in showing their emotions, maybe anger or aggression, yes, but not necessarily love and empathy of the Moon.

Venus is positively correlated with painters and musicians, and as the ruler of Libra and Taurus it is easy to see why. Venus is not necessarily just the ruler of attraction, she rules negotiation, cooperation, art, and beauty, all strong in Taurus and Libra.

Jupiter, is seen positively correlated with actors, politicians, playwrights, executives and journalists, if we consider the planet Jupiter as the ruler of freedom and expressive speech we can see him strongly involved with all of them. Jupiter as the Ruler of the 9th house and Sagittarius demonstrates his ability and desire to bring others along on his adventures. He is persuasive and has the charisma to sway people's minds, their beliefs and attitudes. This is very much a Jupiterian quality.

Jupiter is negatively correlated with scientists, doctors and the military, possibly because these professions are straight down the line, direct thinking, no imagination or mixed attitudes, just do what I say in the proscribed manner. I think this shows just how tricky and charismatic Jupiter really can be which is an incredible insight into the biggest planet in our Solar System.

Saturn, is positively correlated with doctors and scientists, and this again is a stroke of luck for astrologers, we see just how powerful Saturn is in his role to create structure and organisation. These are both very important qualities in these two professions. Science preaches the importance of empirical evidence, and this is based on the Saturnian traits of organisation and structure. I think we should add, Public Servants to Saturn's list: *"stand in line", "wait your turn", "go to the end of the line and fill in these forms"*. Saturn is negatively correlated with painters, writers and actors who need freedom to express their feelings, certain not a Saturnian trait.

SUMMARY
- Astrology can be used to help understand the themes and trends that flow through our psyche over time.
- Predictive astrology uses planets in transit as well as Progressed and Directed planets.
- Outer planets travel slowly and with their powerful psychological qualities they transform us in specific ways when they Apply or Separate or from natal planets.
- Orbs are important, tight orbs (½ to 2°) are more powerful and immediate than wide orbs (up to 15°).
- Aspects between natal planets can be influenced by transits from the powerful outer planets.
- Unconscious change or transformation is particularly related to Houses 4, 8, 12.
- By observing your own personal transits we can better understand those of your clients.

Chapter 9: Co-dependency—Three Stages of Projection and Romantic Love

There is a buzz word that has been going around for some years now and it is 'co-dependency'. It means that two people with their own personal problems live together in a 'domestic violence' situation unable to separate and heal. If you have major personal emotional problems and you meet someone who also has major personal emotional problems, and you get together, then what will be the result? That's easy = relationship problems.

Your anxiety or depression won't go away just because you fall in love. Many people believe that their partner will save them, rescue them from boredom, suffering and loneliness. This is called 'projection', projecting our internal needs onto those outside, especially those closest to us. When working with people experiencing relationship problems it is essential that I come up with a model that I can draw upon to help them. Something that is simple, sensible and something that worked. This is one that I came up with and it works fine.

Stage One—Honeymoon
When two people meet they look at the other and say to themselves:

A - *'You are so gorgeous, you are going to make me so happy.'*

They each say the same thing unconsciously to themselves. Thus they have given away their power to create their own happiness, they now rely upon their partner to provide happiness. What happens? After a while, the honeymoon phase wears off (*see the chapter on Romantic Love*), and they start to fight, the dysfunction and personal issues which have been on hold to impress and snare their partner, have been released. They each now begin to resent the fact that when they met it was the 'other' who promised to make them happy.

B - *'What?! I never promised to make you happy! You promised to make ME happy!'* and so it goes on.

This is the first stage of projection, the unconscious thought that 'the other' will provide for your inner love and nurturing needs. This is the stage of giving away your power. Most relationships stay at this stage.

Stage Two—Awareness of Inner Needs
If things settle enough, or they decide on a break, one or the other will go and seek counselling or talk to someone about their problems. Once they begin to talk they soon realise that underneath their strong exterior is a

mass of pain and hurt, of loss and grief. At this second and important stage the individual realises that they have needs, big emotional needs that their partner is unable to help them with. This stage is only reached by about 10% of all couples but can be the springboard for enlightenment in love and romantic relationships.

The conversation now evolves to this:

A - *'I have been thinking, darling. I have realised that I have some enormous problems associated with my childhood that need healing. All that is happening here is that I am dumping them onto you and expecting you to heal them for me. It just isn't working. I need help and you are not the one to do that, I need to go to a professional counsellor for that.'*

The partner is confused.

B - *'You have been dumping your emotional baggage onto me? But I can heal you my love.'* The partner is going to drag his lover back to stage one, *'I will make you happy: which means that I will make you dependant (*for happiness*) on me again.'*

A - *'No, you are my lover, you provide support when I need it, love and sex. When I need emotional healing I need someone who is trained in that sort of thing.'*

B - *'So what you are saying is that I am not a good lover, that I don't make you feel good or happy, that I am letting you down?'*

A - *'What I am saying is that when you try to heal me, when you talk to me and tell me what I should be thinking and feeling, I get resentful, You take my power away from me, you become my father / mother who always told me what to do and think.'*

B - *'Oh, I didn't know that, sorry. But how can I help?'*

A - *'By letting me get some counselling, by being there when I need a shoulder to cry on and to make me a cuppa when I feel down. But not to take over my mind or tell me what I have to do.'*

B - *'Okay, I can do that, maybe I'll go and talk to that person too about my problems. Then we will both be healed.'*

What is happening now? The first lover has made the BIG realisation that she needs help, professional help, because what she is doing is not working. Secondly, she has realised that when they had tried to heal each other in the past all that happened was that it ended in a fight. They each had opinions and neither listened to the other. When lovers try to take on the role of healer, it changes the romantic relationship to one of power and dominance, rather than one of support and love.

A 'love' relationships is between two equals, but when one or both need healing it requires a professional who has the power to heal over and above the skills of their patient. The healing relationship is a power relationship, the patient accepts the power and knowledge of the healer / counsellor. We listen to our healer, but rarely to our partner.

When a lover takes on the mantle of healer, it can come across as:- *'I know what you need and you have to listen to me otherwise you are stupid.'* It creates resentment. The wise person seeks healing from a healer, love from a lover and coffee from a cafe.

Stage Three—Negotiation and Compromise

Our lovers have gone their separate ways for counselling and have found that they have deep emotional needs left over from their childhood. The domestic violence situation is easing, they have separated for some 2 months while they sorted themselves out and are now far more wiser and aware of their triggers and wounds. They have decided to get back together and sort out a relationship based on support, not on healing and resentment.

A - *'Let's sit down and talk, let's re-establish this relationship, make new rules and set boundaries so it has a greater chance of success.'*

B - *'Okay, let's do that, I'll go first. I have a need that I am working on in therapy right now, and I need you to help me with it.'*

A - *'Okay, I promise not to judge you while we talk about it, not to butt in or put you down. I know that it takes great courage to tell me and trust me.'*

B - *'All right then... ah, I need to be hugged every morning before getting out of bed.'*

A - *'Oh dear, I hate being held, you know that. I get this feeling of being trapped, Umm, what can I do here? I am feeling trapped just by talking about it.'*

B - *'Well, I am prepared to compromise.'*

A - *'Yeah, okay, I have the need not to be trapped, and that means that being held too long makes me panic. So what about a short hug each morning?'*

B - *'Hmm, I like long hugs, but yes, I can compromise on this. How about we hug for 10 seconds every morning?'*

A - *'Done, I can handle that, but you must promise that we only hug for 10 seconds. I might even get used to it you know and maybe we could hug for longer. Now for my needs: I need you to say 'hello' to me when you come home from work. I feel so rejected when you ignore me.'*

B - *'Okay, I can see what you are saying, yes, I would like that, but how about if you remind me, you know, say something like, 'hey, what about a hug', how's that? You know how forgetful I am, and I do like to hug you but when I get home after work I am so tired I just want to sit down.'*

A - *'Okay, our first round of negotiations have gone down well. Let's write down what we agreed to and sign it, then we'll stick it up on the fridge for us to see and be reminded of the commitment we have to our relationship.'*

We have now reached the third and final stage of enlightenment in the relationship: the negotiation and compromise of our needs. This is a stage where each partner is trusting enough to share their innermost needs and to then negotiate with their partner to have these needs met. They still go for counselling for their traumas, but have a better working relationship with each other at home. This final stage is continuous, it moves around in circles at times, is constantly in need of renegotiation as needs change. It must be dynamic, not stagnant. Most importantly it has rules: no butting in, take turns to talk, no put downs and then write it down, sign it and display it.

Summary of Projection in Relationships
Stage 1—Honeymoon, *'you will make me happy'*, giving away your power.
Stage 2—Awareness of Inner Needs, *'I have needs that you can't help me with, I will go and get some counselling.'*
Stage 3—Negotiation and Compromise, *'I now trust myself to seek your support in getting my needs met. Let's work out how we can relate better, I am prepared to help you with your needs, will you help me with mine?'*
Write it down, sign it and stick it where you can see it, then there is no room for arguments later. There are however, three essential ingredients for a successful relationship: honour, respect, and trust.

I must mention that very few couples will ever get to this final stage. Their measure of success is how mature they are, their commitment to their agreement and the respect that they show for each other. In my counselling practice I use this model a lot. It does work, very well, but if there is damage to either individual and they don't seek further counselling then their chances of success diminish. If one or the other does not hold up their side of the bargain it will crumble. You might want to try this if you are having trouble with your relationships.

> **Stage One** - accepting that there is a problem. *"I'll stop projecting my issues on to my partner and make an effort to fix it."*
>
> **Stage Two** - telling your partner and seeking help. *"Ah ha, I see what the issues are. I will set a time to do my daily homework sessions and work solidly on them."*
>
> **Stage Three** - coming back to your relationship and trying to resolve issues within it. *"Will you help me with some of my issues? Yes? Okay, here is one I struggled with..."* Meeting them in the middle.

The Theory of Romantic Love

Rubin (1970) mentioned in his study of love that there is not enough known about love. *"Although interpersonal attraction has been a major focus of social-psychological theory and research, workers in this area have not attempted to conceptualise love as an independent entity."* According to Rubin (1970), *"Love is generally regarded to be the deepest and most meaningful of sentiments. It has occupied a pre-eminent position in the art and literature of every age, and it is presumably experienced, at least occasionally, by the vast majority of people. In Western culture, moreover, the association between love and marriage gives it a unique status as a link between the individual and the structure of society... An initial assumption in this enterprise is that love is an attitude held by a person toward a particular other person, involving predispositions to think, feel, and behave in certain ways toward that other person."*

Rubin goes on to mention that love is not a single characteristic or attitude but a complex combination of many attitudes and that its attention to the one individual rules it out as a personality trait. In the conclusion to their study of love theories, Hendrick and Hendrick (1989) state, *"...most would agree that love, in an inclusive sense, cannot be defined by any single characteristic."* They further state, *"Love is simply too unruly to be categorised so easily. It means different things to different people in different relationships at different points in time. Only with patient, open-minded exploration of several of the current approaches to love will we have any possibility of developing the overarching theory of love that still eludes us."*

So what is love? John Lee published his book of love styles in 1973 which describes love as being composed of 6 styles: **Eros** (passionate, romantic love); **Ludus** (game-playing love); **Storge** (friendship-based love); **Pragma** (practical love); **Mania** (possessive, dependent love); and **Agape** (altruistic love). After much study and experimentation Hendrick and Hendrick (1989) finally state..."*a question has justifiably been raised as to whether love exists as a personality tribute or as an aspect of a relationship. It does not seem to us that current love research is sophisticated enough to give a definitive answer to the question.*"

The Macquarie Dictionary says love is, "*A passionate affection for another person, a feeling of warm personal attachment, strong liking for anything.*" It can be seen here that the general construct for love is multidimensional as Rubin and others admit. This multidimensional aspect of love makes it difficult to measure.

It can be seen that defining love is not an easy task. Sternberg

(1986) mentions the role of learned behaviour, "*Love is a complex whole that appears to derive in part from genetically transmitted instincts and drives but probably in larger part from socially learned role modelling that, through observation, comes to be defined as love.*"

This is presented as a report on romantic love based on Sternberg's **Triangular Theory of Love** (1985) which proposes romantic love as being formed from three components: **Passion, Intimacy, and Commitment**. These components were judged to be strong indicators of romantic love.

Passion is the motivational force that leads to arousal of sexual needs as well as the need for self-esteem and self actualisation. Passion may come after the development of intimacy in a relationship or it may be the initial driving force of romance. Psychological arousal can easily be the precursor of physiological arousal in romantic love but not so in a filial one. Passion, therefore, is the driving or motivational component in the Sternberg theory of love. Like a match bursting into flame, passion flares brightly at first, then slowly it fades. Many relationships are like that, they rise and fall with the flame of passion, they end when the flame dies out.

Intimacy is the close feelings and bondedness that occurs in a love relationship. That love relationship could include parent / child, sibling / sibling or friendship relationships. Sternberg classifies intimacy as not being bound only by romantic love but also a component of other close love relationships. It is the sharing of close personal memories, wishes and dreams.

Commitment is the final component of the triangle theory and it consists of two aspects: short-term, and long-term commitments. The short-term is the decision to love a specific person and the long-term is the decision to maintain that love. Marriage is seen as the conscious decision to commit ones love to another for life.

Sternberg stresses that the three components are all important parts of a loving relationship but that they may differ in importance over time, across and within relationships. Furthermore there are eight subsets of loving experiences: Non-love, Liking, Infatuated love, Empty love, Romantic love, Companionable love, Fatuous love and Consummate love.

Love is not all that easy to define or measure and Mars and Venus, though a great analogy for gender roles, is a little too simplistic for us. Sternberg's idea of a three way split for love is interesting, I like to describe it as a three legged stool. It starts off with one leg, **Passion**, which is the first thing to happen when two sets of eyes meet, it is the driving force behind love, lust. But, passion is like a match stick, you strike it and it roars into life, but is quickly extinguished. If we add some **Intimacy** and sharing we have allowed the match to continue to burn a little longer, but not as brightly or passionately. Then we add the final ingredient **Commitment**, which allows the match to burn as long as it is fed fuel. If one of the legs is removed or shortened then it becomes very uncomfortable to sit on, and requires great compromise to stay upright.

For instance, passion is easily extinguished, so we remove part of that leg, we now have to rely on Intimacy and Commitment to remain seated. If we then find that our relationship lacks the passion for sex or fun or play, then the other legs may begin to weaken. We are less inclined to talk about ourselves, our deeper intimate selves, we feel less inclined to stay committed, we begin to seek passion elsewhere. A healthy romantic relationship requires commitment in all three areas, not one, not two, but three.

Gender & Power—astrologically

Do you believe astrology creates a philosophy or does philosophy create astrology? For example, regarding relationships, marriage is ruled by the 7th house. Why is it ruled by the 7th house? Why is a long term partnership (7th) separated astrologically from sexual relationship (8th)? Why are romantic affairs (5th) separated astrologically from marriage and the 7th house?

I don't always relate the sign Libra to long term and socially serious relationships like marriage, but there it is, ruling the natural 7th house. What else does Libra and its ruler, Venus, mean to us? The old key words ATTRACTION / HARMONY / BEAUTY are the 1st words that comes to mind. Astrology subtly conveys to us that 7th house relationships are connected up with those realms as well as open enemies and lower courts.

Astrology is a language and it has different signs, houses, and planets ruling different facets of human behavior. Those signs, houses, and planets also have other meanings and we are affected by those other meanings. For example, Pluto scares many of us but it rules the sexual function and sexual relationships. We are afraid of its mercilessness, its power and lust, but the deepest and maybe finest moments of our life may also be ruled by it - the birth of our children.

Indeed, why the traditional rulerships for such complex things as relationships? I can't answer that, there is so much traditional astrological interpretation that doesn't hold water today. The 7th house as the ruler of relationships is such a small part of its nature.

I see the 7th house as the energy or people that are drawn to us, or we draw to us. The 1st house is 'us' and what we project. We learn about us, 1st house, through others, 7th house. So I don't really like to call the 7th the sole ruler of lovers, it is, I believe, the house of 'others'. We would say that companions, customers, clients, the guy that opens the door for you, the cashier at the supermarket, the lady in the car next to you while driving, the person selling door-to-door, etc. are all 7th house people.

The 7th house represent what we need to find in another person to complement our own personality (at least the persona that we are projecting onto the world). What are the characteristics of that partner or the opposite, the open enemy. If the Ascendant is the way we project ourselves, the 7th house is it's opposite and complement, it is what we receive in return. Since it is the opposite sign, it is someone different. Like the axiom that "*opposites attract one another.*" It is the type of person we need to get to know, to understand, or to fulfil those characteristics we find lacking in ourselves. Actually, the 7th house is also known as the marriage partner, the 5th would be lovers.

Back in the Dark Ages our anglo-saxon-celtic ancestors were patriarchal, men, dominated most walks of life. The local Baron, Lord or Knight, or the local Bishop for that matter, wished they could claim their vassal's new wife on their wedding night. What does astrology say about that? Old age and Capricorn / Saturn go together, Jung called the archetype of old age and grumpy old men the 'senex'. Women with these significators strong in their charts may seek older men for the security it brings. What does this say about men? What significators indicates that a man seeks a much younger woman – insecurity or lust to impress other men? The questions just keep coming.

~

Chapter 10: Composite and Synastry charts for Lovers

Finding the midpoints of each chart then putting it into one chart is a common method for comparing charts. This technique involves calculating the midpoints for each planet and cusp for each chart. The computer will do it for you.

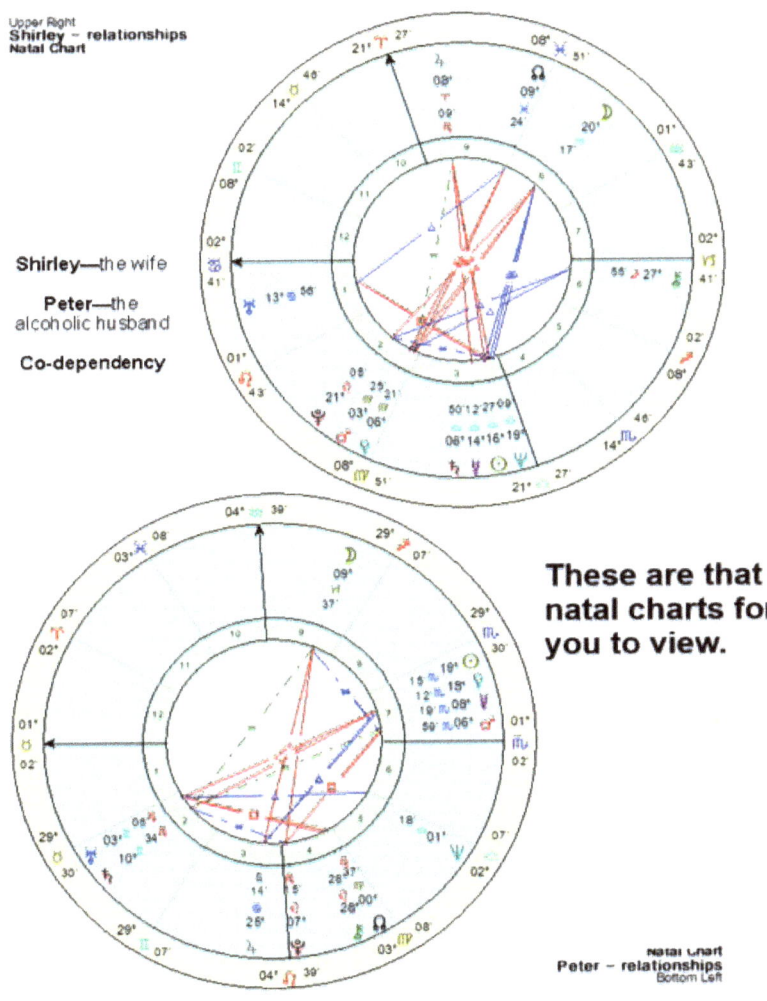

Shirley—the wife

Peter—the alcoholic husband

Co-dependency

These are that natal charts for you to view.

For example **Peter's** Sun is 19° Scorpio, Shirley's is 16° Libra
The difference is 30 - 16 = 14
14 plus 19 (Peter's) = 33

Half 33 is 16° (this is the midpoint degree between the two Sun's, it is midway between them)

Therefore we go to the lowest number, which is **Shirley's** 16 Libra, and we add 16° = 32°. Now 32 is 2° bigger than Libra (30°) so it becomes 2° Scorpio, give or take a few minutes. I don't generally bother doing minutes, I just run it to the closest number. So we do this for all the planets and house cusps.

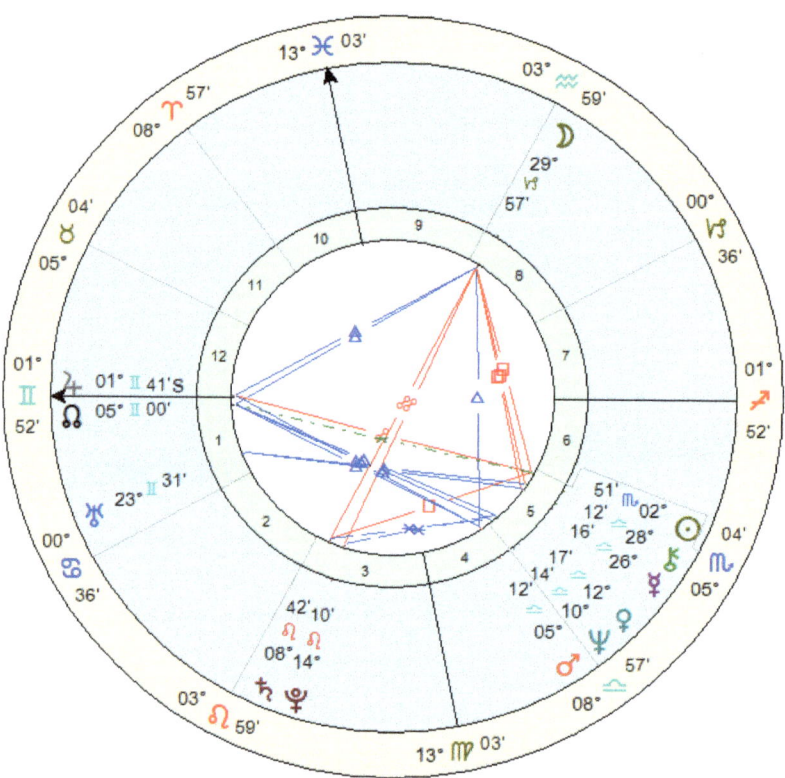

Here we have the midpoints of each chart, it shows the midpoints of the two people in a relationship creating a single chart. To interpret it we just read it the same as for any other chart, we can even use transits as well. **It reflects the relationship, not the individuals**. Of course you first need to know the natal charts of each individual, you already know that don't you. Only use composite charts and synastry charts as a part of your reading for a couple or prospective couple.

Let's look at the midpoint composite chart:
There are 9 points in Air signs, and you know what that means don't you, its Defense is Air = Denial: *'I'm alright, our relationship is fine, we've got no problems. Well if we do we can sort them out, and you know, we don't need help, and it will be right in the end, we have soul love, we love each other, s/he'll get better, s/he promised.'*

Next we ask, *'Where is the passion and intimacy?'*

With so much Air there will be talk but little action. This is not a good sign. Jupiter on the first cusp from the 12th, applying too, and Uranus in the first house, and it's an Air chart with Moon in Aquarius, etc. What do we have? ADHD, alcoholism, gambling, addictions, escapism, criminal behaviour, antisocial personality, narcissistic personality, magical thinking... Overall you would advise this couple to be honest with themselves and deal with any issues they might have with each other.

Composite charts – use the midpoints of both to combine the charts. I have kept the them in their Placidus charts. But first, we have their natal charts to look at and then the Composite chart.

Synastry—putting each chart into the others chart.
This means that you place the first person, say **Shirley**, on the inside and then place the planets and Ascendant and MC of **Peter** into her houses. This shows how **Peter influences Shirley,** how she sees him. We do this for both, **Peter in Shirley, Shirley in Peter.** We use the biwheel to make it easier.

The influence Peter has on Shirley (Shirley on the inside and Peter on the outside)
For a start his **Asc** is in her 11th conjunct her 12th house cusp. This shows that **Peter** makes her feel insecure, in fact she may even fear him. On a positive side it may be that **Peter** pushes **Shirley** to face her innermost fears.

Peter's MC is in **Shirley's** 8th house suggesting that he promotes **Shirley's** spiritual growth and sexuality. **Shirley** sees **Peter** as motivated to grow through crisis. It may also suggest that **Shirley** sees **Peter's** motivation for love is driven by sex, though this is a long shot.

Peter's Sun is in her 5th, ah ha, fun, gambling and parties, it shows that he 'shines' in her 5th house of play. A good sign I would say, unless there is also a tendency for gambling and alcohol. Shows where **Peter's** personality has the most impact on **Shirley**, in her 5th house.

His **Moon** in her 7th, another good compatible aspect, shows where **Shirley** feels **Peter's** emotions lie. Capricorn, as we know is not very good at showing affection, so although there may not be outward displays of affection there is commitment and she likes him dearly, love is even indicated.

Mercury— how they communicate, interests, movies, hobbies, parties too. **Peter's** Mercury is in **Shirley's** 4th, shows that he makes her feel a homebody, he is interested in keeping home, family and ties are shared with each other as home becomes the major source of recreation and communication between them.

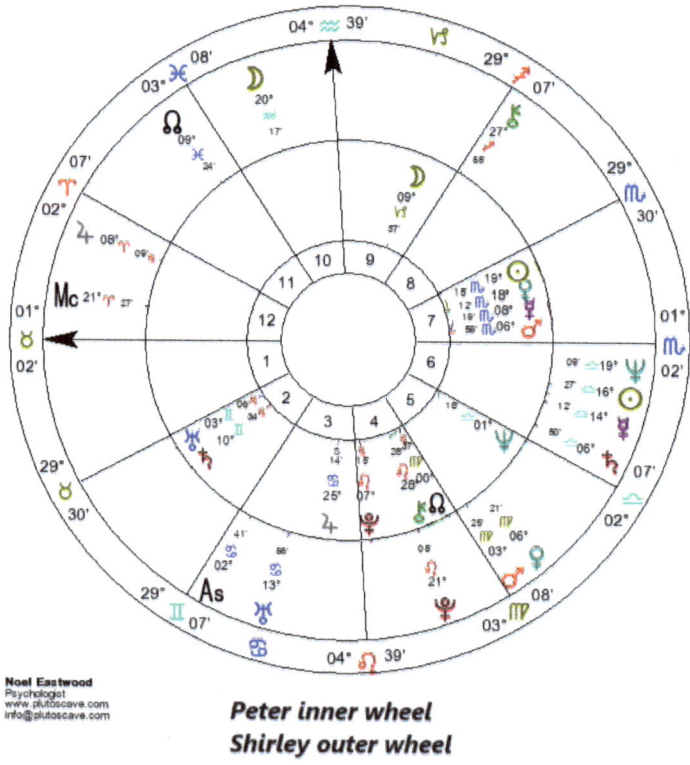

Peter inner wheel
Shirley outer wheel

Venus—shows where **Peter's** sense of socialisation and relating with others and with **Shirley** appears. Venus is in **Shirley's** 5th, again we see fun and play as the major areas of compatibility, **Peter** influences **Shirley** strongly here. They both enjoy partying and perhaps, if other signs exist, a swinging lifestyle with sex and other couples, or an open relationship.

Mars—where **Peter** shows his sexuality and drive, and perhaps his temper and mood swings. His Mars is in her 4th, so despite all their compatibility at home and having fun at parties there is conflict at home. *'This is my house and you just sleep here!'* The sexuality would now be seen better when we look at its aspects to other planets later as this house placement says nothing about sex.

Jupiter—shows where Peter adds wisdom to Shirley, it is in her 1st house, so this is good. He is very wise in her eyes and he impresses her very much. However there appears to be an emphasis on the 5th house as well, so watch for alcoholism, gambling and drug addictions.

Saturn—where **Peter** inhibits or makes **Shirley** work harder, it is in her 12th house, so perhaps this shows that **Peter** inhibits **Shirley** spiritually, or that she is fearful of him. He brings out her worst fears.

Chiron—where he wounds her, is in **Shirley's** 2nd house, and she is perhaps wounded in her physical, spiritual, emotional and mental security, maybe he prevents her expressing herself, she may feel that he prevents her from speaking up about how he treats her.

Uranus—where he creates tension, but also expresses his own needs for freedom. This is in her 11th house conjunct the 12th cusp, perhaps showing **that Peter** creates internal tension, and also that he promotes her humanitarian ideals, they both see the need for love on a global level.

Neptune—where **Shirley** feels abandoned by **Peter**, or that it is where she feels that she has no control in that area of her life, it is in the 3rd house, and again he inhibits her self expression. Perhaps she feels that **Peter** has too much say and does not let her express herself enough.

Pluto—very deep fears, sexuality and growth through crisis, **Peter's** Pluto is in **Shirley's** 2nd house suggesting that she feels quite insecure, that **Peter** does not provide a strong sense of security and safety.

North Node—where **Peter** promotes **Shirley's** growth, destiny and fate, it is in the 2nd house suggesting that **Shirley** feels that this is not a secure relationship, that **Peter** is not going to provide security in the long run.

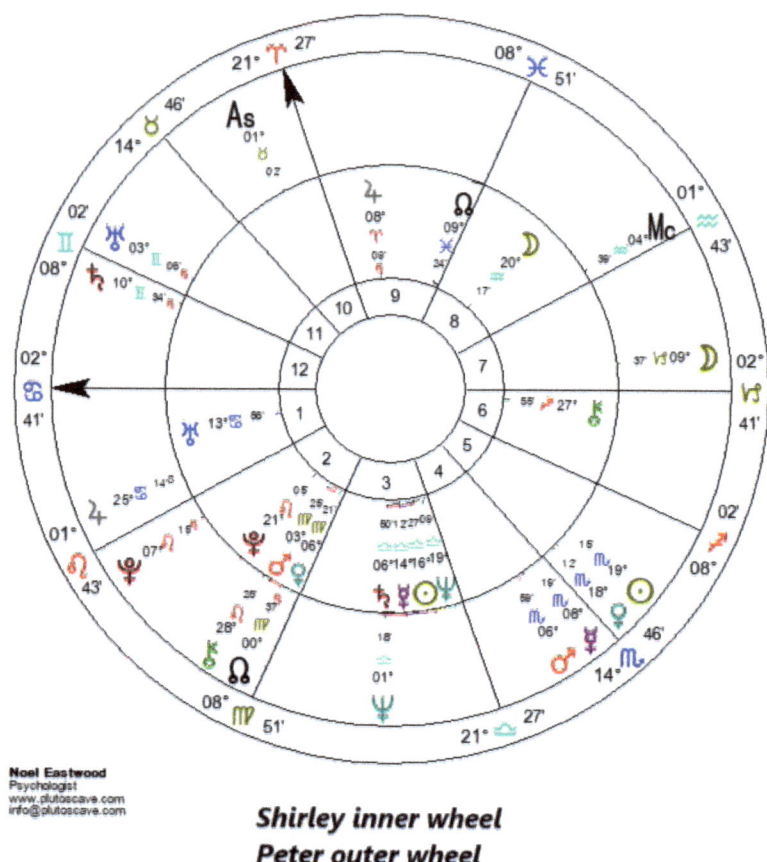

Shirley inner wheel
Peter outer wheel

Peter's chart, how Shirley affects him - (Peter on the inside and Shirley on the outside)

    Ascendant—Shirley's Asc. is in his 3rd house, he feels that Shirley is comfortable with his communications.

    MC—her MC is in his 12th house, suggesting that **Peter** feels as though **Shirley** is pushing him towards a confrontation with his deepest fears, not supporting his growth.

    Sun—her Sun is in his 6th house, **Peter** sees **Shirley** as a good worker, responsible and dedicated, perhaps a good servant.

    Moon—emotions, **Shirley's** Moon is in **Peter's** 10th, conjunct his MC suggesting that Shirley nurtures his career and ambitions. Now this may also suggest that **Shirley's** mood swings adversely affect his career and ambition.

Mercury— is in the 6th house, **Peter** sees **Shirley** as oriented towards an interest in helping others. There may be jealousy here, but we would have to see it in the aspects between planets to confirm this.

Venus— 5th, she provides a nice warm home environment for him.

Mars— also in the 5th, she is inspired by his party going antics.

Jupiter— 12th house, **Peter** sees **Shirley** as perhaps interested is learning about the world but he keeps this hidden. Not an open person.

Saturn— 6th, may mean that **Peter** sees **Shirley** as supporting his work ethic.

Chiron— 8th, **Shirley** wounds **Peter's** sexuality and promotes person crisis within him.

Uranus— 3rd, may show that all their arguing and talking creates stress, that he needs freedom from her chatting / arguing.

Neptune—in the 6th, may show that **Peter** feels that **Shirley** just gives everything to everyone else, and not him, and that he has no control over that.

Pluto— 4th, Shirley makes **Peter** face his childhood fears, that she promotes his exploring of his background and past psychological wounds. He may also fear that she will not provide a safe home environment.

North Node— 11th, suggesting that **Peter** believes that **Shirley** provides 'good luck' for his ambitions in helping the planet.

Peter across - Shirley down

Synastry Grid

Synastry Grids
Now that we have explored these house placements, our next task is to then look at aspects between each planet. We use a synastry grid for that.

Peter—how he experiences her
Moon—Square **Shirley's** Sun - we are not connecting emotionally. A very heavily aspected Moon is not a good sign for long term love. May indicate emotional co-dependency.

Squ. Me - not compatible in our general interests, we argue, creates intellectual tension.

Trine Ve - compatible sexually in some ways, we get on well socially and together, I like her.

Trine Ma - sexual attraction and compatibility, I like her drive.

Squ Ju - I dislike her being so smart, perhaps some incompatibility in their general energy levels.

Squ Sa - I feel inhibited by her, she holds me back.

Opp Ur - she is stressful to live with.

Squ Ne - I can't trust her, I feel abandoned by her.

Sex NN - she helps me in my ambitions, nice compatibility.

Opp Asc - she is always ignoring me and paying attention to others, conflict, incompatible.

Sun—Squ Moon - again, same thing, emotions missing their mark

Trine Ur - she is exciting.

Squ Pl - she frightens me, she makes me feel bad things and bad thoughts.

Quincunx MC—she is a hindrance in my career interests and holds me back in my ambitions, she's hot and cold and inconsistent.

Mercury—mostly compatible, she has similar interests to me, I find her interesting.

Venus—conflict with Moon and Pluto, emotional disturbance, I fear what she can do to me emotionally.

Mars—well aspected, she is great in bed and has great drive for work and career.

Jupiter—she is too smart, a smart ass, or she is not bright enough for him, not compatible on an intellectual level.

Saturn—some good some bad, shows an up and down relationship, inhibited but needs to be kept on task, she is good for me but...

Chiron—close aspects, perhaps we get too close to each others emotional wounds without actually helping to heal them, we push each others buttons, co-dependency.

Uranus—mostly stressful, we stress each other out and need time out from each other.
Neptune—mostly negative, I fear she will leave me, I feel out of touch with myself when we are together.
Pluto—positive, perhaps sexual compatibility.
North Node—intense but generally we get on OK and support each other in our dreams.
Asc - stressful, we fight a bit.
MC - she is a good supporter of my ambitions, a good worker.

Shirley—how she experiences him
Sun—we generally get on well, we are generally up front with each other.
Moon—he is mostly unsupportive of my emotional needs.
Mercury—we don't think the same way but we get on well enough... I suppose.
Venus—we generally get on well socially, I like him.
Mars—he gets too involved with sex and he is sometimes too aggressive with me.
Jupiter—he is pretty smart but he gets too intense and over involved with his ideas.
Saturn—although we don't have similar emotional needs we do make a good partnership and do well in our business.
Chiron—I don't trust him to support me emotionally, he may abandon me but generally we help each other through those tough emotional times, he might be my soul mate (some mixed aspects here suggests that she is uncertain as to where she stands with him).
Uranus—he stimulates and excites me.
Neptune—I feel abandoned by him at times.
Pluto—he is frightening at times and I fear his violence.
North Node—mixed as well, we might be soul mates, and we do support each other, just that, well, its just...
Asc—we do get along and have similar personalities.
MC—he sometimes helps me with my dreams, but we don't always pull in the same direction.

Relationships, Astrology and Jung's practice of psychotherapy

Carl Jung conducted a series of investigations into astrology and relationships, he found that there the three most common points in the natal chart were the Ascendant, Moon and Sun. He also found commonly that both the husband and wives Moon was in the same sign. Jung states, "Yet in my statistical investigation it happened that precisely the three conjunctions stressed by astrological tradition came together in the most improbably way."

Jung himself used astrology to build a bridge of understanding between himself and his patients. During the preparation of his essay on synchronicity he examined the birth charts of 180 apparently happily married couples, he wanted to find their astrological correlations. He then went on to examine another 966 charts of 483 couples, altogether 32,220 pairings were examined.

Jung states, "You take three matchboxes, put 1000 black ants in the first, 10,000 in the second and 50 in the third, together with one white ant in each of them, shut the boxes, and bore a hole in each of them, small enough to allow only one ant to crawl through at a time. The first ant to come out of each of the three boxes is always the white one. The chances of this actually happening are extremely improbable. Even in the first two cases, the probability works out at 1:100 x 10,000, which means that such a coincidence is to be expected only in one case out of ten million. It is improbable that it would ever happen in anyone's experience. Yet in my statistical experiment it happened that precisely the three conjunctions stressed by astrological tradition came together in the most improbable way."

A Modern Approach to Relationships—the Personal Planets

Ascendant and MC—common direction and projection
Sun—shows the reason for incarnating, the essence of the personality. It is strong because it denotes self-esteem, but still only part of the story, as you know.
Moon—shows the emotions and feelings of the native, if both are in the same element or mode or sign there is stronger compatibility.
Mercury—shows the intellectual interests and hobbies, their communication skills and compatibility.
Venus—shows their basic social and relating skills, how well or interested each is in socialising and relating with others.
Mars—the drive and sexual potency or libido of each, it is also aggression and temper.
Jupiter—shows the hyperactivity and wisdom, or lack of, perhaps even the ability to hold a conversation deeper than that of a Mercurial one.

The personal planets show the immediate personal attraction and compatibility, because they sit on the surface and are easily seen by others. As we get closer and more intimate we begin to share our other archetypes, the deeper 'self'.

When we move away from the personal inner planets we begin to see deeper and often darker secrets and issues arising. It is often not as noticeable when we meet strangers, we don't see or aren't allowed to see the outer planet effects on their psyche. Co-dependency is due to the unrealised deeper issues, which of course are the outer planet's impact on our psyche.

If we just had inner planets we would see the person and that would be it. When we add the outer planets it becomes more difficult, they are deep psychological elements which have the potential, if poorly aspected, to disrupt our lives and loves.

Definition: A Marriage chart
This is the time, date and place of the marriage ceremony, the formal / legal 'birth' of the relationship, I don't use these.

Chapter 11: A Marriage That Didn't Succeed

Stephanie (not real name) married **Sam** (not real name). As you can see, when you have the chart drawn up, both have very similar patterns, configurations. strong 1st house, same Asc (Pisces), both 12th house Sun / Mercury, Pluto in the 7th and their Moon is ruled by Mercury (Gemini and Virgo Moon).

Stephanie - natal

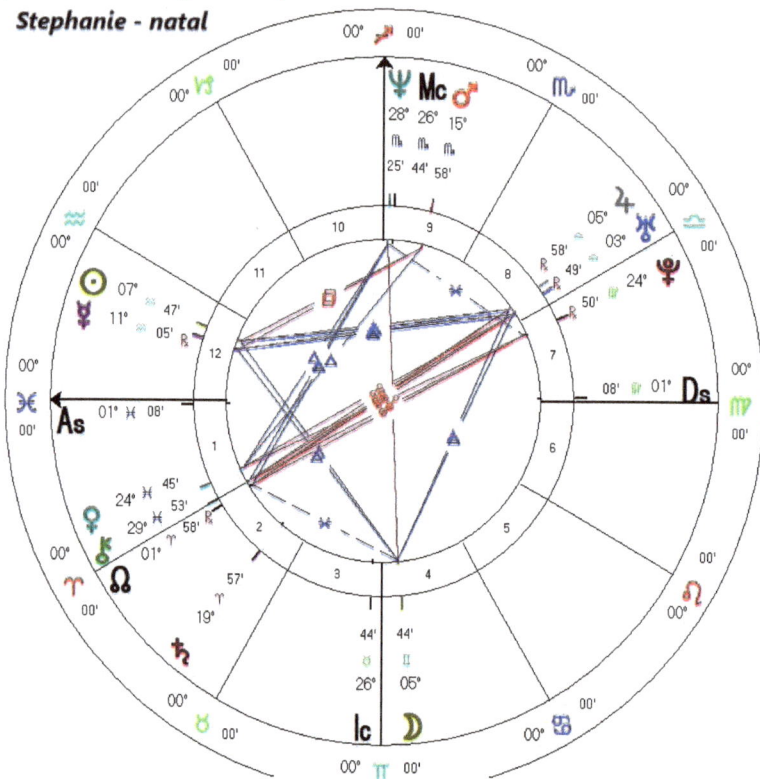

I would say that the 12th house Sun shows a possible absent father and perhaps some unresolved grief over this. First house shows a competitive nature, arguments. It's the strong Mercury as ruler of their Moons, suggesting a tendency to worry (and headaches with Mercury in the 12th). Both are very sensitive with Pisces Asc., one of their spiritual lessons is to come to terms with Water, as both have Aquarius Sun in the 12th and Mercury ruled Moon so too much Air. They need to understand emotions, then learn to handle and express it, rather than go into denial as an Air chart has a tendency to do.

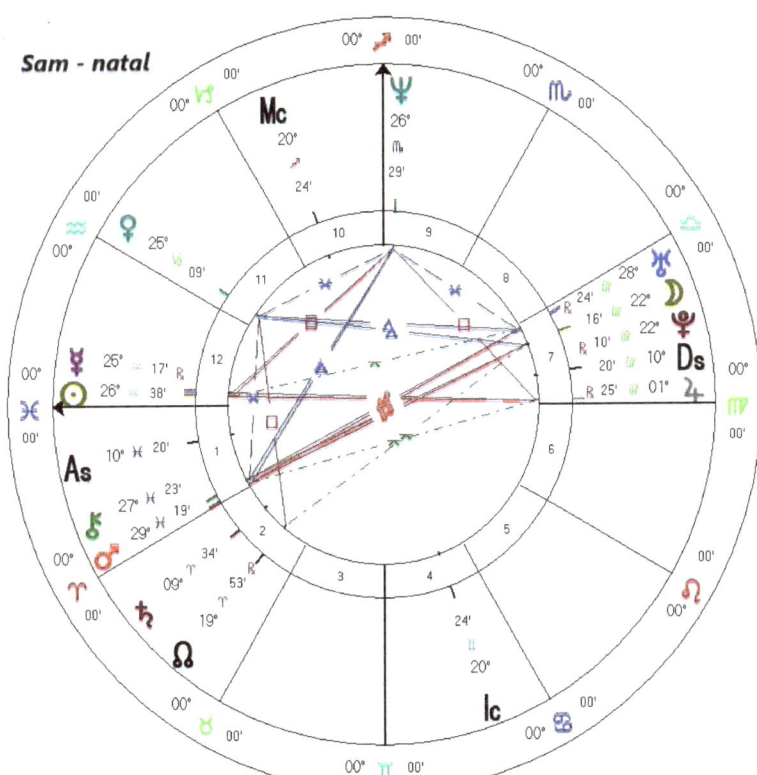

I ran a synastry grid to see how **Sam** and **Stephanie** related to each other. Initially it does look like an extremely compatible match especially with Venus Sextile Venus, Venus conjunct Mars, Venus trine Neptune to name just a few.

Even the more difficult aspects are initially exciting for the two of them. I suspect it was like spotting someone across a crowded room and the attraction was so intense and destined that everyone else in the room evaporated and the two were swept into each others arms for eternity. However, too much of a good thing can eventually not be a good thing. Planets that combine unfavourably in personal relationships can either produce sparks, which excites both people, or friction. The sparks can turn into friction if the couple don't work at maintaining the pleasant side of each aspect.

Synastry Grid

Stephanie (columns) / **Sam** (rows)

Sam \ Stephanie	☽	☉	☿	♀	♂	♃	♄	♅	♆	♇	⚷	☊	As	Mc
☽						□ 4S18	✱ 3A49	△ 7S19					□ 4A35	
☉							✱ 1A46							
☿							✱ 1A30							
♀	☍ 2S29			✱ 0A23	☌ 4A33		☍ 3A39	△ 1A44	☍ 2S34	☌ 2A38			□ 4S20	
♂												△ 5S38		
♃				☍ 6A38			☍ 3S36	☌ 7A33						
♄	⚻ 2A19			□ 5A11			⚻ 2A13			☌ 0S04	△ 0A27			
♅				☍ 4A30			☍ 5S44	☌ 5A24		☍ 6A26				
♆	□ 1S46	□ 3S07	✱ 3S16	△ 0A54	□ 3A00		✱ 0S00	☌ 1S55		△ 1S01				
♇	☌ 2A34	⚻ 1S47	⚻ 0S26	✱ 0S18	☍ 4S28		☌ 3S33	✱ 1S38	☌ 2A40	☍ 2S32			□ 4A26	
⚷	☍ 7S37			☌ 0S34	⚻ 1A31		☍ 1S29	△ 3S24		☍ 7S43	☌ 2S30			
☊	☍ 9A42			☌ 2A39	⚻ 0A32	☌ 7S35	☍ 3A33	△ 5A29		☌ 4A34				
As		☌ 4S30	☌ 5S51		☍ 0A17		⚻ 2S43	□ 4S38						
Mc	✱ 4S28	□ 0S06	□ 1S27	✱ 1S35	△ 2A34	□ 4A41	✱ 1A40	☌ 0S14		△ 0A39				

They were initially very attracted to each other, but after awhile the friction develops, they split, but after awhile they long to be together again, and so the cycle goes. They had several difficult aspects that can cause sparks then friction.

Here are a couple from their natal charts: with Stephanie's Venus opposite Pluto, and Sam's Venus trine Pluto, there is initially a strong bond, especially sexually. But after a time, the warm fuzzy bond can become intense. **Sam** has a strong 1st house, plus he has Pluto conjunct Moon which makes him very intense. **Stephanie** could interpret that as him being domineering. That's when the friction sets in. If they were to direct some of their passion to a shared creative project then maybe that friction would lessen, still Sam would need to be conscious not to be so intense.

With Stephanie's Venus opposing Uranus there are instant sparks, but that is hard to maintain over the long haul. Eventually Stephanie's Venus can feel her love is rejected as Uranus (**Sam**) becomes interested in and distracted by other things. Ah, the age old scenario of "*he spends more time watching sports on TV than he did* *when we first got together"* turns into *"he doesn't love me anymore"*. Somehow they need to find a balance between his need for freedom and her need for intimacy.

Sometimes even a nice aspect can lead to stress because of the nature of the planets. Stephanie's Sun is sextile Sam's Saturn which we've all read makes for a lasting relationship. But there is the potential for the Saturn person to appear authoritative which can make the Sun develop a lack of self-confidence.

Actually the example of Stephanie and Sam may have shed some light on the original question about why love turns sour. It's probably a case of getting swept away by love, but not working to develop it. I suppose too that a transit could trigger the friction to begin.

The bottom line in Compatibility is that we seek a partner who is similar to us. The more similar the more chance of success. We see this in the inner planets, the more inner planets that share the same sign, house, element, mode, or are conjunct, the greater the chance of compatibility. When we add the outer planets to a compatible inner planet chart, we add unknown elements.

There could be two very compatible people, with inner planets all showing a high degree of compatibility, but if the outer planets show dysfunction through conjunction to inner planets such as the Sun or Moon, or Ascendant or MC, then the stage is set for co-dependency. The more psychological issues that arise between two people the greater the co-dependency.

Compatibility with Stephanie and Sam
Let's look at their Composite chart. This chart shows is that Venus is conjunct from the 12th house to the Asc by 11 degrees. It is a little over the 10 degree limit but it is still a useful conjunction. I want to emphasis that the two do love each other but that they failed at securing a compatible relationship.

Venus in Aquarius is a seeker of new adventures, new conquests and fun times. But, it lies in the 12th house, the hidden house. It is conjunct Mercury and Sun so it isn't a singleton, but it isn't strong. The shine of a Venus conjunct Ascendant is only going to shine every now and then.

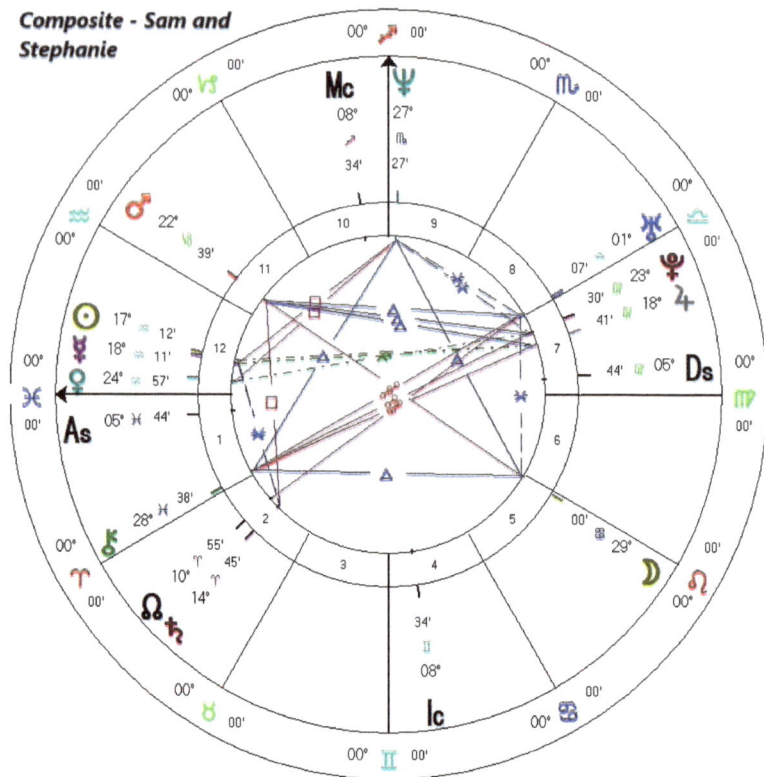

Sun and Mercury are sextile Saturn and quincunx Jupiter while Venus is quincunx Pluto. These planets are all personal planets, they define the personality of the native. As a compatibility chart the natives are hidden, hiding in the 12th house. The 12th house wants to rest up the planets inside there, and these three should be resting, waiting for rebirth into the 1st house. Instead they are held down by these aspects that are weak and held by outer planets.

We also have Chiron in the 1st house in their natal charts and in their Composite chart. It is a planet that brings Stephanie and Sam's wounds to life when aspected by transit – quite a nasty placement. It is opposite Pluto, Uranus and Jupiter which is quite awkward too. Chiron in the 1st house is always waiting to let off steam and this will occur at any time.

Then we have Moon opposite Mars which is even more awkward as it involves the emotional regulator, the Moon. Moon in Cancer and in the 5th house is very emotional and wants to be embraced, hugged and held, with a little bit of fun time - unfortunately it doesn't really happen.

Mars is nicely placed with trines to Jupiter, Pluto and Uranus, but then it is held in a square aspect with Saturn which is frustrating. Mars opposite Moon is very tough to live with, frustrating and with big, over-sized tantrums.

Fortunately there is a Grand Trine between Moon, Chiron and Neptune. It is fine being in Fire houses and Water signs, so a mix of two elements that don't mix well. However, it does try its hardest and will be one the better aspects in the chart.

The Lord of the Chart is Neptune which sits right at the top of the chart making it the Planets of High Degree too. It is square Sun, Venus, Mercury and that makes it somewhat of a locking device for the Sun light to shine. The sextile to Uranus and Pluto is fine.

What does the Composite chart show us? It shows us that for there to be success the two will have to work very hard in resolving their issues.

SUMMARY
- Love can be seen in the natal chart especially when triggered by inner and outer planet transits.
- Codependency is aligned with projection and needs and so there is a way to help move a relationship forward.
- Using Synastry and Composite charts, biwheels and grids you can see the influence each person has on the other.
- Astrology shows where couples are compatible and where not so compatible.
- Even Carl Jung used astrology extensively in his work with couples.
- Successful marriages are not much different to unsuccessful marriages, however, successful marriages rely on certain personal traits particularly on Commitment.
- Romantic Love needs certain qualities that include but are not limited by Passion, Intimacy and Commitment.

An extra feature: Asteroids—Relationship Values and Sexuality (from Solar Fire)
Relationship and Sexuality have been much studied through planetary symbolism in the past. Many astrologers are interested in sex. More detail and insight on this topic may possibly be gained by studying the gods and goddesses of various cultures, and the attitudes and behaviours which is part of their mythology as represented in the astrological wheel by the asteroids of their name. Here is a small sample

of possibilities and the descriptive ideas just scratch the surface. Keep the orb tight, maybe 2° at the most.

Achilles Greek hero & lover of Patrocolus, cross-dressing.
Adonis Youth loved by Aphrodite, Persephone & Dionysus.
Aglaja One of the Graces - three women dancing - female companionship and sensuality.
Amor Roman equivalent of Eros.
Amun Egyptian creation god by masturbation, oral intercourse.
Antiope Amazon queen; Amazons in general - men for procreation and women for intimacies.
Aphrodite Patron of prostitutes; sensuality; all kinds of erotic love; libido plus.
Apollo Musical & predominantly gay; male lovers include Admetus, Hylas, Orpheus, Hyacinthus, Troilus; jealous of Orion, the lover of his sister Artemis (Diana); lacking style with women and resorting to force to meet his desires on occasions.
Ariadne Abandoned by her lover Theseus.
Artemis Huntress, lesbian, same sex companionship/relationship, hide and seek, don't pin me down, guardian of virginity, tom-boy, private, close relationship with sibling Apollo.
Astarte Love and war goddess similar to Aphrodite; worshipped by Egyptians, Canaanites, Phoenicians, Greeks & Romans.
Atalante Huntress, catch me if you.
Bacchus Orgiastic, drunken revelry, bisexual, ecstasy, cross-dressing.
Chione Chione was so beautiful that she pleased a thousand men by the time she reached the marriageable age of twice seven year. Under-age Beverley Aadland began an affair with Errol Flynn aboard his yacht.
Circe Femme fatale - making fools of men; finds few men (Odysseus) to match her intelligence.
Cybele Oriental goddess introduced to Rome; her Galli priests were eunuchs; modern day - a woman often in the company of effeminate men; of interest- historically Bangkok has been a centre for the leading (razor) edge of sex-change operations; Cybele could show a preference for intimacy with Asian partners.
Diana Huntress, lesbian, same sex companionship / relationship, hide and seek, don't pin me down, guardian of virginity, tom-boy, private, close relationship with sibling Apollo. Did not associate with men with few exceptions.

Dike Obviously strong and dominant female
Dionysus Orgiastic, bisexual, wine, ecstasy, cross-dressing
Echo One way love for Marcissus who was in love with his own reflection.
Eros Passion, the urge to create form, the life force.
Euphrosyne One of the Graces - three nude women dancing - female companionship and sensuality.
Eurydike Her fate totally depended on what her partner did.
Freia Norse goddess of sexual love (also known as Frigg); her sacred day is Friday.
Frigga See **Freia**
Ganymed Young prince abducted and loved by Zeus; *** young actor James Dean is known to have slept with several directors to further his career - his Ganymede conjunct the MC by 17 minutes arc. John Lennon Sun conjunct Ganymede also had a one night stand with manager Brian Epstein.
Hebe Young maiden who served drinks to the gods; modern day equivalent - high class young barmaid or woman in service of high status males, high class escort girl
Hera Faithful and veangeful wife - takes revenge on her husbands lovers and his children by them.
Heracles (Hercules) forced to become slave of Amazons for three years and married dominatrix Omphale = role reversals; cross-dressing; male lovers include Abderus, Admetus, Dryops, Hylas, Iolaus, Nestor, Philoctetes, Polyphemus.
Hippolyta Amazon queen; Amazons in general - men for procreation and women for intimacies
Hylonome Grief stricken Centauress whose grief for her slain lover leads to suicide; modern day - someone whose life goes off the rails when a partner leaves.
Irene One of Aphrodite's Horae (Hours)
Ishtar Babylon the great, mother of Harlots; *** Linda Lovelace (porn star) - parallel Jupiter (7 minutes) & parallel Venus (1 minute) *** Christine Keeler - square Pluto (8 minutes) *** Jodie Foster – 1st role as teenage hooker in "Taxi Driver" – trine Moon 13 minutes, sextile Jupiter 0 minutes.
Jokaste Mother & husband of her son Oedipus; *** Elvis Presley – conjunct Pluto in Cancer; Sigmund Freud – square Sun (39 minutes)
Lilith Femme fatale; sexual assertiveness born from anger; abortion; no emotional attachments to multiple partners; rejection of gender role stereotypes in love making.

Loreley Femme fatales similar to Sirenes of Greek/Roman mythology; lured by victims to their deaths.
Minerva Very close bond with her father - daddy's girl; career woman with great intelligence whose public persona strong but sexless.
Nestor Eloquent & a strategic planner in the Trojan War; lover of Heracles.
Odysseus A husband who has to travel abroad for extended periods; intimacies while abroad - helped by powerful women.
Orpheus Musical. Inconsolable grieving for his lost beloved bride Eurydike, after which he turned away from women and sought young boys as lovers. *** John Lennon – conjunct Mars.
Pallas Very close bond with her father, career woman whose public persona is sexless.
Parthenope One of the Sirenes who drowned herself when Odysseus didn't fall for her charms
Patroclus Achilles' male lover slain in the Trojan War.
Penelope Odysseus wife - absolute fidelity in marriage, but lacks the vengefulness of Hera.
Penthesilea Amazon queen; Amazons in general - men for procreation and women for intimacies.
Persephone Daughter/wife in a tug of war between her mother (Demeter) and her husband (Hades/Pluto).
Philoctetes Trainer of heroes, lover of Hercules.
Proserpine Daughter / wife in a tug of war between her mother (Ceres) and her husband (Pluto).
Psyche Relationship at deep soul level; Greek word meaning butterfly or soul.
Sappho Poetess of Lesbos, lesbian, amongst her female lovers were Atthis & Anactoria.
Sirene Femme fatales; lured sailors to a watery grave.
Siva/Siwa Hindu phallic god, husband of Parvati, relationships with male gods - Agni and Vishnu.
Thalia One of the Graces - three women dancing - female companionship and sensuality.
Ulysses A husband who has to travel abroad for extended periods. Much assistance for achievement of goals from powerful women.
Vesta Vestal Virgins; rites with sacred phallic object Palladium; dildo; unmarried; celibate
Zeus Bisexual; many children with different women. Philanderer and paedophile.

A quick word about asteroids: I love them but they take a lot of time to delineate properly. I only use them sparingly. I can see that Sam's Orpheus is within 1° of Stephanie's Eros, quite a powerful combination – but it is in the 12th house so somewhat subdued. There is also a Persephone and Pan conjunction, not a close aspect, I like 1° to be good, but this is close. Sam's Eros is close opposite to Stephanie's Medusa – not so good.

What this says is that the love asteroids are mixed but they draw them oh, so close. No wonder they are entangled, I supposed that Sam and Stephanie will be '*on-again off-again*' lovers, they can't keep their hands off each other.

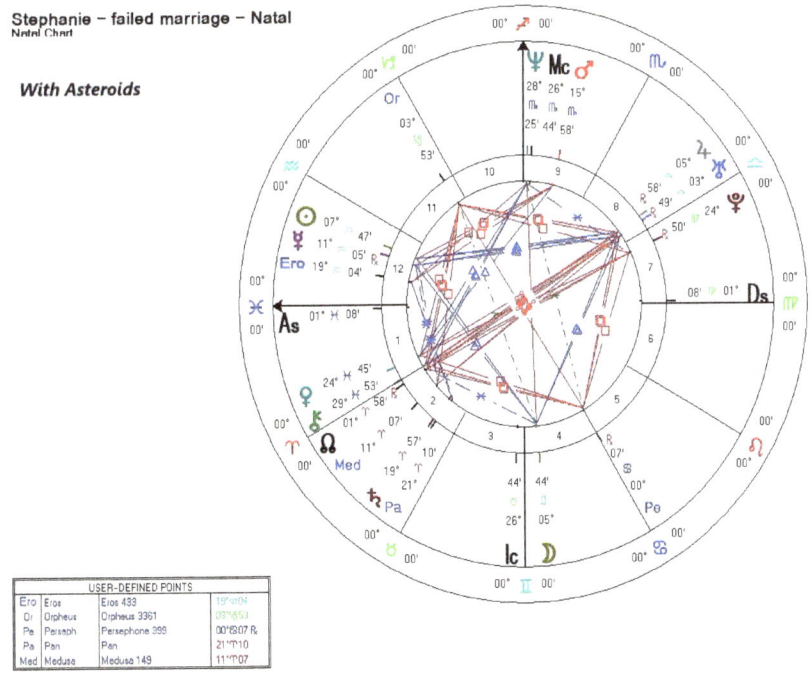

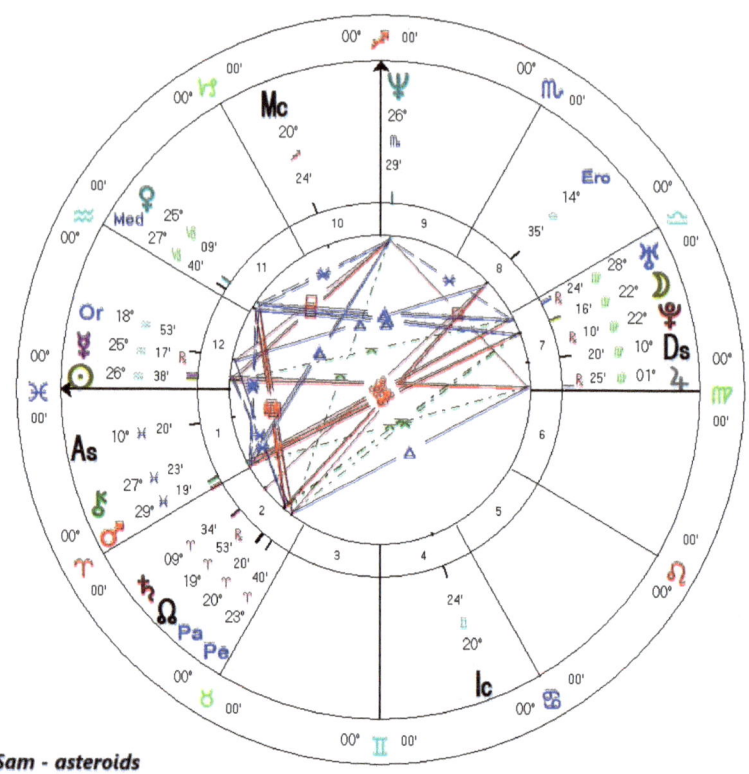

Sam - asteroids

Chapter 12: House Systems

For beginners and even experienced astrologers, the question of which astrological house system to use is a complicated one. To make it a little easier to get your head around two of the most important factors in any astrological chart are the Ascendant and the Midheaven. The angle of the Ascendant shows the degree of the zodiac that is rising on the Eastern horizon at the moment of birth. The Midheaven (MC) indicates the degree that is highest in the sky above the horizon at the place of birth. They stay the same for every house system.

Obviously, these two angles differ considerably depending upon where the birth takes place. Exactly on the equator the Ascendant is always square (at 90°) to the MC. But the further north or south you go, the more slanted the MC is to the Ascendant. For instance people in Norway experience very long winter nights and very short summer nights. In such a case, the MC is clearly not square the Ascendant. How does this influence the house size and position and is it important?

Astrological house systems were designed to take the environment into account in drawing up a natal chart. Each house is a specific sphere of life, and the planets and points express themselves in matters related to that house. So the house cusp and size are very important.

Most of our early astronomers were court astrologers by trade, they knew both science of astrology and astronomy. These ancient astrologers had devised a division of the zodiac called 'mundane division' in order to explain the personality and strengths and weaknesses and opportunities shown by the signs and planets. For instance, Claudius Ptolemy was concerned with the problems of house calculation as the size would vary according to their birth place north or south of the equator.

Some house systems are thousands of years old and some were developed just recently. This diversity is one of the main points of contention between astrologers, all systems are astronomically valid, but their standpoints vary, and therefore so do the degrees at which the houses fall. Many astrologers are unaware of the conceptual differences in the various house systems, and tend to stick rigidly to the one which they were taught.

How then does an astrologer choose a house system? The most common is the Placidus House system. The reason for this is that it was the first system that the average astrologer could easily calculate without being a mathematician. The astrologer would consult the ephemeris and the tables and logarithms that were sold with it, the Placidus house system tables. Even though Placidus provided the necessary tables to calculate the house cusps, it still took between 4 and 8 hours of hard work to draw up the chart. I know because that's how I learned astrology, slaving away over tables and logarithms.

We now look at house systems and how the chart changes accordingly. The following are most, but not all, of the house systems available. Note that they all have something different to the rest. If in doubt stick to the one you know, or use Whole Sign house system which I use for all my charts these days. You will observe that the house systems are all slightly different.

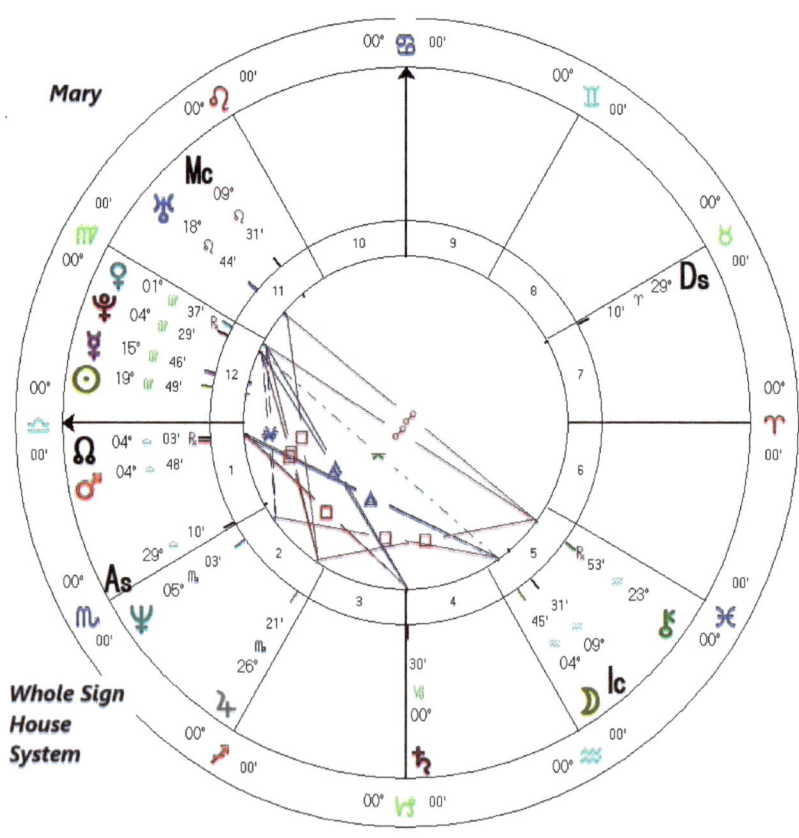

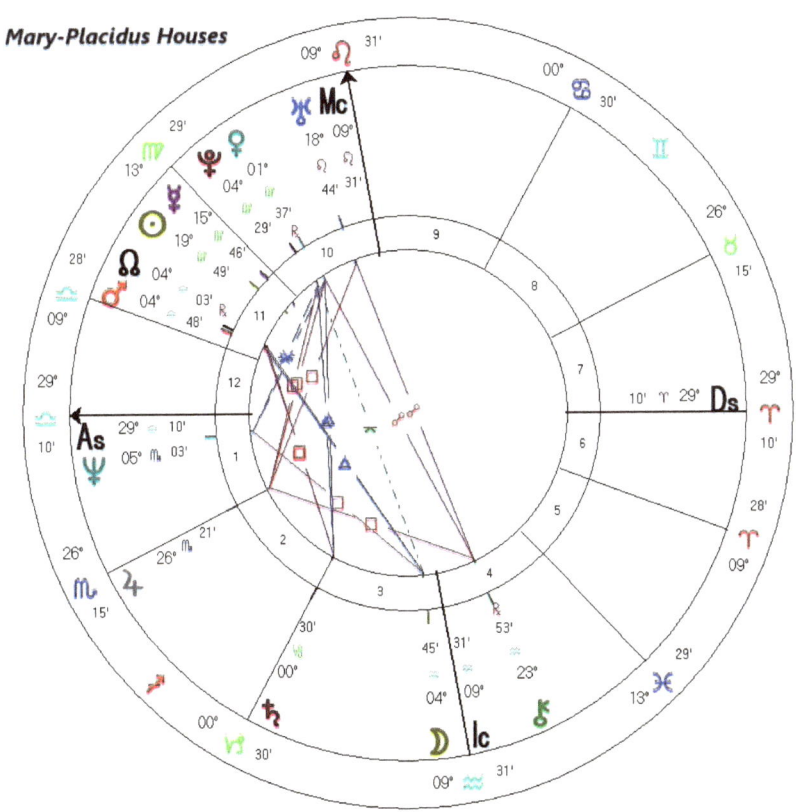

Mary-Kock Houses

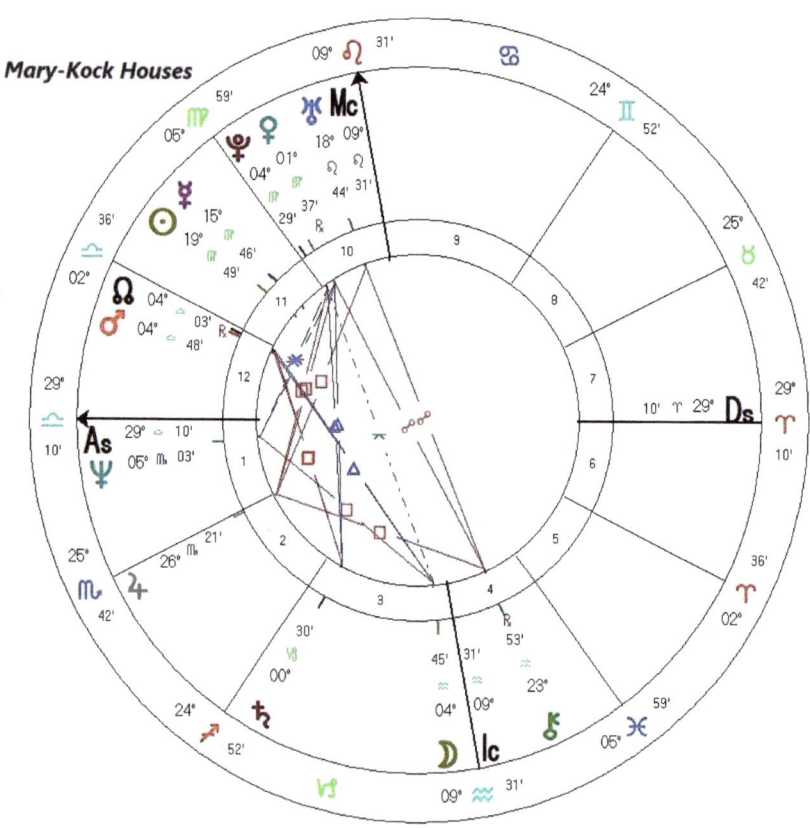

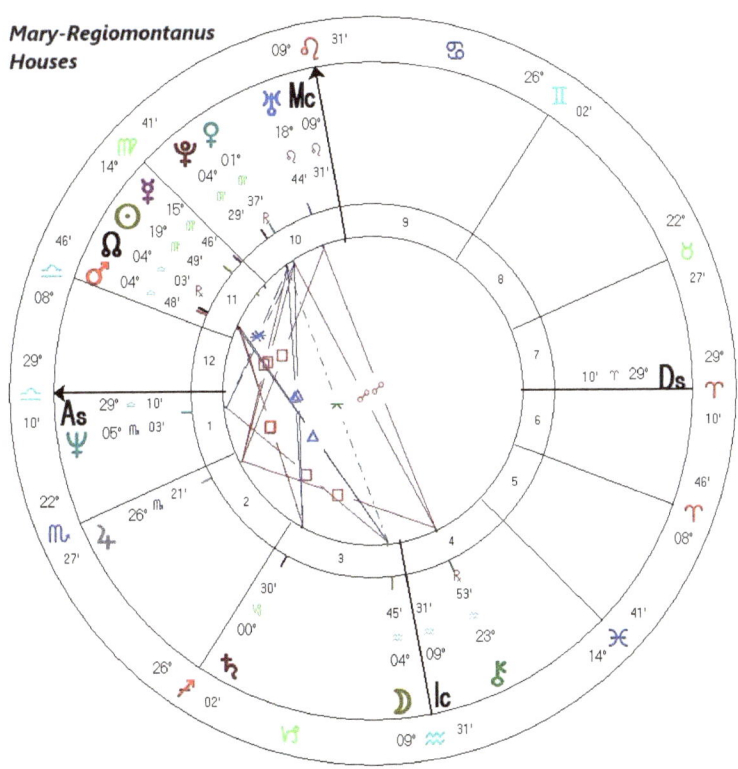
Mary-Regiomontanus Houses

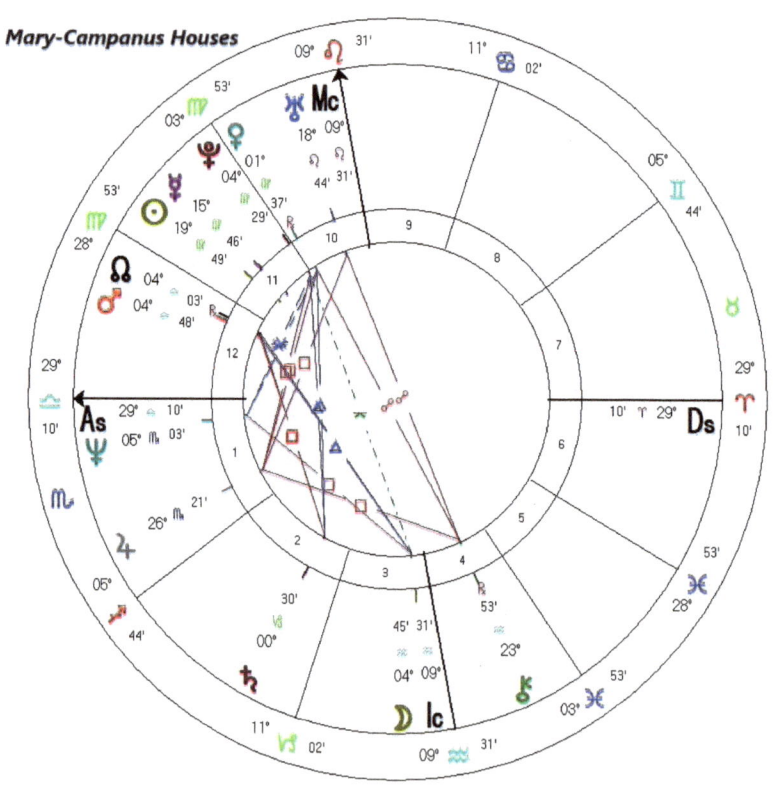

Mary-Equal Houses

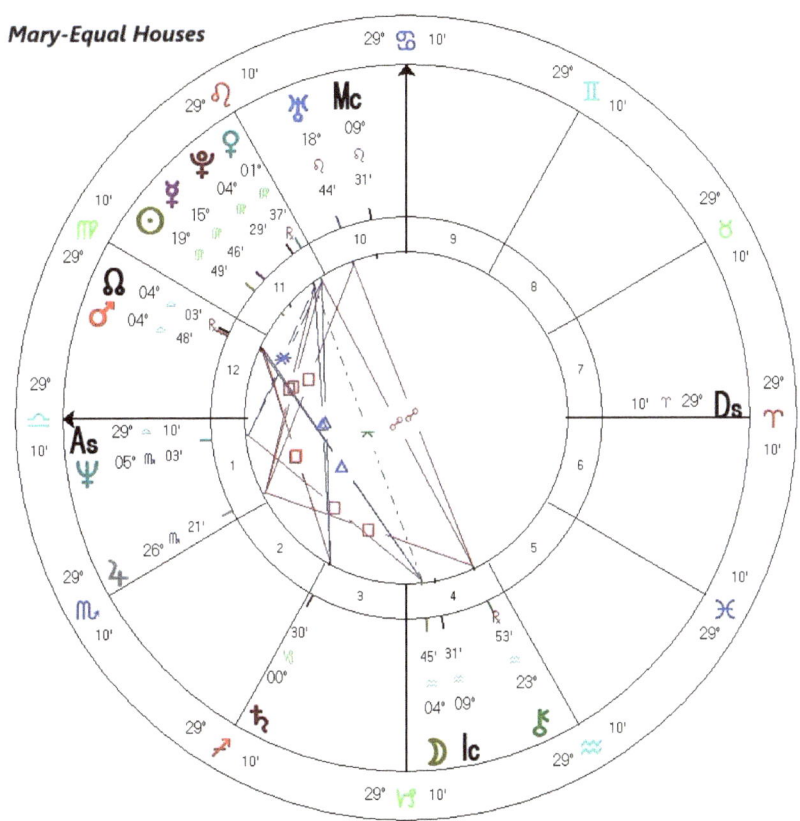

They are all different in their own way, you can make up your mind which one to use.

~

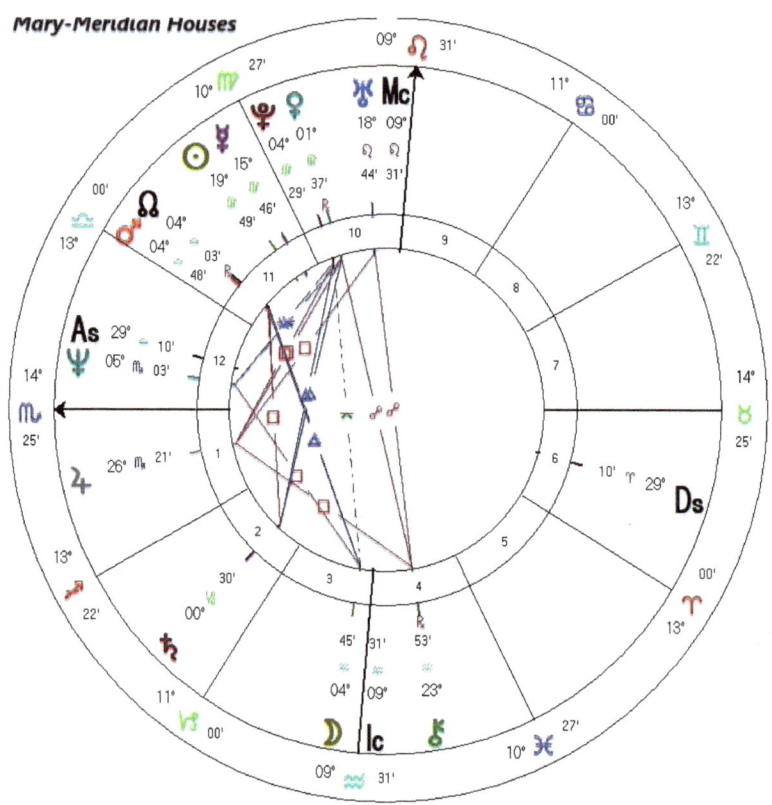

Chapter 13: Personal Myths and Astrology

"All plots are myths. But myths are more than plots. They are tales told about the interaction of humans and the divine. Myths link together human capacities with divine powers. To be in a myth is to be in mimesis with those powers (Hillman). But, what are these divine powers and who is this god? How did we enter this world of wonder? How did we enter this world of imagination speaking to us with its own kind of outside reality?" Stephanie Pope,
www.headlinemuse.com/videoofthemonth/womanontop.htm

"Meaning makes a great many things endurable - perhaps everything. No science will ever replace myth, and myth cannot be made out of any science. For it is not that "God" is a myth, but that myth is the revelation of a divine life in man." Memories, Dreams, and Reflections, C. G. Jung

The Magician seeks beyond the veil of consciousness in her vision quest.

The Importance of Myth

Mythology is an organised collection of stories which helps explain our beliefs and our history. Beneath the story-lines, myths usually confront major issues such as the origin of humanity, its traditions, cultures and society and the way in which nature and humanity interacts. The standard style of myth narrates the deities' daily activities, their love affairs, pleasures, their jealousies and rages, their ambitions and schemes, and their arguments and battles.

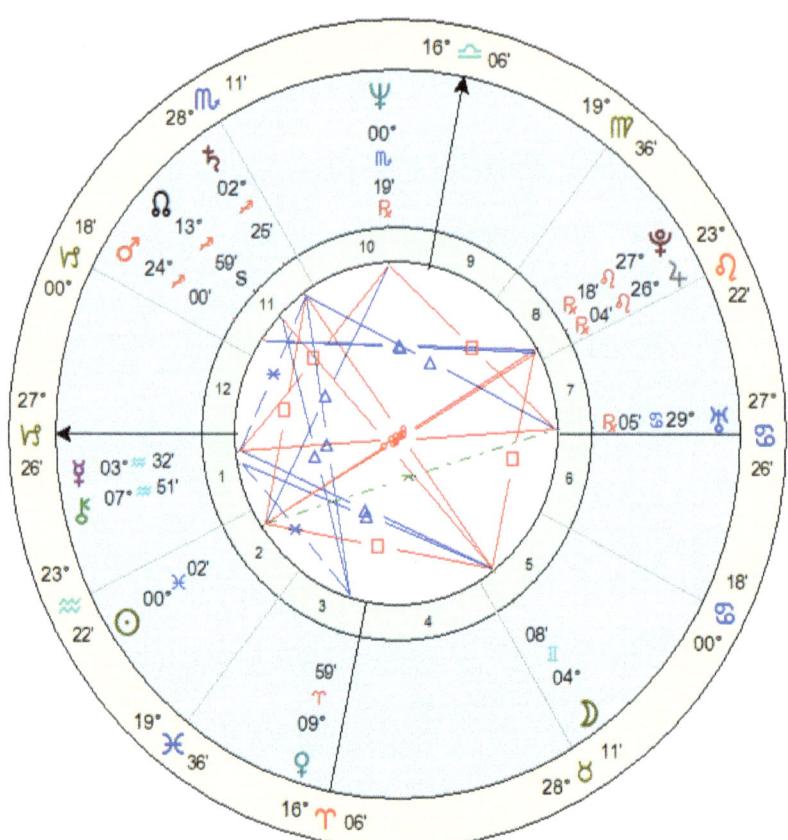

Mitch - using the Placidus house system

Personal Myths—Using the Chart can Help you

These are myths that represent your history, your culture and your current story of where you are now. Mitch needed the inner space to find meaning using astrology and I was able to find a way to help him to do just that. **Guest chart Mitch**—an analysis of his natal chart shows T-square pattern with Neptune focal point of Mercury and Uranus, another T-square with focal planet Moon from Sun and Jupiter / Pluto conjunction, plus a third T-square with Sun focal planet to Moon and Saturn. He almost has a Grand Cross. These 3 T-squares shape his behaviour, his beliefs and the people he attracts and is attracted to. He also has a lot of trines which tend to ease the hard T-squares.

His is a busy chart, when one point is triggered by transit the whole chart vibrates like a spiders web. This would increase his sensitivity as well. Have you already noticed how many Fire and Air planets there are? Six planets in Fire and three in Air. While the Earth Asc is a godsend, he needs as much Earth as he can get to stabilise him. His Air Fire activity stimulates him to learn, study, he is a healer with university qualifications. The excess Air and Fire will also increase his internal agitation and irritability. Of course, he doesn't show it, there's too much conflict in his chart to even think to cause more. Is he a classic Air / Fire, no, not really, but he has a charged, energised chart that shows signs of it.

Looking at his Luminaries (Sun and Moon), Moon is in Gemini in the 5th house, a Fire house, aspecting Mercury and Chiron nicely; but there are hard aspects to Neptune, Jupiter, Pluto, North Node and Sun. This suggests that he will withdraw into silence when challenged, either his Gemini Moon will shout and yell, or it will withdraw. Moon is emotions, with so many challenging aspects it is going to find that too much vibration sends it into a spin. Stress would be a good word to use, that and racing negative thoughts. I would say that he internalises rather than externalises his Moon or emotional qualities.

Sun is in Pisces in the 2nd house, an Earth house; it has a nice aspect to Neptune and challenging aspects to Moon, Jupiter, Pluto and Saturn. I could say that both his parents dominated him. He finds it safer in the 2nd house, being a sensitive Water sign, and so can hide, working hard avoiding conflicts, yet with Pluto / Jupiter in the 7th opposing his Sun he cannot hide from his wife. Yes, the Moon in Gemini and in the 5th house also represents his wife.

With Capricorn Ascendant, Chiron and Mercury close to it's cusp is a good Earthy quality but he needs more Earth. Unfortunately both planets (Chiron and Mercury) are in Aquarius. Especially difficult would be Mercury as its his conscious mind, too busy, lots of thoughts and ideas racing through his mind. This will be triggered by Moon in Gemini, his own sign. The Asc is ruled by Saturn, The Lord of the Chart, so Saturn is a very important player. Although under pressure from Moon and Sun, it tries its hardest to make his life as easy as he can. Oh, and it is in Sagittarius, the sign of his protagonist (Jupiter) and thus not so comfortable for him.

He has Uranus conjunct his Descendant which shows some stress and hyperactivity from his wife, and others. Mars and Venus are the only planets with no heavy aspects. Venus is in Aries in the 3rd looking out for love and hot passion. His wife is an Aries so I am sure he has a physical relationship, but the conflict in his chart means that she is also the one who contributes to his stress and worry. His Mars is in Sagittarius and the 11th house, he expresses his Martian energy and urges by helping people – which he does.

Over all, he has a difficult chart, too much stress, internalised in the mind (Gemini Moon and Mercury); but hard aspects of the T-squares may actually help him stabilise, but they also add to denial.

In therapy he took a long time to be able to articulate his problems, basically because he was in denial of his situation. His wife was a true matriarch and a domineering one at that. Her expectations of him were somewhat over the top. He could not do anything without her permission. Don't forget that this is a sensitive Pisces Sun who needs love and nurturing, it hurt for him to be bullied daily, his hard external shell was almost gone.

Mitch came to therapy when Transiting Neptune crossed his Ascendant, this was like Water washing away the Earth - I know that feeling myself. Plus, Transiting Pluto was opposing his Moon. Two devastating transits, absolutely frightening, and triggering the 'spiders web' network throughout his psyche setting off alarm bells. You don't need me to tell you what these transits were doing, but I will. Neptune, his Planet of High Degree and ruler of Pisces his Sun's sign, wanted to wash away his self esteem. His rock solid Capricorn was the only thing he had that stood solid and tall in his life, it was a pillar of strength for him, he needed it to survive.

He had one single strategy in his tool kit which he relied on too much, when it came time to shift a gear and use another, there weren't any. This was happening while Pluto decided to challenge his emotional stability, and with that Moon in Gemini so unstable and erratic. He was in a bad way as this was about his mother and his wife. Disillusioned and abandoned - his wife didn't believe that he couldn't work so hard, that he needed time off, he was having a real breakdown and his wife didn't believe it.

In therapy he found his archetypes and he found a way to survive. I asked him about his dreams, his internal myths, what was it that he really admired? His myth was quite unexpected, it was an imaginary Indian Village, it was his saviour. After four years of unsuccessful therapy with Neptune and Pluto doing their terrible yet valuable thing, he made his way to psychotherapy with me. There he developed a safe place to do his therapy and develop more strategies.

Pluto transits to the Luminaries and Ascendant are horrors and Neptune really completes the feeling of helplessness and hopelessness. Mitch really needed astrology and psychotherapy, there is no question of that.

Mitch survived, he even made a warriors room in his house

where he placed his weapons, his native spear and shield, drawings and sculpture's he had made himself, none of this were allowed previously in the house. The home was his wife's home, nothing of his was permitted to be on display. Now that he found his inner warrior, it became their house. He even told her he was using the spare junk room for his den. She couldn't stop him, he had found his mojo and their marriage eventually improved. Mitch's mythology, and living his myth, made him whole.

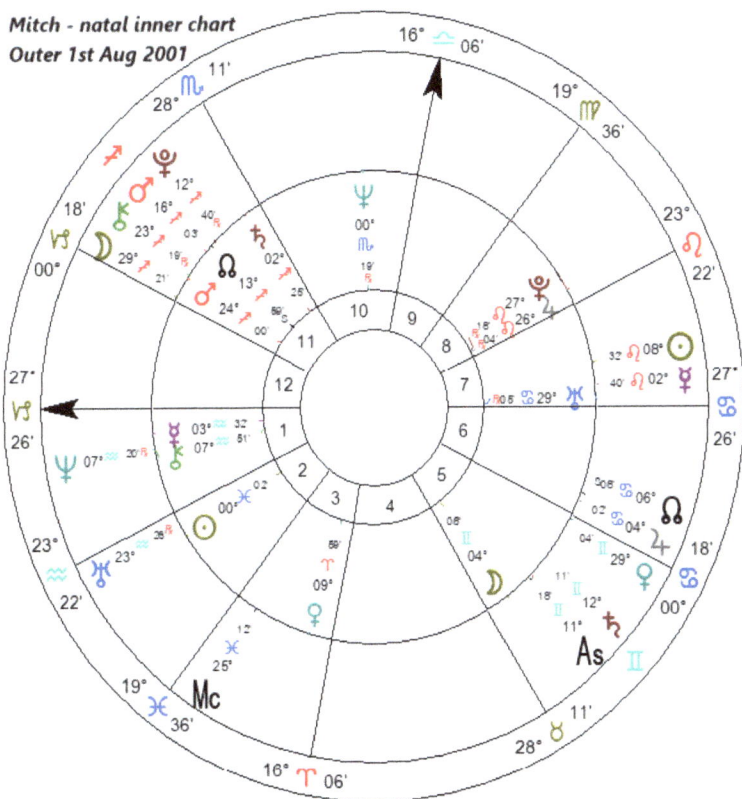

Another client, **Ronnie.** She is amazing, she has done incredible things in trance so far. She has a lovely Leo Sun, 8th house of transformation and evolution which is ideal for her inner work. It is nicely Trine to Jupiter Uranus. Moon is in fiery Aries and it's in the 4th house of home and family, so very important to her. Capricorn Asc adds some solid stable Earth to guide and direct her, she is reliable and dependable. MC is Virgo, also Earth, she liked to give and serve others, was generous and Venus is in Virgo in the 9th house with Mars is in Cancer in the 7th house.

Ronnie wanted to stop being afraid, afraid of heights, afraid of water, afraid of people, afraid of just about everything. She wanted a world where there were answers just for her, honest answers she could rely up – she chose the world of archetypes.

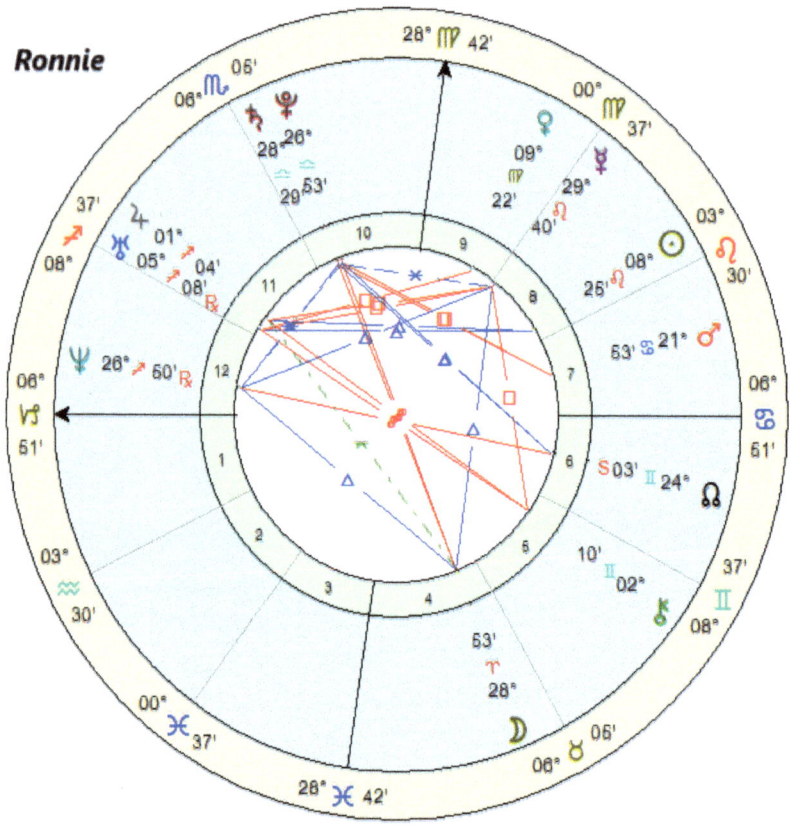

Ronnie

Let's look at her chart. Both Venus and Mars are poorly aspected, Venus in particular is a Singleton, only the one aspect, no wonder she is not in a relationship, in fact they never last. Her mood swings and frustrations means she can't focus or concentrate on them. She has a lovely Kite focus on Moon, she gets on great with father, not as well with mum, but as they both get older they enjoy each others company more.

Let's look at her transits for counselling. Transiting Pluto has finished crossing her 1st house cusp, no wonder no one could live with her for very long. Even though it is out of the 2° to 4° orb I normally use, he is still sitting there, he is a powerful dude. She has finished a North Node transit, and remember North Node goes backwards, clockwise to

Ronnie counselling

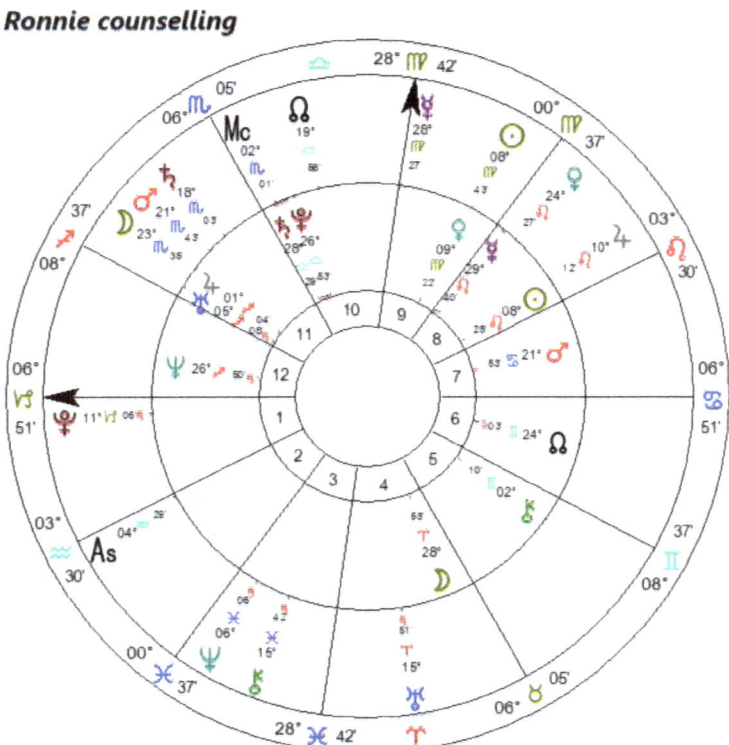

the chart, the planets travel anticlockwise. North Node would have initiated her seeing me, someone who has been able to take her on a journey into her inner world, and no anti-psychotic drugs. Transiting Jupiter has finished crossing natal Sun, that would have been wonderful, and it was during a holiday with her beloved family, a time to rest and relax.

In therapy I asked her where she would like to start her therapy. She said that she would like to be in a place that had no water, her big fear was water whether that would be a beach, a swimming pool or a river. She started to meet up with the Sun and Moon archetypes on a planet somewhere, the sky is different to ours. She has worked hard to get the Sun to participate, he prefers to sit back and watch, observe, which must be his 8th house placement, he acts quite Scorpionic. The Moon is easy for her to work with although I would have expected it around the other way but the inner world has its own rules.

She asked the Sun and Moon to bring to her those facets of her psyche that maintained an awful energy at work with two of her supervisors. She asked: *"What parts of me are responsible for the poor relationships at work with my supervisors?"*

She learned that her own jealousy was part of the problem. So Sun and Moon brought the energy forms together and helped heal them. The Moon was the main character that helped her sort that out. Moon said that she knew that she was jealous, so it wasn't unconscious and could be worked with now.

Then she asked the Sun if he would take her to his home and he did. He lived on a cliff edge, a huge Tibetan Monastery, high up in the mountains with clouds drifting below her. He took her to walk to the edge of the cliff and told her to sit down and dangle her feet over the edge. She is, was, terrified of heights, so this was deliberate. He asked her to close her eyes and just sit there, to feel the moment and hold on to it. She felt herself beginning to feel a calming breeze and finally was able to sit there with her eyes open and enjoy the view.

He then took her to walk into his pool. She is terrified of water, truly, she can't go near open water at all. However, she walked into the pool at his monastery with the Sun beside her. He told her to sit in the bottom and to close her eyes. She did, she sat at the bottom of the pool and was mildly surprised that she could relax. That was an amazing session. The Sun was taking her through her fears, one by one, and healing them.

She has started to work with Pluto too, she can certainly feel his power. Although she knows she needs to work with him she will get there soon enough. Mythology and dreaming are a marvellous way to heal.

Chapter 14 - The Four Elements as Defences

I know I have written about the four elements in astrology in my first book but I have new material that I wanted to mention as this is one of the most important tenets of astrology.

The elements help explain the powerful connection between astrology and Psychodynamic Theory as developed by Sigmund Freud, Carl Jung and expanded upon by their followers. They reflect and enhance Freud's theory of the psychosexual stages of personality development. He proposed that people develop defences to protect their very sensitive and soft emotions, they provide the necessary barriers to the harsh realities of the world. Defences are necessary but if they are too well developed they become a problem, we withdraw behind these defensive barriers preventing us from participating fully in the world around us.

We see defences in the chart when planets, signs, houses, Ascendant and chart dominants planets highlight an element in the natal chart. Often there is more than one element highlighted and not every one will have a single dominant element but we all have defences, no-one is free of them. We look at planets in elements, planetary signature, house emphasis, Ascendant element, most aspected planet, etc. until the most dominant element shows its defence – but even then we need to be careful because there may be more than one defence.

Defences also work in closely with complexes and projections. If there is a deficit with an element this too is considered important in defence formation though nowhere near as important as the dominant element. An understanding of the four elements in astrology will be one of the most important things that you will learn in preparation for professional practice.

Oral Defences - Water
Defends against abandonment, betrayal, emotional rejection and loneliness by attaching and connecting to others and love objects, e.g. pets, houses, and significant objects like a car or lover: *"I need you, don't leave me, I can't live without you!"*

Our first reflex at birth is to suckle at our mother's breast, the feelings of warmth, security, love, joy, nurturing, satisfaction and fulfilment come from this initial experience. If there are emotional needs not being met at this age (especially around weaning time) the child can become 'fixated' at the oral stage of development. They then seek, throughout life, objects to replace the breast – toys, possessive friendships, cigarettes, addictions of all sorts (drugs, sex, food & alcohol), excessive crying, whining and talking, require a dummy/pacifier, thumb sucking, gum chewing and an unnatural need for affection.

The oral reflex is a natural phenomenon, it is fundamental and thus the first and most powerful experience for a newborn child. It is much like our first meeting with a stranger – first impressions last. A child's first impression of what to expect from life is at childbirth and the first nurturing experience afterwards. If the nurturing breast is withdrawn before the child is fulfilled and satisfied then a yearning takes place, a yearning that may manifest as a defence. One form of defence that can form at this stage is a resentment of those who remove the 'breast' or comfort. This may then lead to passive-aggressive behaviours whereby the child then begins to sabotage efforts by those around him to pacify him.

An oral defence can also develop when a child experiences abandonment and trauma which may fixate them in the oral defence stage. When a relationship breaks up a huge amount of energy is given to grieving the loss. Oral, abandonment issues are seen in many people especially those that seek counselling and provides therapists with most of their work. Sometimes, especially with a powerful but poorly aspected Sun or Moon (being in a Water sign or house), Pluto or Neptune, the native will seek revenge when their emotional needs are not being met or when they feel betrayed, rejected and abandoned.

Oral defences are seen with a dominance of Water signs, when the Sun or more commonly the Sun or Moon is in a Water sign, is in a Water house, or is in poor aspect with the outer planets Neptune or Pluto. To find an Oral defence in the chart we look for Water dominance, a poorly aspected Sun or Moon, often it is not in a Water sign but is in conjunction with the outer planet Pluto or Neptune. We look for signs of abandonment, a focus on the 4th house, possibly the 7th, and on the 8th and 12th houses as well as a Water signature and aspects to Neptune, Pluto and Moon. Most commonly it is seen when the Moon is particularly poorly aspected.

Anal Defences – Earth
Defends against change and insecurity by exerting control, often through power struggles with authority figures, and by hoarding and collecting, not letting go: *"I'm not shifting! I can't handle change & I am feeling very anxious & insecure."*

Freud called this defence Anal, suggesting that it began at the potty training stage. The Earth issue is one of power and the control of the child's pace of change. The child finds that he/she can control the flow of urine and faeces, which also stimulates the erogenous zones, producing a nice feeling. Freud was into nice feelings when he came up with this one but it holds quite true when explained as control of 'good feelings' and control of 'the pace of change' to reduce anxiety and insecurity. Just imagine a child just discovering what it felt like to be in control of those pleasurable feelings of letting go of a 'nappy full' of faeces. The child wants to be in charge of this activity, but no, Mum or Dad puts him/her on the potty and makes them stay there until it is finished.

Then there is the transition from an ignorance of defecating and then finding out that, "*Hey, I am not feeling so safe here, things are rushing along far too fast for me to handle. I am feeling afraid and confused, what do they want? Do they want me to sit here all day?*" This can then set up power conflict between authority (Mum or Dad) and the child.

Sometimes involved with this defence are power plays which are sometimes used to control the child. To defend against these feelings of 'powerlessness' the child enters into power conflicts with anyone that represents an authority figure. This is then projected onto the step-mother or father, school teacher, police, the neighbour and anyone that tells them what to do and when to do it. This is their way of controlling their insecurity and anxiety, by controlling the pace of change. Other negative anal activities include collections, hoarding things, an inability to give or let go of things, meanness, pettiness, money-hoarding, revenge, over orderliness, and a degree of passive-aggressive sabotage.

You can imagine the battles at home with this one, the child wants to take command of their pleasure activities be it toilet, bath, playing with toys or being with their friends, it becomes a constant battle to control this child. The defence gets interesting when it comes to relationships. The anal person learns to control through the giving and withholding of affection, much like Mum or Dad had to do to instil discipline. The withholding of and then the giving of affection in a relationship creates a battle ground in the marriage (conditional love), it is usually the recipient that seeks counselling.

Anxiety and insecurity are both major emotional wounds that Earth people use to defends against. Change that comes too fast is confusing and frightening for the Earth signs, they feel terribly insecure. To defend against insecurity they slow down, go to ground, escape into a cave, avoid situations, leave their job, sabotage, become anxious, become depressed and try to control their lives through preventing change, hoarding, or not letting go of friends. They can also order and structure, like the Public Service, by controlling others and they control the fear of losing control.

Anal defences are seen with a dominance of Earth in the chart, the Moon or Sun in Earth signs, when the Sun or Moon is in an Earth house, 2nd, 6th or 10th, poor aspects to Venus (in Taurus), Saturn and Mercury (in Virgo). Most particularly we see it with Saturn. These planets in negative aspects to Moon and Sun, especially the conjunction to Saturn, may make anal defences along with an Earth signature.

Dissociation Defences – Air

Defends against confusion, ambivalence and restricted freedom of expression by denying that anything is wrong, by dissociating and escaping into fantasy instead of facing the real issue, escaping into intellectual explanations and magical thinking: *"It's an omen so I don't have to go to counselling now. I know how to handle this situation, I just ignore it and it goes away. The aliens will save us."*

When Sun or Moon are in Air signs it is easy for them to ignore emotions, to turn off or to rationalise and make logical any emotional issues that arise. There is nothing more powerful than a good argument, and it is in the Air signs and houses that this is most commonly used to avoid real life issues and conflicts. This is often seen when a person will argue with their partner to understand why they acted that way. Often they will argue well into the night until they are satisfied that they have found out the why's and the wherefore's behind the perceived problem with their partner.

Air dominant signs 'dissociate' which basically means that the individual is so overwhelmed by anxiety or abandonment that they seek to avoid these painful feelings by rationalising and arguing, strongly denying that they have any emotional problems. They have great difficulty expressing feelings, they appear cold and are most comfortable talking about love and affection than in actually doing or expressing them. This is the classic politician, accountant or lawyer, no emotion and a closed heart.

Disassociation is also common amongst abuse victims, when confronted by aggression (verbal or physical) they freak out, they disassociate often leaving their body to escape the trauma. They also use magical thinking and escape into fantasy more than the Water signs —everything becomes 'magical' or 'mystical'. It's a great way to deny their inner anxieties and losses, thus they avoid talking about their issues.

These people come for counselling because they get stuck in their heads and can't sleep. These defences are the worst of all problems because once they get into the habit of thinking instead of feeling they begin to experience life as a thought, they live in their heads all the time, disturbing and preventing them from sleeping. This has the potential to make people go crazy. In my experience the Air signs have a predisposition to experience psychosis most so than any other sign. A combination of Water (Oral) and Air (Dissociation) is really hard to treat.

People using this defence require order and knowledge in their lives to make life comfortable. They seek order through information, objectivity and the ability to predict what is coming up next. Sometimes they require a sense of independence to make their life ordered and safe. They will escape into fantasy, mystical and magical explanations or omens to make their life more predictable. They also turn up as the classic academic and sceptic who find security in intellectual pursuits to thus avoid emotional experiences.

We look for a dominance of Air in the chart, Sun or Moon in Air signs, an Air signature, a predominance of planets in Air houses, and poor aspects to Mercury (in Gemini), Venus (in Libra) and Uranus. The Air signs Gemini, Aquarius and Libra may be highlighted along with the Air houses (3rd, 7th and 11th) and planets, especially strong is Uranus conjunct Ascendant, Moon or Sun.

Oedipal Defences – Fire
Defends against insignificance, inertia, personal meaninglessness, impotence, criticism, vulnerability, rejection and humiliation, and the feeling of being totally ignored and worthless by seeking or competing with others for attention, rivalry, jealousy and envy: *"Hey, look at me! Pick me! Pick me! I'm the best player, pick me!"*

Liz Greene and Howard Sasportas, in *The Development of the Personality*, describe the Oedipus Complex as the defence for Fire signs. This is a defence from being overwhelmed by feelings of worthlessness and insignificance to gain attention and recognition. This can be in the form of one-up-man-ship, seeking to be better than the other, it can also be seen as bullying and fighting to gain the upper hand and to prevent being overturned or conquered, ridiculed or humiliated. The classic attention seeking behaviour of some children (and adults) can also be an Oedipal defence.

The Oedipal defence also defends us against a meaningless existence. Fire signs need to be special, they love being the centre of attention, anything that takes this feeling of special significance away will be strongly defended against. *"I just want to be special, would somebody just notice me!"* The Heroes Quest is one of the Fire signs ways to gain recognition and also to give meaning and significance to their existence.

This defence stems from King Oedipus of ancient Greece, who unknowingly killed his father and married his mother. In psychodynamic theory this is seen as a boy child seeking to kill or conquer his father so that he can have mother all to himself. This in itself is a common process in childhood, mother is the boy's first love and Dad gets in the way. The child then tries to manoeuvre and gain power or colludes with mother to get Dad out of the picture. This is seen as a triad (two against one) whereby mother and the child gang-up on Dad. Once Dad is gone he has effectively been 'castrated', impotent, dis-empowered, but if the child loses then he becomes the one who is 'castrated' instead.

'Castration' was Freud's way of saying 'impotence' or 'loss of power'. This struggle is not confined to boys and fathers, it can be between any family members. Castration or loss of power can occur between brother and sister (sibling rivalry), mother and son or daughter, father and daughter or son, etc. He who is castrated loses his / her power to another more powerful family member, this occurs in most families to varying degrees.

To prevent being castrated or to seek revenge for being castrated by the family, the child becomes somewhat of a bully, seeking to re-establish their position of dominance, or they become broken in spirit. It can also be seen as throwing tantrums, excessive competition for attention and through passive-aggressive behaviours (sabotage). They can also seek revenge for being deposed and being pushed off the pedestal.

One of the most common manifestations of the Oedipal Defence is seen with sibling rivalry and the previously mentioned triads, joining forces with another or group of others to defeat a single foe - the 'other'. As part of this competition is the need to be protected from criticism and humiliation. This is Fire's biggest fears, that they are not good enough. In other words to be humiliated or criticised in front of others is one of the Fire signs biggest fears.

Read R.D. Laing's *The Divided Self,* it is basically an Oedipal defence and one of needing recognition and living a significant and meaningful life. Oedipal defences are found with a dominance of Fire, when there is a focus on Fire signs, houses and planets. Sun, Mars and Jupiter, 1st, 5th and 9th house focus and Ascendant in a Fire sign and chart signatures. Especially strong is the conjunction between Sun or Moon with Jupiter or Mars in a Fire house or sign.

Margaret Thatcher (1925 – 2013) – was the Prime Minister of Great Britain through the heady years of the 70's and 80's. She expressed some powerful defences as seen by the elements of Fire and Air in her chart. As the first female Prime Minister she went to great lengths to be more commanding than her underlings, she sought speech therapy to deepen her voice and gave the world a proud, domineering yet feminine presence. Margaret Thatcher will long be remembered for sending British soldiers to the Falkland Islands to die for their country, something many could not believe a mother could ever do - send their sons to war.

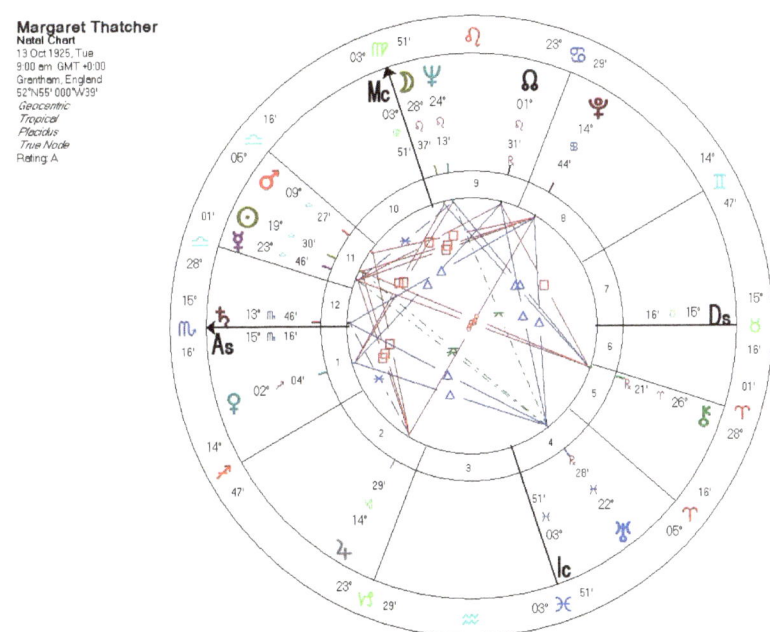

This chart shows a predominance of the element Fire: Moon, Neptune and North Node in Leo and in the 9th house (also Fire); Chiron in Aries and Venus in Sagittarius in the 1st, the first house is always important. We see immediately that Margaret needs to defend herself, her self esteem (Fire quality) by being the best by defeating her opponents to gain attention from her party and the people. Margaret also has Saturn conjunct her Ascendant making Earth moderately strong. She then has some Water with Scorpio Ascendant and Neptune conjunct Moon with some Air (Sun, Mercury and Mars in Libra).

There is obviously a mixture of elements, it is up to our professional skills to determine what is the predominant element. I would go with Fire, followed by Water and Air/Earth a close 3rd. With such a powerful personality as Mrs Thatcher we see almost all of her elements at play. Margaret's weakness (Fire) is through fear of humiliation and embarrassment, with a fear of abandonment (Water - Neptune Moon). To defend against this she competes and bullies others to get to the top and to stay on the top. Water is also strong but in this case it manifests as steam - Fire and Water together can be explosive.

Mechanisms of Defence

In order to cope with painful anxiety the ego had to develop some kind of defence. The most important of these defences is *repression*. In repression the ego forced the unpleasant thoughts down into the Id (deep unconscious). Conflict results between the repressed emotional need to expression > and the ego which wants to bury it deeper because it hurts.

Early in his career, Freud had used hypnosis to unearth repressed ideas. Later he depended on the process of "free association" or 'talking therapy'. Freud placed great emphasis on the process of repression. Repression shows that what we thought was forgotten was really only repressed. Many of our ideas and memories of past events were not really lost but repressed. Some of these memories cause significant distress and are hard to repress thus you seek therapy to overcome, resolve, or express it safely.

Freud placed a great deal of significance on the importance of early childhood experiences that affected the development of the personality. Often these experiences were very traumatic and they become repressed in the id where they might remain for years, only to rise later into a neurosis such as a phobia.

His patient Fraulein Anna O, clearly illustrates the repression concept. Please read the whole story at: wikipedia.org/wiki/Anna_O.

Period of life	Freud	Erikson
Ages First year of life	*Oral Stage* Sucking at mother's breasts satisfies need for food and pleasure. Infant needs to get basic nurturing, or later feelings of greediness and acquisitiveness may develop. Oral fixation results from deprivation of oral gratification in infancy. Later personality problems can include mistrust, rejecting love, and fear of and an inability to form intimate relationships.	*Infancy: Trust Vs Mistrust* If significant others provide for basic physical and emotional needs, infant develops a sense of trust. If basic needs are not met an attitude of mistrust towards the world, especially towards interpersonal relationships, is the result.
Ages 1—3 years	*Anal Stage* Anal zone becomes of major significance in formation of personality. Main developmental tasks include learning independence, accepting personal power and learning to express rage and aggression appropriately. Parental discipline patterns and attitudes have significant consequences for child's later personality development.	*Early Childhood: Autonomy Vs Shame & Doubt* A time for developing autonomy: basic struggles is between a sense of self-reliance and a sense of self-doubt. Child needs to explore and experiment, to make their mistakes and to test limits. If parents promote dependency the child's autonomy is inhibited and capacity to deal with the world successfully is hampered.

Period of life	Freud's Psychosexual Stages	Erikson's Psychosocial Stages
Ages 3—6 years	*Phallic Stage (Astrological Oedipal Stage)* Basic conflict centers on unconscious desires that child develops for parent of opposite sex and that, because of their threatening nature, are repressed. Male Phallic Stage, known as Oedipal Complex, involves mother as love object for the boy. Female Phallic Stage, known as Electra Complex, involves girls striving for their father's love and approval. How parents respond, verbally and nonverbally, to their child's emerging sexuality has an impact o sexual attitudes and feelings that child develops.	*Preschool age: Initiative Vs Guilt* Basic task is to achieve a sense of competence and initiative. If children are given freedom to select personally meaningful activities, they tend to develop a positive view of self and follow through with their projects. If they are not allowed to make their own decisions, they tend to develop guilt over taking initiative. They then refrain from taking a active stance and allow others to choose for them.
Ages 6—12 years	*Latency Stage* After the torment of sexual impulses of preceding years, this period is relatively quiet. Sexual interests are replaced with interests in school, friendships, sports and a range of new activities. This is a time of socialisation as the child turns outwards and forms relationships with others.	*School age: Industry Vs Inferiority* Child needs to expand understanding of the world, continue to develop appropriate sex-role identity and to learn the basic skills required for school success. Basic task is to achieve a sense of industry, to set and attain personal goals. Failure to do so results in a sense of failure and inadequacy.
Ages 12—18 years	*Genital Stage (astrological Air)* Old themes of phallic stage are revived. This stage begins with puberty and lasts until senility. Despite societal restrictions and taboos, adolescents can deal with sexual energy by investing it in activities such as forming friendships, engaging in art or sports and preparing for a career.	*Adolescence: Identity Vs Role Confusion* A time of transition between childhood and adulthood. A time for testing limits, breaking dependant ties and establishing a new identity. Major conflicts over clarification of self-identity, life goals and life's meanings. Failure to achieve a sense of identity results in role confusion.
Ages 18—35 years	*Genital Stage Continues* Core characteristics of mature adult is the freedom to 'love and to work'. This move towards adulthood involves freedom from parental influences and capacity to care for others.	*Young Adult: Intimacy Vs Isolation* Developmental task at this time is to form intimate relationships. Failure to do this can lead to alienation and isolation.
Age 35—60 years	*Genital stage continues*	*Middle Age: Generation Vs Stagnation* There is a need to go beyond self and family and to help the next generation. This is a time of adjusting to the discrepancy between one's dreams and one's actual accomplishments. Failure to achieve a sense of productivity can lead to psychological stagnation.
Age 60 + years	*Genital stage continues*	*Later Life: Integrity Vs Despair* If one has few regrets and feels personally worthwhile, ego integrity results. Failure to achieve ego integrity can lead to feelings of despair, helplessness, guilt, resentment and self-rejection

Earth – Anal

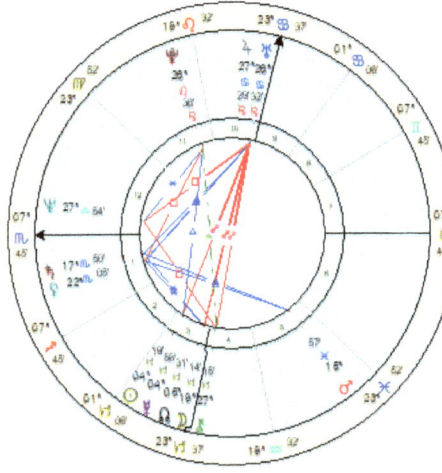

This man had health problems, his duodenum was closing up. We see issues with control in his Scorpio Ascendant and a large stellium in the 3rd house in Capricorn. We could safely say that this fellow has issues with power and control.

There are also issues with siblings and some abandonment with Cancer strong. We could venture to say that there may be some mother issues with Cancer so strong in the chart at the MC with Uranus conjunct and the Moon poorly aspected. Moon is conjunct Chiron, the wound from mother and opposing Uranus and Jupiter, a Mother Complex? He spent a lot of time with his mother throughout his illness and he is experiencing problems in his marriage.

Air – Dissociation

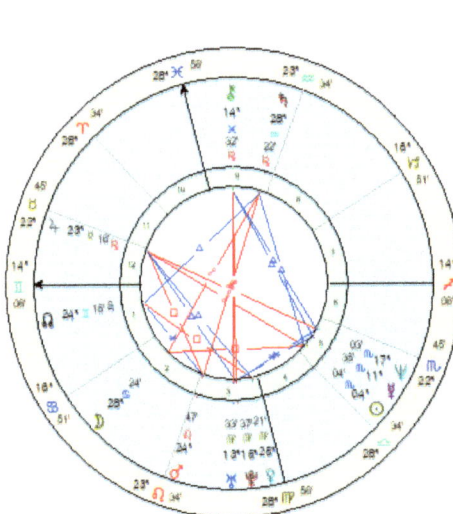

This man came for counseling after two months of restlessness, not sleeping, confusion as to direction in his life, worrying all night, too many thoughts, can't sleep. He has some classic significators for Air defenses:-

Dissociation - Gemini Ascendant, Mercury Lord of the Chart conjunct Sun in Scorpio which intensifies the defense, Mercury conjunct Neptune which confuses the mind, Mercury well aspected and maybe too well with 5 aspects. As you can see not all that much emphasis on Air but enough to spin him out.

Abandonment issues? Moon square Sun, Yod to Saturn, Jupiter in 12th poorly aspected and rules the 7th house, he feared losing his wife as well.

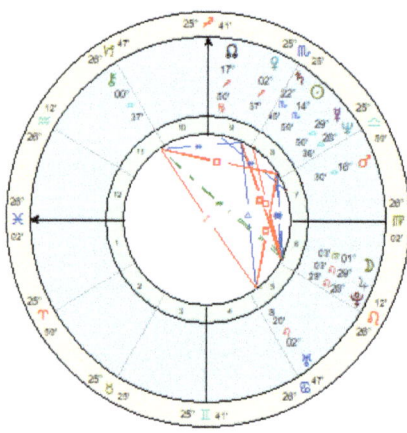

Water—Oral

This fellow was counselled for relationship issues, he couldn't let go of his lovers, just in case one left him he always had a back up lover. Got himself into all sorts of unhappy situations which devastated his partners.

Look at Sun in Scorpio in the 8th House, Pisces Ascendant, 4 planets in the 8th House.

His Water defense is compounded by his Earth Defense to stay in control – his Moon in Virgo and 3 planets in his 6th House act as Earth Defenses too.

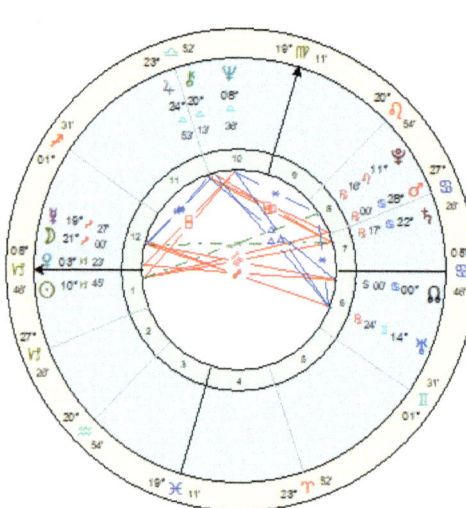

Fire – Oedipal

This lady came for relationship counselling, from the placement of the Sun in the first house (Leo characteristics), Moon and Mercury in Sagittarius, even Venus in Capricorn and Capricorn Ascendant and Sun signs may elevate them into active principals, similar to Fire.

Not an overly Fire chart, as it has elements of Air and Water (Moon 12th, Cancer 7th) it does demonstrate that this lady, an ex-Kindergarten teacher and brothel owner likes to be in command and competes with her partners for attention and in business.

Issues of abandonment arise in relationships when she gets too carried away with her need to be on top.

SUMMARY
- The Four Elements are Keys to understanding your client's psyche.
- We can use some of Freud's teachings to guide us.
- Water illustrates Oral traits and qualities—fears abandonment.
- Air illustrates Denial traits and qualities—fears reality.
- Earth illustrates Anal traits and qualities—fears loss of control.
- Fire illustrates Oedipal traits and qualities—fears insignificance.
- We find these keys by locating the significators, signatures, focal planets, dominant signs and houses.
- Elements are our first and greatest psychological keys in astrology.
- Psychological defences can arise from astrological conflict, repression is one way of understanding this conflict.

Chapter 15 - The Mythology of the Seasons

The Capricorn Myth and the Winter Solstice

The arrival of Capricorn announces the Winter Solstice, midwinter's day, the shortest day of the year in the northern hemisphere. People in Europe and the Middle East celebrated this day which heralded the sun's return. This day announced the coming of warmth, sunshine and the wealth of produce at harvest time. Here in the southern hemisphere, we celebrate the Summer Solstice (midsummer's day), when we embrace the start of our glorious summer holidays.

Zodiac - Public Domain, https://commons.wikimedia.org/w/index.php?curid=66...

    The Winter Solstice marks the sun's victory in the celestial dance of the seasons swinging between the privations of winter and the bounty of summer. It heralds the end of winter's long, cold nights, boredom, depression, limited food choices and inactivity. There was always the spectre of starvation as our ancestor's stores of food threatened to run out towards the end of winter.

    Several pagan gods of interest to astrologers were celebrated at the Winter Solstice: Sol Invictus, Mithrais and Saturnalia (Saturn). Sol

Invictus was elevated to God status in Rome in 274 AD. Sol Day or Sunday, was decreed by the Roman Emperor Constantine in 321 AD. An illustration of how important the Winter Solstice was to our ancestors is seen in the label given to the solar god, Mithrais. Mithraism was the most popular pre-Christian religion of the Roman Empire. At that time the Winter Solstice was called: "the birthday of the unconquered sun". This was the day when Mithrais emerged from his cave, or birthplace, witnessed by two shepherds.

Mithrais - By Jona Lendering - Livius.org Provided under CC 0 license., CC0, https://commons.wikimedia.org/w/index.php?curid=73...

The festival of Saturnalia deserves mention as it was one of the major celebrations of the pre Christian era. Saturnalia is of course, Saturn, who, back in ancient Roman and Greek times, was primarily revered as a god of agriculture. The Roman festival of Saturnalia was held from the 17th - 25th December. It was a time to celebrate the Winter Solstice. In Rome the courts were closed as no one could be punished for harming people or property during this week long festival.

"*In Roman mythology, Saturn was an agricultural deity who was said to have reigned over the world in the Golden Age, when humans enjoyed the spontaneous bounty of the earth without labour in a state of innocence. The revelries of Saturnalia were supposed to reflect the conditions of the lost mythical age... As a deity of agricultural bounty, Saturn embodied prosperity and wealth in general... Unlike several Roman religious festivals which were particular to cult sites in the city, the prolonged seasonal celebration of Saturnalia at home could be held anywhere in the Empire. Saturnalia continued as a secular celebration long after it was removed from the official calendar. As William Warde Fowler notes: "[Saturnalia] has left its traces and found its parallels in great numbers of medieval and modern customs, occurring about the time of the winter solstice.*" https://en.wikipedia.org/wiki/Saturnalia

Saturn, as we know, rules Capricorn, as such it holds a special place in astrology as the active and forthright Cardinal Earth sign. The links between Saturn, the celebrations of Saturnalia, Sol Invictus, Mithraism, Christianity and the myths of Capricorn, calls for closer examination. Jack Finegan in 'Myth & Mystery: An Introduction to the Pagan Religions of the Biblical World' (1989) writes: "*...But the worship of the sun-god continued widely throughout the empire, and under Aurelian (A.D. 270- 275) the cult was restored to its former high estate. In the year 274 Aurelian declared the god - now called Deus Sol Invictus - the official deity of the Roman Empire; he built a splendid temple of the sun in Rome... and set the sun's birthday celebration (naturalis solis invicti) on December 25th, the date then accepted for the Winter Solstice (also in his solar character was the God Mithrais). In the time of Constantine the cult of Deus Sol Invictus was still at its height, and the portrait of the sun god was on the coins of Constantine....Likewise it must have been in this time and with the intent to transform the significance of an existing sacred date that the birthday of Jesus, which had been celebrated in the East on January 6th... was placed in Rome on December 25th, the date of the birth of Sol Invictus. This date appears in a list of dates probably compiled in A.D. 336 and published in the Roman city calendar.*" Finegan, p. 211-212).

The upper half of the Capricorn glyph shows the head and torso of a goat. This, perhaps, reflects the goat's tendency to climb to higher ground where it can gain a better view of the landscape to locate food and avoid predators. Its lower half shows the tail of a fish linking it to water and spirituality. Thus we might say that one half of Capricorn is related to our conscious mind and the other half to our unconscious. Perhaps the ancient astrologers intended for Capricorn to symbolise our ascent to the peak of human achievement while remaining spiritually grounded.

There are a number of myths this complex sign draws upon:

Amalthia, a sea-goat nymph, was the baby Zeus' nurse (nanny). His mother, Rhea, hid him in a cave to protect him from his father, Cronus, who was in the habit of eating his babies. We use the word 'nanny' as the label we give to a mother goat as well as to a child's female carer when the mother is absent. When Amalthia assisted Zeus to rescue his siblings he placed her in the heavens as the constellation of Capricorn. The word 'Capricorn' means goat (caper) and horn (cornu). The magical horn of Amalthia was taken by Zeus and was known as the 'Horn of Plenty'.

The Babylonian goddess, **Ea**, watched over the land by day but at night she returned to the oceans. Her upper half was of a goat and the lower half a fish. Around 5,000 BC in Sumer and Babylon, their god, Enki, was represented as a satyr as well as a sea-goat. He was also known as the god of nature which is the same designation as the Greek god, Pan. Like Pan, Enki was known to bring life to the fields.

The god, **Pan** was the son of Hermes, he ruled shepherds and nature (animals, the soil and trees). Pan was part goat and part human. It is possible that Pan is Capricorn. Aegipan was one of the Panes. Panes were goat-legged shepherds of ancient Greece said to be descended from the god, Pan. In one version of the Capricorn myth appears a deadly monster, Typhon, flung Zeus' body parts into a river. Aegipan transformed into part goat and part fish to rescue the body parts and returned them to Zeus. He was rewarded by being placed in the skies as the constellation of Capricorn. Aegipan's name means Goat-Pan.

Another Greek myth involves **Pricus**, the king of the magical sea-goats. When his children crawled onto the land they would lose their fish tails and transform into ordinary goats. King Pricus had a special magic, he could reverse time. It seemed that whenever he turned his back on his children they would crawl onto the beaches and turn into hairy goats. He was constantly rescuing his children by rewinding time to before they climbed onto the beach. Eventually he gave up, kids are inquisitive and impossible to control. Eventually Pricus lost all of his children and became a lonely king. He asked the God of Time, Cronus, to let him die. Cronus placed him in the heavens as the constellation of Capricorn. From there he could watch his children climbing to the highest peaks of the mountains below.

The Origins of Santa Claus - an interesting article on one of the most popular feast days of modern times.

This appeared in the December 2018 edition of the **Federation of Australian Astrologers** journal, Vol. 48, No. 4

The Aries Myth and the Spring Equinox

On the 21st March the Sun reaches the equator on its journey north thus signalling the start of Spring in the northern hemisphere. This is the exact moment the Sun enters the sign of Aries and is called the Spring or Vernal Equinox. Here in the southern hemisphere it is the Autumnal Equinox.

With the arrival of Spring you can see new-born lambs frolicking in the fields and a multitude of gorgeous flowers clamouring to attract bees to pollinate the next generation. It is a time to celebrate the fertility of the fields.

In countries where Winter is particularly harsh, visitors delightedly join in with the locals in their celebrations. The saying, '*as mad as a March hare*', is still used today to describe people's exuberance at the start of Spring. In ancient times the Roman Spring festival of Kalends was an opportunity to party, spend freely and to give generously. Even today we evoke ancient myths to welcome the pleasant weather of Spring after the cold grip of Winter.

In the Mithraic religion followers celebrated the death and rebirth of the God Mithrais at the Spring Equinox. This religion appears to have formed the foundations for some of the traditions and beliefs of Christianity. Mithraism was the popular choice of religion of the Roman military. To this day much of the Mithraic religion remains shrouded in secrecy as followers were not permitted to record their rituals.

The Venerable Bede, a British monk of the 8th century, wrote that Christianity had borrowed the pagan festival of Eastra (Eostre), the Saxon Goddess of Spring, and called it 'Easter' to celebrate Christ's death and rebirth. The only reference we have to this Goddess is his commentary: *"Eosturmononath has a name which is now translated as 'Paschal month,' and which was once called after a goddess of theirs named Eostre, in whose honor feasts were celebrated in that month. Now they designate the Paschal season by her name, calling the joys of the new rite by the time-honoured name of the old observance."* (De Temporum Ratione, 725 AD).

Eastra may be Ishtar, the Babylonian and Assyrian goddess of love and fertility. The names of the two Goddesses are similar in pronunciation but unfortunately we do not have enough information on Eastra to know if they are one and the same. The Easter Bunny's gift of chocolate rabbits and eggs on Easter Sunday is most likely connected with the Eastra pagan celebration.

During the 17th and 18th century many American Puritans and Protestants considered Easter (and Christmas) as far too 'pagan' for them to celebrate. They complained that it was simply an excuse for revellers to party, drink and engage in lascivious behaviour.

The most celebrated Greek Goddess attributed to Spring is Persephone, the daughter of Demeter and Zeus. Hades, the God of the Underworld, fell in love with Persephone. In an act of desperation he drove his chariot out of his underworld kingdom and kidnapped the young and beautiful Persephone. When her mother, Demeter, discovered what had happened she petitioned Zeus to force Hades to release her daughter.

Alas, Persephone had eaten a seed while in the Underworld thus condemning her to remain with Hades as his wife. Hearing this news, Demeter, the Goddess of fertility, withdrew her blessing from the people of the earth. Their crops failed, people starved and everyone blamed Zeus. Zeus succumbed to the people's outrage and permitted Persephone to live with her mother from Spring to Autumn. Persephone and Demeter, rulers of fertility and agriculture, also presided over the Eleusinian Mysteries of the cult of Demeter which promised the believer a joyful and fruitful afterlife.

In examining the myth of Aries we can see how the ancients would consider Winter as a form of death. Spring arose with all its glory as confirmation of the renewal of life. The modern celebration of Easter evokes similar themes: death and rebirth. It is an allegorical triumph of light over darkness, of good over evil. This theme also parallels the hero's journey which forms the foundations of the Fire element - Aries, Leo and Sagittarius.

The ancient Babylonians celebrated the Spring Equinox by recognising the importance of agriculture and in particular, the farm worker. The symbology of the ram came later with the Persians and Egyptians who saw him as a symbol of fertility.

The zodiac sign of Aries is represented by the ram, the virile male sheep. In the rutting season he bursts with an abundance of libido and vigour to single-mindedly inseminate his flock of up to fifty ewes. It is during this period that he is aggressive and preoccupied in securing and servicing his ewes. He becomes so fixated in fighting off competitors that he will often forget to rut and even to eat.

Any sheep farmer will tell you: never let children enter a paddock or enclosure if there is a ram present. Rams have a reputation for butting, often causing severe injuries and sometimes death. Rams have been known to fight each other until one or the other is injured, some die.

Rams are born to assume a position of dominance, humans are therefore considered subservient to them, particularly if ewes are present. Rams will interpret a touch, push or tickle of their head as a challenge to a fight. Farmers will warn anyone entering a paddock containing a ram to continually note its location while they work. A ram can butt without warning or provocation.

Like an Aries child, rams are boisterous and impulsive, but they can be trained, or, more correctly, they can be 'socialised'. We do this with our puppies by sending them to 'puppy school' and then giving them access to other dogs in supervised play areas. Socialisation is an important part in training a headstrong Aries to get along with others. Why did our ancestors assign the ram to the constellation of Aries? Was it his impulsive, aggressive and single-minded nature that they had in mind? Although I agree with the virility of the libidinal ram as their preferred option, I can't help but wonder why they didn't chose a flower or a bee, or something that more closely represented the obvious fertility of Spring.

I need to remind myself that the ancients lived closer to nature than we do today. Many would have been farmers and many would have had direct personal contact with their animals, particularly herd animals like sheep.

It is believed that sheep were the first animals tamed by humans. They are placid, smallish herd animals and their behaviour is quite simple: they will follow the leader. A flock of sheep will follow their shepherd because they know he will protect them and lead them to water and sweet grasses. The shepherd becomes their leader.

The myth of Aries has been passed down to us from the ancient Greeks, immortalised in the legend of 'Jason and the Argonauts' and his quest for the Golden Fleece.

The myth goes like this: Hermes was asked by Zeus to send Aries, the magical flying ram with the golden fleece, to rescue the son and daughter of Athamas, the King of Boeotia. Aries carried Phrixus and his sister Helle on his back to escape their vengeful step-mother.

To celebrate his successful escape to the city of Colchis, on the far eastern coast of the Black Sea, Phrixus sacrificed the ram and gave the golden fleece to his protector, King Aeetes. Aeetes hung Aries golden fleece in a sacred grove guarded by a fierce dragon. When Jason learned of such a treasure he set out on his quest to steal this magical golden fleece and lay claim to his own kingdom - and so a legend is born.

As reward for his brave act in rescuing the children, Zeus placed Aries in the night sky as the constellation of Aries.

It is important not to get Aries the Ram confused with Ares the God of War - please note the subtle difference in spelling. Ares was the son of Zeus and Hera, he wasn't too bright but he did love to fight. His sister, Athena, was the Goddess of War but was far more strategic than her rash brother. Bloodthirsty Ares had few friends but what he did have was the bed of Aphrodite. The Roman God of War, Mars, is the Greek Ares.

This article by Noel Eastwood appeared in the **Federation of Australian Astrologers** March 2019 Journal - Vol. 49 No. 1

The Libra Myth and the Autumn Equinox

Autumn is the season when most of the crops have been harvested and the serious business of distributing the bounty of the fields begins as the community prepares for a cold and often depressingly hungry winter. In ancient times the end of harvest saw the taxman arrive for his tithe and the merchant seeking to purchase what was left over. Carrying their trade-mark set of scales each arranged for the distribution of the kingdom's bounty.

    Trade has always relied upon an equitable transaction and any dishonest dealing was treated just as seriously then as it is today. The Babylonian 'Code of Hammurabi', 1754 BC, was composed of 282 laws. The code covered such things as trade dealings as well as marriage and work contracts, criminal justice and the treatment of slaves. The oldest recorded complaint was by a Babylonian copper merchant who, in 1750 BC, complained of the poor quality copper ore he had received.

    Issues of injustice applies equally to food: "*The deliberate adulteration of food had been a problem for millenniums, inspiring government regulations in ancient Egypt, Sumeria and Rome. By the late 1870s, the Industrial Revolution... provided a variety of new techniques and ingredients useful for committing fraud... Ground-up insects were sold as brown sugar. Children's candy was routinely colored with lead and other heavy metals. Beef hearts and other organ meats were processed, canned and labeled as chicken. Perhaps one-third of the* butter for sale wasn't really butter but rather all sorts of other things — beef tallow, pork fat, the ground-up stomachs of cows and sheep — transformed into a yellowish substance that looked like butter… They also faked the look of rich cream by using a yellowish layer of pureed calf brains." From: 'The Jungle', Upton Sinclair, 1906. As you can see the scales of measurement and justice merge for a very good reason.

The mythology of Libra
Libra is the only astrological sign that does not represent a living creature. This is because Libra's scales are held by Astraea, the Goddess of justice, innocence, purity and precision who resides in the constellation of Virgo. Astrologers Arielle Guttman and Kenneth Johnson, provide us with this insight: *"Libra constitutes something of an enigma, inasmuch as it appears to have been inserted into the zodiac at a rather late date. Early Babylonian zodiacs, for instance, contain only eleven signs: the constellation we call Libra was known as the claws of the scorpion, hence a part of Scorpio rather than a separate sign. The Greeks saw this star group as the scales held by Astraea, goddess of justice (see Virgo); here we find it linked with Virgo rather than Libra, but beginning to assume the symbolism which is familiar to us today."* 'Mythic Astrology: Archetypes in the Horoscope' (ebook version, 2016).

Libra was also a valued constellation of the early Romans: *"'Italy belongs to the Balance, her rightful sign. Beneath it Rome and her sovereignty of the world were founded', said the Roman writer Manilius. (Marcus Manilius, 1st century AD). He described Libra as, 'the sign in which the seasons are balanced, and the hours of night and day match each other.'… the idea of a balance in this area goes back much further than the Romans. The Babylonians knew this area as ZIB.BA.AN.NA, the balance of heaven, around 1000 BC…"*
http://www.ianridpath.com/startales/libra.htm

Dike – the Greek goddess of justice, fairness, moral order and the individual's rights by custom and law. She was one of the three Horai, her sisters were Eunomia (good order) and Eirene (peace). These goddesses were also the keepers of the gates of heaven. Dike is depicted as a young woman holding a set of scales while in Roman mythology she is depicted similarly but blindfolded (blind justice).

Tyche – the Greek goddess of fortune, chance, providence, fate, luck, success and prosperity. She guided the affairs of the world and was known as one of the Moirai (Fates). Nemesis, in some respects Tyche's alter ego, provided a balance to Tyche's habit of gifting good fortune to her favourites. Tyche became the Roman 'Dame Fortuna', known today as 'lady luck'. Tyche was very popular in the Mediterranean region up until Christianity took hold when 'good luck' became associated with virtuous behaviour, faith and prayer. We evoke Tyche's favour when we bid one another "good luck".

Ma'at – is the Egyptian goddess of truth and justice. Anubis, the scarab-headed god, weighed the soul of the newly dead against one of Ma'at's feathers to judge if they were worthy to enter the afterlife.

Pagan Autumn Equinox festivals
Many wicca and pagan festivals were held at this time to celebrate and give thanks for the gifts of the harvest. Prayers of thankfulness and special thanksgiving ceremonies are common after harvest throughout the world.

Michaelmas celebration – the feast of Saint Michael was held on the 29th September. It often included aspects of older Pagan harvest customs such as the cooked stubble-goose (the goose was fed on the stubble of the harvested fields), dolls woven from the threshed grain stalks were placed in the centre of the dining table. The horse bringing the last of the harvest was decorated with garlands of flowers while fruit and vegetables were brought to the church for distribution among those in need. The feast of Saint Michael disappeared from Britain around the 1700's.

The Gods of the Vine – harvest was a time to celebrate the grape and its beverage - wine. The Roman God Bacchus, his Greek name was Dionysus, and the Druid's Green Man, were the main archetypes celebrated at this time. According to the Roman historian, Livy (born c. 60 BC), the original Bacchanalian festival was a mysterious three-day, women only celebration, which later became a time of drunkenness and sexual debauchery.

Nutting day – celebrating the harvesting of nuts, an important winter food which is stored wrapped in its own protective covering.

Celtic festival of **Samhain** – a festival at the end of harvest when the livestock were brought from their highland pastures as winter approached. This was a time when faeries appeared and the partition between the living and the dead was thinnest. Bonfires were lit and food and wine were made in offering of thanks and to ensure a safe winter for the community and their livestock.

Oktoberfest – held in late September to the first weekend of October celebrating the alcoholic beverage made from hops – beer.

Scarecrows – have been used in various forms to keep birds from eating the farmer's seeds at sowing time and the ripened crops at harvest. Ancient Egyptians erected wooden frames covered in rags to frighten the birds from their fields. Greek farmers made scarecrows that looked like the hideous god Priapus. The Roman's spread scarecrows throughout the known world. In recent times scarecrow festivals have become popular to celebrate our humble agricultural past.

Libra and its ruler Venus

Venus (the Greek Aphrodite) was an attractive and alluring yet quite dispassionate goddess. Although Venus could draw lovers together she lacked the spark of passion and intimacy that comes with romantic love. Libra is an Air sign which perfectly describes the complex nature of Venus.

There are many Libran people who are attractive, engaging and charming yet lack the empathic warmth that one would expect to reside within such beauty. This is one of the many facets of the esoteric element of Air which seeks intellectual engagement without emotional complications.

One side of Libra is cold and dispassionate which we consider an essential asset in negotiations be it in marriage counselling, brokering a business deal or when selling fruit at the markets. The other is the overwhelmed pacifist which can arise when Libra feels confronted with excessive emotion, aggression and/or passion. This can cause them to compromise their own needs 'just to keep the peace'.

From a psychological perspective I have counselled many Libra types who compromise their needs when faced with disharmony in relationships be it at work or in the home. This can sometimes happen with parents who are unable to discipline their children and become the victim of their child's bullying.

I see these issues in people with a dominance of 3 or more planets in Libra or the 7th house. This is particularly strengthened if the Sun and/or Moon are conjunct Venus while also residing in Libra and/or the 7th house.

Libra corresponds to the 7th house, its importance can't be understated as it holds up a mirror, the Shadow archetype of Jungian psychology, which allows us to see what we really are. Without the 7th house we are blind to our faults and failures thus stifling insight and the ability to grow spiritually.

Astrologers and counsellors can assist these sensitive yet sometimes confused Librans by supporting them through the process of setting boundaries and limits to the behaviour of their 7th house 'close others'.

The scales of Libra may have also been the model for two of the Tarot Major Arcana cards: Justice and Temperance. Both represent fairness and balance while Justice can also represent the ancient law of 'an eye for an eye' present in the three religions originating in ancient Mesopotamia and the Fertile Crescent – Islam, Judaism and Christianity.

This article by Noel Eastwood appeared in the **Federation of Australian Astrologers,** September 2019, Vol 49, #3.

The Cancer Myth and the Summer Solstice

The first day of Cancer marks the Summer Solstice, midsummer's day, which in Latin is called *sol sistere* meaning 'sun stands still'. At midsummer the flowers are in full bloom, the pastures green and small children expectantly wait for the sweet fruits to ripen.

Midsummer was considered an ideal time to celebrate the union of the nature Gods and Goddesses by getting married. The first full moon after the summer solstice was called the 'Honey Moon' which was said to be the best time to harvest honey. This day remains with us today as a reminder of those bygone days as newlyweds go on their 'honeymoon'. Interestingly, a child conceived in midsummer is born in spring the following year giving it the best chances of survival. Midsummer's Eve was also an occasion to enjoy lovemaking. "*Midsummer Night is not long but it sets many cradles rocking,*" goes an old Swedish proverb.

Midsummer also marked the time for the men to sharpen their tools and their spears and prepare for warfare. The men went off to war whether it be for revenge, to take someone else's harvest, or to lay claim to new and better land and its resources. Generally there was little opportunity for fighting before seeing to the needs of the village which meant that agriculture, and therefore the seasons, ruled life and death in the ancient world.

Pagan midsummer festivals
The Summer Solstice is the longest day of the year in the northern hemisphere. It also heralds a time when communities prepared to come together and share the burden of bringing in the harvest. After harvest, the villagers would gather to process and divide their produce for the coming barren, long months of winter.

Midsummer's Eve was seen as the night when stone circles would come alive with faerie folk only to melt away with the dawn. The ancient Celts would light bonfires and lovers would leap through the flames to bless their union and ensure they bore many children. Ancient Romans celebrated the festival of Vestalia, the Goddess Vesta, which ran from the 7th to the 15th of June. This was the only time that married women could visit its shrine to return to their home with the 'sacred flame' of the Goddess Vesta.

The festival of Litha was a period of the giving of gifts and food; when bonfires would remain lit throughout the night; torch-lit parades wound through the streets amid other forms of community celebration. This day was known as the 'Gathering Day' as many medicinal herbs were at their peak ready for harvesting. In Ireland, pagan worshippers would clasp a pebble in their hand and whisper their wishes as they circled the Litha bonfire. At the third circling they would throw the pebble into the fire.

On midsummer morn the sun is perfectly aligned with the Heel and Alter stones at Stonehenge. Many other locations were used by pagans to celebrate the summer solstice such as gardens, woodlands, parks and beside lakes. Bonfires would drive evil spirits away from the villager's crops and livestock, while youths jumped back and forth through the flames for good luck. Married couples would wait for the flames to die down before doing the same thus ensuring a fruitful marriage. In some areas, a wheel stuffed with straw was lit and rolled down the hill after dark to awaken the fertility spirits to ensure a bountiful harvest. Farmers would drive their animals through the smoke of the bonfires for good health and in the morn would walk them through its ashes.

The Christian religion claimed the summer solstice festival as St. John's Day in the 4th century AD. Interestingly St. John The Baptist's birth was celebrated on the Summer Solstice while his cousin, Jesus, was celebrated at the Winter Solstice, 6 months later.

St John's Day remains an important day for the peasant folk of Europe:
"... in France and England, the countries where the sway of the Druids is known to have been most firmly established, Midsummer Eve is still the time for culling certain magic plants... Indeed all over Europe antique fancies of the same sort have lingered about Midsummer Eve... of all the festivals for which the merry bells ring out there is not one which has given rise to a greater number of superstitious practices than the festival of St. John the Baptist. The Eve of St. John was the day of all days for gathering the wonderful herbs by means of which you could combat

fever, cure a host of diseases, and guard yourself against sorcerers and their spells. But in order to attain these results two conditions had to be observed; first, you must be fasting when you gathered the herbs, and second, you must cull them before the sun rose. If these conditions were not fulfilled, the plants had no special virtue... the person who gathered the magic herbs before sunrise at this season had to walk backwards, to mutter some mystic words, and to perform certain ceremonies. The plants thus collected were carefully kept as an infallible cure for fever; placed above beds and the doors of houses and of cattle-sheds they protected man and beast from disease, witchcraft, and accident." The Project Gutenberg EBook of 'The Golden Bough: A Study in Magic and Religion' (Third Edition, Vol. 11 of 12) by James George Frazer, 1913.

Cancerian links to motherhood, home and family
Our most intimate social engagements have always been associated with food. Comfort eating is emotionally driven and illustrates why Cancerian mothers enjoy feeding their family and visitors. It is a form of nurturing as well as of acceptance, security and safety from the harsh world outside.

In the Middle Ages, women had a 10% chance of dying in childbirth. Many women chose to make out their will prior to birthing. Child mortality from birth to 5 years was very high: 30-50% died either during childbirth or by illness and accidents in infancy. Then, as now, some mothers experienced episodes of Post Natal Depression (PND), starvation, physical illness, and loneliness.

In periods of war or famine when the men were absent for long periods of time, mothers who were disconnected from their extended family, were often left to fend for themselves. We recognise that social isolation contributes to our growing mental health crisis today. We also know that strong family ties are protective factors, providing emotional and social support through the hardships of raising a family.

Astrology and myth – Cancer the crab

Cancinus the crab – the Greek Karkinos or Carcinus, was sent by Hera to annoy and thwart Heracles in his 2nd Labour against the nine-headed Hydra. Heracles had been sent to kill the flame-breathing Hydra, defender of the entrance to Hades, the land of the dead. Hera had a particular dislike of Heracles and sent the giant crab Carcinus to stop him. Carcinus latched onto Heracles heel but the hero easily crushed it. In recognition of its loyalty and courage, Hera placed Carcinus in the sky as the constellation of Cancer.

Khepri and the scarab beetle - from Egyptian mythology the god Khepri was the god of sunrise and therefore of birth, he was depicted with the face of a scarab beetle. The scarab beetle's ball of dung was seen as a perfect sphere representing the sun rolling through the sky. Although there is no reference to Cancer or the summer solstice the scarab beetle represents birth and rebirth which appears to have influenced early astrologers.

Crios the giant crab - a Greek myth that is perhaps the best illustration of many of the Cancerian traits we recognise today. Crios was appointed protector of Poseidon's sea nymph daughters. Poseidon fled his home when the god Typhon roamed the oceans leaving Crios alone to defend his daughters. Crios fussed over the sea nymphs not letting them out of his sight. Alas, one day some of the nymphs left their ocean home putting Crios in a panic. He asked his giant squid friend, Vamari, for help. Sadly, the squid ate the nymphs instead. Crios fought the squid for many long hours but although he won the fight he was terribly wounded. As reward for his bravery and loyalty, Poseidon placed him in the sky as the constellation of Cancer. In this myth we see some of Cancer's key traits: the drive to nurture and protect family and loved ones.

Early astrologers accepted all forms of the Cancer myth be it crab, tortoise, turtle, scarab beetle, and even lobsters. Eventually, they settled on the crab in its simple yet comprehensive representation of the primary Cancerian trait we celebrate today: a hard exterior protecting their soft emotions within.

Interestingly, there appears to be a connection between Cancer and the Mithraic tradition whereby the Solstices were considered *'gateways'* allowing the soul to gain access to the sect's mysteries. The Greek philosopher, Porphyry (c. 234 – c. 305 AD) wrote that Mithraism considered the Solstices to be associated with the entry and exit of souls. It seems that this theme goes back to Babylonian, Chaldean and Egyptian times.

This article by Noel Eastwood appeared in the **Federation of Australian Astrologers Journal,** June 2019, Vol.49, No. 2

Chapter 16: My Newsletter Has Just About Everything

Here's an example of what I write in some of my many newsletters. It's not always about astrology or tarot, maybe there's some psychology, whatever, but it is interesting. Please be mindful that not everything happens in the earth plane and that I sometimes tap into it and have some weird experience. Anyway, you've done enough astrology so here's something different for you as a reward for getting to the end of the book.

What happens when we die? I don't have the answer to that question, I don't think many people do. I'm pretty sure though, that I'll find out one day. I have previously written about some of my out-of-body experiences and meeting ghosts. The following stories are from recent encounters and might help answer some of the questions we all have about the afterlife.

One night I was meditating, as I do when I go to bed (and then again around 4.00 am). It's a habit I have had for many years now. I find that these times are perfect for my dreaming experiences, out-of-body and astral travels. I also do a lot of problem-solving and even compose my books in these meditations.

(Image: wounded Australian soldiers walking back to an aid station behind the front lines, Kokoda Campaign, Papua/New Guinea, 1942.)

I had spent the day reading up on Australian history, particularly the 2nd World War action in New Guinea, north of Australia. I had worked with a veteran, many years ago, who was there. On this particular night, I did what I always do: build the chi (energy) in my navel chakra, a standard tai chi and Taoist alchemy practice.

As I fell asleep I felt the ball of chi at my navel move down to my feet, and this is very unusual. I normally create a ball of light at the top of my head (Omega point) and the soles of my feet (Alpha point) but not like this. The ball of chi forced itself down to the Alpha point at my feet and then zoomed off, at speed, away from me. At the same time my double or clone self, which one day I'll explain in more detail, raced off with it. I was a bit perplexed but as I was almost asleep I ignored it.

Only a few seconds later the ball of chi and my clone returned, again at speed. With them came 10 or so Australian soldiers from their action in the New Guinea campaign of WW2. They were horribly thin too, their clothing in rags, decimated in body and spirit. They had been dead for nearly 80 years, frozen, in a state of shock and bewilderment.

I didn't know what to do, I'd not rescued anyone who had passed on before. I have visited, and have had many visits from deceased friends and family but I've not rescued those who had died. So I did what came automatically to me - I let go and allowed my unconscious, my 'body wisdom', to do what needed to be done. I completely trust my innate wisdom when on the astral planes, it does things I have no idea how to do consciously, so these days I just 'let go'.

At that moment my aura glowed a brilliant white light, a white I'd never used before. Within seconds the soldiers all disappeared, like bubbles popping in the air. I scanned my bedroom to check if they were still there, but they had all gone. I relaxed and fell fast asleep. In the morning I scanned my room again and it was empty of the ghosts from the night before. I believe that they were empowered in some way, to move out of their state of shock and on to the next stage of their journey of existence.

The next experience was a ghost in my cranio-sacral therapist's room. During my first session I sensed others in the room but said nothing. Then a session or two later something strange happened: I was lying on S's table in a lovely blissful state when BANG! someone hit the table next to me. I jumped in shock and saw an alien standing next to my right shoulder. It had a very ugly face too. I'm fairly comfortable these days with strange things like this so I didn't freak out, but I sure did when they first started happening many years ago. Still, this was a bit of a shock.

My therapist, S, asked me what had just happened and I told her that someone else was in the room and had hit the table to get my attention. I didn't want to frighten her so I didn't say that I'd just seen an Extra Terrestrial (ET). I thought that maybe I was seeing things, so I went back to my blissful state. At the end of the session we talked. S doesn't see ghosts, so when she said that two other patients had seen a stranger with a beak-like face, I was a bit freaked out. This now made sense of what I had seen. The alien's face was in fact a mask, like that worn by nurses from the times of the 1918 Spanish Influenza pandemic. What I had seen was a mask made of white canvas, a full-face mask with two glass windows for the eyes. It had a pointy front that was used to pack cotton wool soaked in eucalyptus oil and other remedies to kill the virus.

Look at the picture below and imagine seeing that standing next to you. She had an off white, worn and faded dress, like they wore at that time, and an apron which had a faded Red Cross which was almost gray. I felt that the frequent washing made it faded and turned it into a soft gray.

(Image: the type of mask I saw, typically worn by medical staff in hospital plague wards c.1919.)

This ghostly nurse from the past was there for the next five or so sessions and even though she stood next to me she rarely did anything. Twice she patted my arm but I never experienced healing from her. I told S that maybe the nurse was not there to help heal her patients but rather to watch and learn what S was doing. You see, my cranio-sacral therapist is an incredibly gifted healer.

At her last session, this ghostly nurse showed me an image of why she was there. I was given an image of a hospital ward full of plague victims. The nurse wasn't there to help S heal her clients or to learn how to heal, she was still traumatised, 100 years later, and she was the one in need of healing.

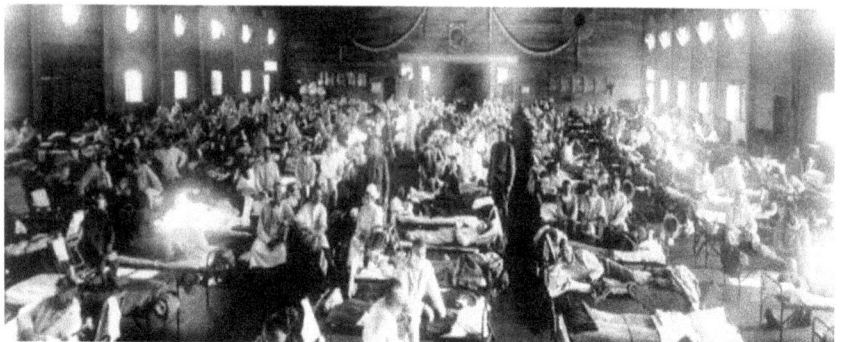

(Image: a packed plague ward, 1918. Conditions like this can easily overwhelm nursing staff.)

The image was horrible, it really stressed me out, but I calmed myself and let my body wisdom take control. As I'd done previously with the ghost soldiers from WW2 I unconsciously glowed the same brilliant white light. When the light faded she was gone. She's not been back since. I like to think she found healing and moved on.

It happened again. I was meditating early in the morning when a man in his thirties entered my dreaming space. He was upset as he told me that his wife and daughter had been involved in a car accident and that his wife was in a coma in hospital in a very serious condition. He then said that his daughter was, '*allowed to go early*'. Those were his words, I thought that was strange.

As I tried to work out what he wanted I noticed a little girl, maybe eight or nine years old, standing beside me. She had freckles, and reddish hair, it was long and straight, she smiled up at me as though saying, '*Can we go now, please?*'

She was clearly very happy and excited to get going. She took me by the hand and together we walked forward into a golden mist. Yes, I know, it sounds like everyone else's death experience, but that's what happened. After a few metres the little girl became really excited, she kept glancing up at me expectantly. In a few more steps, we stopped. I heard voices and then faces appeared from out of the mist. The little girl looked up at me, her smile was of a happiness that only comes with the recognition of a loved one. She looked at me once more, smiled brightly then dropped my hand. She quickly stepped into the mist and disappeared.

I came back to consciousness and lay in bed pondering the experience. These are spontaneous and just happen, I don't have a great deal of control over them. This was such a nice experience too, there was no sadness, no pain, no fear, just complete joyfulness. The golden light? Well, it came from the mist that appeared around us. I haven't heard from the man who came to me that night, nor do I know what happened to the girl's mother. This is just one experience, an interesting one too.

Just when I thought that I wouldn't see any more spirits during my cranio-sacral therapy, there, off to my left, next to where S was sitting, appeared a young woman with short brown hair, eyes closed and squirming about on her bed. My first impression was that she had cerebral palsy and was blind. I didn't know what to do, was she dead and looking for release? Was she living and had connected with me for some reason? I tried to white light the room to see if it would help but nothing happened.

I told S that we had visitors again and she replied that she would clear the room so that we could do our healing without interruption. But no, the girl wasn't going to let that happen. She came right up to my ear and whispered, *"I just want to ask you a question."*

That shocked me, her voice was as clear as a bell in my ear. Once I recovered I began to wonder what her question might be. I told the girl that I would let my higher self answer her question because I was busy with my healing. I offered to see her that night in my sleep if she wanted more. When the session ended, S and I chatted about it and shrugged our shoulders. The gods and spirits I saw during our sessions were all different, none have been the same (and I saw a few there).

When I went to bed that night I visualised the girl and told her that I was ready to answer her question and would give her all night to talk with me then fell asleep. I think it was around midnight when she arrived and asked me to tell her about my 'division'. I wasn't sure what she meant... then it clicked, **clones**, she was asking about my clones. I had three clones: a black me who looks after external issues that might arise; my white and gold clones assist in my health and spiritual growth.

As soon as I explained what I was doing she cloned a **knight protector** for herself. I was initially a little confused because the people I have helped in the past had cloned images of themselves. But hey, there are no rules to this sort of thing - so why not a knight protector?

I showed her what I did by adding another clone to help me with my gardening. Because she had a clone that wasn't a direct clone of herself, I made my new one a blend of Pan, the earth God, and The Seer (High Priestess) from the Wildwood Tarot. I called him the Green Man no doubt influenced by my love of Celtic mythology. I spent the rest of the night till about 5:30 am talking with the girl and her clone.

Spending most of the night on the astral planes takes it out of me so I took my time to process what had happened before getting out of bed. I wonder, will she ever visit me again?

~

The End

About the Author

Noel Eastwood is a retired psychologist with over forty years professional experience in psychology, counselling and education. Now a full-time author, Noel shares his lifelong passions of Taoist Alchemy, Jungian psychotherapy, meditation, tai chi, astrology and Tarot. A gifted storyteller, his fiction and nonfiction works blend ancient wisdom and contemporary themes. His unique blend of hands-on experience and knowledge, rollicking good storytelling, and the wisdom of esoterica is evident in his writing.
He lives in Brisbane, Australia with his wife and family.
You can visit his website and subscribe to his free newsletters on the many diverse topics above.

Web: www.plutoscave.com
Email: info@plutoscave.com

www.ingramcontent.com/pod-product-compliance
Lightning Source LLC
Chambersburg PA
CBHW061747070526
44585CB00025B/2818